ISLAM
AND THE
INSTITUTION
OF
MARRIAGE

Legal and Sociological Approaches

Edited by
Katherine Lemons
Laurens de Rooij

AMI PRESS

AMI Press
60 Weoley Park Road
Selly Oak
Birmingham
B29 6RB

A catalogue record for this book is available from the British Library

ISBN 978-1-915550-02-6 (hardback)
ISBN 978-1-915550-03-3 (paperback)
ISBN 978-1-915550-04-0 (eBook)

TABLE OF CONTENTS

LIST OF CONTRIBUTORS iv

INTRODUCTION 1

PART I
ISSUES IN CONTEMPORARY MARRIAGE FIQH

1. The Existential Perspective on 'God's Bestowal of *Faḍl* upon Men' and Its Implications on *Qiwāma* 9
   Arif Abdul Hussain

2. The Institution of Marriage in Islam: A Case Study of the First Pillar of the Marriage Contract 35
   Mohsen Kadivar

3. Competing Conceptions of Marriage in Islam: Between Tradition and Modernity 54
   Ziba Mir-Hosseini

4. Juristic Principles Governing Family Life 74
   Sayed Mustafa Muhaqqiq Damad & Syed Wajee ul-Hasan Shah

PART II
SOCIOLOGICAL ANALYSES

5. Unregistered Muslim Marriages in Britain: Avenues for Regulation 89
   Fouzia Azzouz

6. A Purposive Approach to Islamic Marriage: A Re-assessment of Q. 30:21 114
   S. Mohammad Gh. Seyed Fatemi, Munzela Raza, Ahmad Kaouri and Abbas Ramji

7. Online Dating for British Muslims and the Relationship with Their Islamic Identities 133
   Laurens de Rooij

8. Marital Disputes and the Pursuit of Justice 164
   Katherine Lemons

LIST OF CONTRIBUTORS

ARIF ABDUL HUSSAIN founded the Al-Mahdi Institute in 1993 and currently serves as its Director. He lectures in *uṣūl al-fiqh* and Muslim Philosophy. For over twenty years, Shaykh Arif has been at the forefront of developing and delivering advanced Islamic studies, tailored toward training students capable of addressing the needs of contemporary societies. Shaykh Arif was educated at the Madrassah Syed al-Khoei, London, where he graduated with Honours and then taught grammar, logic, Islamic law and *uṣūl al-fiqh*. He then pursued Post-Graduate Islamic studies in Iran and attended private training and research studies with leading scholars of the Qom Seminary. After founding the Al-Mahdi Institute he continued his graduate (*khārij*) training in *uṣūl al-fiqh* and *fiqh* under Ayatollah H. Amini, a student of Ayatollah Khoei.

FOUZIA AZZOUZ holds a PhD from The School of Sociology, Politics, and International Studies (SPAIS) at the University of Bristol. She is currently a lecturer at the Faculty of Foreign Languages at the University of Algiers II, Algeria, and teaches on various subjects including British and American studies and research methodology. Her research focuses on the marriage and divorce practices of Muslims in Britain, examining state accommodation of British Muslims, legal pluralism, multiculturalism, and Sharia councils. She has written various papers on these topics and is currently working on a book dealing with Sharia councils and Muslim women's experiences of abuse in the contexts of marriage and divorce.

SAYED MUSTAFA MUHAQQIQ DAMAD completed his seminary studies at the Fayziyyeh School in Qom, Iran, where he achieved the status of a *mujtahid* by the age of 25. Among his notable teachers are 'Allāma Sayyid Muḥammad Husayn Ṭabāṭabā'ī and Ayatollah Murtaḍā Muṭahharī, under whom he studied Islamic philosophy. His studies in Islamic jurisprudence and legal theory were conducted by Ayatollah Muḥammad Riḍā Golpaygānī and Ayatollah Murtaḍā Ḥā'irī al-Yazdī. Parallel to his seminary education, Professor Damad pursued secular academic studies, earning a degree in Islamic Philosophy and a Masters degree in Islamic Jurisprudence, both from Tehran University, before earning his PhD in Law at the University of Louvain-la-Neuve, Belgium. He is the Dean of the Department of Islamic Studies at The Academy of Sciences of Iran and is a Professor of Law and Islamic Philosophy at Tehran University. He is recognised as one of the world's most influential Muslims by The Muslim 500 for his scholarly work.

Laurens de Rooij gained his doctorate at Durham University in England. He is currently an Associate Lecturer in the Sociology of Islam at the Al Mahdi Institute. His research examines how non-Muslim people in Britain interact with news reports about Islam and Muslims and how that affects their interpretation and conceptualisation of Islam and Muslims. Laurens has spent time at a number of institutions across the globe, including The Graduate School of the Syarif Hidayatullah State Islamic University in Jakarta, Indonesia (spring 2013), the Religion Department at Duke University in Durham North Carolina, USA (Autumn 2013), The Centre for Religion, Media and Culture in the Journalism & Mass Communication Department at the University of Colorado in Boulder, Colorado, USA (spring 2014), and at Brazil's Fundação Joaquim Nabuco (summer 2016). In 2017 he was a post-doctoral research fellow at the University of Cape Town for a year, where his research analyses how the media discourse on minorities (particularly Muslims and Islam) affects how they are conceptualised, understood, and treated in South Africa. This work was supported in part by the National Research Foundation of South Africa. He was also a lecturer at the University of Chester (2018), and a researcher at London Metropolitan University (2018–2020), Toulouse School of Management (2021–2022) in France, and Mahidol University in Bangkok, Thailand (2022–2023).

Mohsen Kadivar is a contemporary Shīʿī theologian and jurist and a research professor of Islamic Studies at Duke University (Durham, NC, US). His interests span both classical and modern Islamic thought with a special focus on Islamic philosophy and ethics, Shīʿī theology and jurisprudence, Quranic studies, Shīʿī political thought, and Islam and human rights. He has authored twenty-nine books in Persian and recently published his English monograph *Human Rights and Reformist Islam and Blasphemy* and *Apostasy in Islam: Debates in Shīʿa Jurisprudence* (Edinburgh University Press, 2021). He has contributed several articles and book chapters, the most recent of which include "Democracy and Ethical Values from Islamic Perspective" (March 2020), "Genealogies of Pluralism in Islamic Thought: Shiʿa Perspective" and "Toward Removing the Punishment of Apostasy in Islam" (both March 2021). His forthcoming books include *Governance by Guardianship: Rule and Government in the Islamic Republic of Iran* (Cambridge U. Press) and *Islamic Theocracy in the Secular Age: Revisiting Shi'ite Political Thought of Islamic Republic of Iran* (University of North Carolina Press).

AHMAD KAOURI is a graduate of the Hawza programme at Al-Mahdi Institute. He is currently pursuing his MA in Islamic Studies at the University of Birmingham. He also holds a BSc in Computing and IT and a Master of Business Administration. His research interests span jurisprudence, philosophy, Quranic exegesis, mysticism, theology and ethics.

KATHERINE LEMONS is Associate Professor of Anthropology at McGill University. Her research is in the areas of anthropology of Islam, law, and gender. She is the author of Divorcing Traditions: Islamic Marriage Law and the Making of Indian Secularism (Cornell University Press 2019).

ZIBA MIR-HOSSEINI is a legal anthropologist, specialising in Islamic law, gender and Islamic feminism, and a founding member of the Musawah Global Movement for Equality and Justice in the Muslim Family. She has held numerous research fellowships and visiting professorships (most recently at NYU Law School). Currently, she is Professorial Research Associate at the Centre for Islamic and Middle Eastern Law, SOAS, University of London. She has published books on Islamic family law in Iran and Morocco, Iranian clerical discourses on gender, Islamic reformist thinkers, and the revival of *zinā* laws, and most recently the co-edited *Gender and Equality in Muslim Family Law* (2013) and *Men in Charge? Rethinking Authority in Muslim Legal Tradition* (2015). She co-directed two award-winning feature-length documentary films on Iran: Divorce Iranian Style (1998) and Runaway (2001). She received the American Academy of Religion's 2015 Martin E. Marty Award for the Public Understanding of Religion. Her latest book is *Journeys Towards Gender Equality in Islam* (2022).

ABBAS RAMJI graduated from the University of Birmingham with degrees in Medicine and Behavioural Sciences. He successfully completed a postgraduate certificate and a postgraduate diploma in Medical Education as well as his postgraduate specialist psychiatric training. He has been a Consultant Psychiatrist since 2013 and is also the Deputy Director of Medical Education at Derbyshire Healthcare NHS Foundation Trust.

MUNZELA RAZA is a graduate of Al-Mahdi Institute and a qualified medical doctor. She also holds an MA in Islamic Studies from the University of Birmingham. She is also the founder of ICBL (Islamic Case-based Learning), an innovative way of delivering Islamic education using the popular case methodology approach.

SYED WAJEE UL-HASAN SHAH holds a Bachelor's degree in Religion and Education from York St John University. After graduating in 2016 he dedicated a year to studying Persian in Qom. From 2017 to 2021, he successfully completed a four-year Hawza program in Arabic and Islamic Studies at Al-Mahdi Institute, earning a distinction in his seminary studies. Subsequently, in 2022, he earned a Master's degree in Islamic Studies from the University of Birmingham, receiving a prestigious distinction. Currently, he serves as a Research Coordinator at Al-Mahdi Institute, actively contributing to the Islamic Law Studies Department. His academic interests lie in Quranic sciences, legal theory and the intersection of these disciplines with Islamic philosophy.

Introduction

The present volume is a study of Muslim marriage in modernity. The essays that comprise the volume are written both by scholars of Islamic fiqh and by social scientists. As such, the collection stages an all-too-rare dialogue between practitioners of fiqh – those working with the source texts to derive new interpretations, to authorise rethinking, and thereby to create spaces of possibility for practices to change – and social scientists – who study practices of Islam. The question of marriage and intimate relationships is an important site of internal contestation, as the collection demonstrates. It demands both fidelity to the tradition and its historical modes of thought *and* adequacy to contemporary conditions. The contributors to this volume examine challenges to fiqh posed by the contemporary by critically analysing the practices and resources available to Muslims in a range of national and historical contexts. These critical approaches will enable a wide readership to understand how Muslims engage with the assumptions and epistemologies that underpin marriage and relationships in contemporary Islamic settings.

The volume begins by introducing the reader to several key internal debates about Muslim marriage, including the entailments of the marriage contract, the status of marital rape, and the relationship between spouses. Together, these essays provide insight into dominant Islamic legal and religious discourses about marriage. Discourses, as understood here, have a double valence: they are at once stable and can be challenged and changed.[1] Anthropologist Talal Asad has argued that tradition is discursive: the discourses that make it up aim to teach people how and why to engage in specific instituted practices.[2] Traditions only persist to the extent that they, and the discourses that comprise them, are at once linked to the past and able to change in response not only to present predicaments but also to aspirations for the future. Islam,

1 We follow Michel Foucault's conception of discursive formations in this analysis. Foucault argued that a discourse entailed statements that together constitute a system through which subjects and objects are formed and at times transformed. See Michel Foucault, *The Archaeology of Knowledge*, trans. A. M. Sheridan Smith, 2nd ed. (London: Routledge, 2002), 41–43.

2 Talal Asad, 'The Idea of an Anthropology of Islam', *Qui Parle* 17, no. 2 (2009): 20.

as a discursive tradition is, accordingly 'a tradition of Muslim discourse that addresses itself to conceptions of the Islamic past and future, with reference to a particular Islamic practice in the present'.[3] Part I of the present volume both captures several dominant discourses within the Islamic tradition about marriage and presents loyal challenges to them, challenges that render the tradition dynamic and seek to bring Islamic discourses on marriage into closer proximity to the realities of contemporary everyday life. Thus, the discourses presented here constitute marriage as both an object of analysis and a site of intervention – they indicate how marriage is understood as well as how different scholars and jurists seek to change its normative entailments.

The essays in Part II present and analyse a different aspect of the discursive tradition, with special attention to the ways in which lay Muslims live and understand marriage. These essays are written by sociologists and anthropologists who explore the various ways in which Muslims engage with fiqh and social institutions that structure their daily lived experiences. The essays examine how individuals, jurists, political actors, and civil society organisations respond to the dynamics of specific socio-political domains on questions of marriage and relationships. A major intervention of the collection is that such practices and arguments are not separate from but spur reforms to fiqh. Indeed, presenting these sociological and anthropological essays alongside the fiqh interventions demonstrates that rather than an isolated theoretical and theological project, fiqh is where practical conundrums and lived problems meet legal theory. This is not a new phenomenon. Wael Hallaq has argued that 'the [Ottoman] qadi mediated a dialectic between, on the one hand, the social and moral imperatives – of which he was an integral part – and, on the other, the demands of legal doctrine which in turn recognized the supremacy of the unwritten codes of morality and morally grounded social relations.'[4] Hallaq's argument is that fiqh has always been responsive to moral and social codes as well as to the sources of law. In this way, the work of making fiqh adequate to social conditions is not distinctly modern but instead an integral aspect of it. Yet fiqh is rarely understood to be an effect of daily life meeting legal theory or doctrine, perhaps because lay Muslims neither think of themselves as reformers nor set out to change dominant fiqh concerning marriage (unlike their counterparts in Part I). Instead, they inhabit the tradition in innovative ways that nonetheless have the effect of changing Muslim marriage practices.

3 Ibid.

4 Wael B. Hallaq, *Sharīʿa: Theory, Practice, Transformations* (Cambridge: Cambridge University Press, 2009), 169.

INTRODUCTION TO PART I

Fiqh is a key site for exploring ideas about marriage and relationships in Islam. The four essays in Part I explore the question of how the law can do justice to contemporary lived experiences, each in its own way. The purpose of this part is to provide insight into debates on fiqh with regard to marriage in Islam.

Arif Abdul Hussain investigates different conceptualisations of *faḍl* and explores how they relate to *qiwāma* (governorship). The conclusions of this essay include: (1) 'the status of *qiwāma*' (governorship) can be assigned to both men and women generally with respect to (local) societal gender roles and spousal relations, rights, and responsibilities in collectivities and existential contexts. However, in societies where women have not been given the opportunity to actualise their innate potentialities 'the status of *qiwāma*' (governorship) will be assigned to men. (2) The nature of the marriage contract must be congruent with the different degrees of *faḍl* (existential aptitudes) bestowed upon individuals and their collectivities, and this includes the need to formulate corresponding conceptions of the notion of *qiwāma* to be assigned to either one or both spouses. Hussain argues that in many modern contexts women have actualised their potentialities and therefore 'the status of *qiwāma*' (governorship) can be extended to them as well.

Mohsen Kadivar builds on this and explores the first pillar of the marriage contract. In examining what constitutes a *muʿāṭāṭī* marriage, Kadivar emphasises the importance of an explicit contract. The man recognises himself as a husband and the woman herself as a wife. The manifestation of the marriage contract is in explicit action, namely, living together by consent and recognising themselves as husband and wife. This, he argues, provides the minimum requirement of a Sharīʿa-approved marriage, although it is recommended both religiously and from a civil-legal perspective to take some additional steps.

Ziba Mir-Hosseini's contribution, 'Contesting Conceptions of Marriage in Islam: Between Tradition and Modernity', departs from this and discusses how the classical fiqh construction of marriage, with its patriarchal ethos, and the Muslim feminist vision for marriage as a partnership of equals, should be viewed as a complex double image, as both expressing and moulding social norms and practices. This is because change often comes when legal theory or jurisprudence reacts to political, economic, and ideological forces and to people's experiences and expectations. As this volume demonstrates, Muslim legal theory is no exception.

Sayed Mustafa Muhaqqiq Damad and Syed Wajee ul-Hasan Shah examine 'Juristic Principles Governing Family life'. They seek to highlight that although in both the traditional and current jurisprudential rulings, the concept of marital rape does not exist and *tamkīn* is still valid, there are, however, Islamically valid reasons for acknowledging and prohibiting marital rape. They proceed by showing how women have both the freedom and the legal authority to refuse sexual intercourse and expect mutual consent and respect. Therefore, despite a history of a general, one-size-fits-all approach, one can argue that, in the modern context, Islam and its Sharīʿa are both primitive and discriminatory. Hence the authors argue for a flexible and dynamic framework of *ijtihād* that is crucial in today's world as it can help Muslim jurists answer such questions relating to family life as well as other issues which Muslims need guidance on. However, in order to remain faithful to the tradition, a scholar's *ijtihād* must be Qur'an centric, with him or her primarily relying upon the Qur'an and secondarily on the reported traditions of the Prophet and Imāms. In turn, the authors are carving out a terrain for Muslims to inhabit more equal relationships than required by the state, and advocating for contexts like India where there is no marital rape statute, for Muslims to adopt one based on religious and moral rather than legalistic grounds.

The essays in this part raise several important issues for discussion. These include questions relating to Islam, fiqh, and marital relations. Firstly, in what ways does Islam inform, constitute, and define the relationship between men and women? This is an important consideration for the essays in Part II, as the contexts within which people engage each other are constituted by the parameters set by fiqh. Secondly, given that marriage law is constituted and implemented in a variety of ways, what is the relationship between Islam and the praxis of fiqh in these contexts? Thirdly, what are the implications of this approach to fiqh on jurisprudence? These questions form the framework that shapes these specific case studies and pushes the authors to argue for a flexible approach to fiqh in order to make it compatible with issues facing Muslims today. The essays allow for the jurist-philosophers to pre-empt religious questions based on their observations of how the lived experience of Muslims is developing. In turn, they also propose that the jurist should not look to set boundaries based on state law or in relation to what may guide such law (Muslim-majority/-minority contexts may differ here), but rather strive for the optimal conditions for the believers and ideal moral values to adopt, and thus they should look at using *ijtihād* to push the boundaries beyond what state law considers a minimum.

INTRODUCTION TO PART II

If Part I illuminates legal debates about marriage and relationships in the contemporary world, Part II investigates practices of and discourses about marriage. The central question taken up by these latter essays concerns how Muslims in a variety of national contexts live and understand marriage. All of the contributions investigate marital practices in Muslim-minority states, implicitly highlighting the particular struggles and opportunities to forge religiously acceptable partnerships in places where Islamic law and state law are distinct and in which Islamic communities are understood to follow norms and engage in practices that differentiate them from members of the majority. The essays provide ways to rethink minority conditions and they question whether religious minoritarianism is always the most accurate analytical approach. The practices these essays investigate neither wholly conform to classical conceptions and practices nor absolutely deviate from them; they thereby demonstrate how people negotiate tradition to forge lives and relationships that are compatible at once with it and with the realities and exigencies of contemporary conjunctures.

Fouzia Azzouz investigates the conundrum of unregistered marriages in Britain. Based on sociological research among lay Muslims and scholars, she shows the complex reasons for low rates of marriage registration. Her essay has a number of significant findings. First, she suggests that low rates of registration are not a specifically Muslim phenomenon but that many young English couples do not choose to register their marriages; this finding raises an important question about the extent to which refusal to register is a Muslim or even a religious matter and to what extent other factors unite Muslims and non-Muslims in resistance to state registration. Secondly, Azzouz shows that because of the manifold reasons for refusing to register marriages – ranging from inconvenience of the process to objections to state oversight – a single legislative solution is unlikely to be adequate for everyone. Overall, her work provides valuable insight into the varieties of Muslim marriage while also implying that from the perspective of registration, 'Muslim' marriage may not be the most useful analytic lens. One consequence of this is to urge scholars and marrying couples alike to focus less on religious difference and more on other axes in order to understand resistance to marriage registration in Britain.

Seyed Mohammad Ghari Seyed Fatemi, Munzela Raza, Ahmad Kaouri, and Abbas Ramji have contributed a uniquely multi-disciplinary investigation into the norm and value of *sakīna* (tranquility) in marital life. They seamlessly bring together readings of Qur'anic sources, exegetical works, and findings from clinical psychology to argue that not only is *sakīna* a key good in marriage from an Islamic perspective (something both Muslim scholars and couples alike need to recognise), it is also necessary for marriage to provide a shelter rather than to represent danger for women; rendering *sakīna* a primary rather than secondary consideration of marital life.

Laurens de Rooij introduces another dimension to the discussion of marriage with his sociological study of online dating among Muslim youth in England. De Rooij's research indicates that Muslim dating apps enable young Muslims greater autonomy over their choice of potential marriage partners by connecting them with like-minded individuals for whom Islam and religious commitment are important characteristics in a spouse. The author shows that the dating apps alter the kinds of characteristics young Muslims seek in a future spouse, moving away from family connections and, in the case of immigrant families, national origin, and towards sect, level of practice, and broader lifestyle. The essay provides insight into how Muslim youth seek greater autonomy in the choice of marriage partner while remaining dedicated to forms of meeting and dating that conform to their understandings of religiously acceptable interaction.

Katherine Lemons draws on ethnographic and archival research in another Muslim-minority setting, India, to examine fiqh as a site of encounter between lay Muslims' marital struggles and qazis' practices of adjudication, which rely on Islamic legal sources. She argues that the Islamic courtroom (*dār ul-qażā*) is a good place to observe processes of making and transforming fiqh because it is here that qazis must bring together their knowledge of Islamic law, their accounts of social norms, and their understanding of each unique case presented to them in order to help litigants find a way forwards that is both livable and in conformity with fiqh. In this way, Lemons' essay brings the volume full circle, connecting through her anthropological research the concerns elaborated in Part I by fiqh scholars and those elaborated in Part II by social scientists. If the volume is itself an illustration of the encounter that is fiqh, Lemons' study is an anthropological account of this encounter as a practice in the courtroom rather than in the domain of scholarship.

Together, the contributions to this volume demonstrate the breadth and complexity of questions pertaining to marriage and relationships with which lay Muslims and scholars alike grapple. In so doing, they offer a rich and deep account of a living tradition, one that is dynamic and pushed to change by scholars and practitioners. Finally, they provide insight into the distinct but mutually entangled domains of fiqh scholarship, adjudication, and everyday life, suggesting that these domains together, in the struggles and debates between and within them, constitute the dynamism of tradition.

The papers collected here are edited and expanded versions of presentations given at the Tenth Annual AMI Contemporary Fiqhī Issues Workshop held on 21–22 July 2022. We thank the contributors to the volume, the Al-Mahdi Institute, and the organisers of the workshop for making possible the intellectual discussion presented here.

BIBLIOGRAPHY

Asad, Talal. 'The Idea of an Anthropology of Islam'. *Qui Parle* 17, no. 2 (2009): 1–30.

Foucault, Michel. *The Archaeology of Knowledge*. Translated by A. M. Sheridan Smith. 2nd ed. London: Routledge, 2002.

Hallaq, Wael B. *Sharīʿa: Theory, Practice, Transformations*. Cambridge: Cambridge University Press, 2009.

PART I

Issues in Contemporary Marriage Fiqh

ARIF ABDUL HUSSAIN[1]

The Existential Perspective on 'God's Bestowal of *Faḍl* upon Men' and Its Implications on *Qiwāma*

With the migration of the Prophet to Medina and the increase in the number of his followers, it became necessary to introduce societal regulations and devotional practices to facilitate the moral, spiritual, and rational growth of individuals and the community of believers. The societal regulations were initially provided by verses of the Qur'an and the accompanying oral Prophetic exegeses.[2] These regulations were revealed in response to questions asked to the Prophet or contextual circumstances that required instructions. An example of such a regulation was the bond of brotherhood between non-consanguine Meccan migrants and their Medinan hosts, which allowed for mutual inheritance between them.[3] The majority of these regulations were not original but modifications of existing norms and practices formulated with a sense of fairness and the goal of limiting abuse as much as possible within the given context.[4]

These regulations appealed to the people of that time as being more egalitarian and pragmatic, which are important markers of regulations in any time and place. Regulations and stipulations governing gender-specific societal roles, spousal relations, rights, and responsibilities were supplied during the last ten years of the Prophet's life

---

1 The author is grateful to Riaz Walji for kindly editing and referencing the paper, and colleagues at Al-Mahdi Institute for organising the workshop in which an early draft of this paper was presented and for their efforts in publishing it.

2 For reference to the Qur'an as the initial and main source of societal regulations, see Noel J. Coulson, *A History of Islamic Law* (Edinburgh: Edinburgh University Press, 2004), 10–13; Knut S. Vikør, *Between God and the Sultan: A History of Islamic Law* (London: Hurst and Company, 2005), 20; Joseph Schact, *An Introduction to Islamic Law* (Oxford: Oxford University Press, 1982), 10–14. For reference to the Prophet's exegeses of the Qur'an as a source of normativity, see Q.16:44; and M. Mustafa Al-Azami, *On Schacht's Origins of Muhammadan Jurisprudence* (Cambridge: Islamic Texts Society, 1996), 13.

3 For reference to the creation of the bond of brotherhood, see Martin Lings, *Muhammad: His Life Based on the Earliest Sources* (Cambridge: Islamic Texts Society, 2019), 128; Fazlur Rahman, *Islam* (Chicago: The University of Chicago Press, 2002), 19. For reference to the abrogation of the norm of mutual inheritance, see Q. 8:75; and Faḍl b. Ḥasan al-Ṭabarsī, *Majma' al-bayān fī tafsīr al-Qur'ān* (Beirut: Mu'assasat al-A'lamī li-l-Maṭbū'āt, 1995), 4:500.

4 See Coulson, *A History of Islamic Law*, 13–14; and Schact, *An Introduction to Islamic Law*, 10–14.

in Medina. While not exhaustive and not covering every eventuality, their phraseology yields fundamental principles for understanding these roles and responsibilities, and the associated issues in different contexts.

Sharīʿa regulations and stipulations that enshrine societal gender roles and spousal relations, rights, and responsibilities, as espoused by the Qur'an and the Prophet, were not perceived to be unfair, prejudicial, or discriminatory by the primary audience. They remained optimal in facilitating the functioning and growth of Muslim communities for the duration of the pre-modern era and may still be effective in similar existential contexts in the contemporary world. However, these same regulations and stipulations may be considered inegalitarian and regressive in contemporary contexts where notions of inalienable human rights and human dignity are part of the mindset and worldview of their communities.[5] This has led to various discourses on the conflict between Sharīʿa regulations and stipulations of the revelatory era and human rights and the notion of human dignity.

The basis of this conflict is the assumption that all Sharīʿa regulations and stipulations of the revelatory era are the intended regulations and stipulations of God for all times and places, which is premised on a fixed and static ontology. However, this conflict dissipates with the understanding of an ontology of flux and dynamism, for all such regulations and stipulations are recognised as 'Sharīʿa' regulations that were formulated in and for the contexts of the revelatory era and other similar contexts only.[6]

This paper embarks upon a comprehensive exploration of the multifaceted notions pertaining to *qiwāma* (governorship), *daraja* (degree), and *infāq* (provision) in conjunction with *faḍl* (existential merit). By means of the following analysis, I endeavour to elucidate that *faḍl* is far from being an immutable or universal phenomenon. Instead,

5 See Vikør, *Between God and the Sultan*, 20–21. For reference to the Qur'an and the Prophet modifying pre-Islamic norms and praxis, see Coulson, *A History of Islamic Law*, 14–18.

6 For reference to the verses of the Qur'an having general or universal principles, see Abdullah Saeed, *Interpreting the Qur'ān: Towards a Contemporary Approach* (Abingdon: Routledge, 2006), 24, 127–28. The following quote is pertinent: 'It is often argued that the *shariʿa* was not given in a finished form. The Prophet's method was a flexible dynamic adaptation of general principles to specific situations as they arose ... after the death of the Prophet Muhammad in 632 AD, his first four successors carried on the tradition of flexibility. They believed that laws had to be understood and interpreted to remain true to their purpose. During their time, laws were continually developed, and the successors to their secular authority were fully empowered to preside over and guide that process. Under Umayyad rule, the law became more rigid as it was employed by the rulers as a theoretical justification for state control. It was then that the religious scholars collected and organised the various rulings of the Prophet and his first successors and created a legal system – from which all four Sunnī schools of law emerged and the main collections of the Prophet's sayings, *hadith*, were compiled." Munira Fakhro, 'Gulf Women and Islamic Law', in *Feminism and Islam: Legal and Literary Perspectives*, ed. Mai Yamani (Berkshire: Ithaca Press, 1997), 251.

it undergoes modifications commensurate with the changing existential aptitudes of both individuals and groups. My contention is that these fluctuations in *faḍl* bear significant ramifications for gender roles within societies. For instance, designating men as governors based solely on their presumed superiority resulting from God's bestowal of *faḍl* becomes problematic when one takes into account the mutability intrinsic to such concepts. As women advance in developing their own skills and abilities at a pace equivalent – if not exceeding – those traditionally assigned only to men under *qiwāma* principles, societal expectations regarding gender must change. In summary, this paper demonstrates the following:

1. The Sharīʿa regulations and stipulations of the revelatory era governing societal gender roles and spousal relations, rights, and responsibilities were formulated in accordance with God's bestowal of existential merit upon men and women of the revelatory era.
2. The notion of God's bestowal of existential merit signifies the existential aptitudes He bestows upon individuals, collectivities, or genders in any given time and place.
3. The existential aptitudes of individuals, collectivities, or genders are subject to change with the growth of humankind.
4. Therefore, the Sharīʿa regulations and stipulations of the revelatory era governing said roles and responsibilities, which were formulated in accordance with the existential aptitudes of the people of that era, are neither universal nor eternal.
5. These roles and responsibilities enshrined in the Sharīʿa regulations and stipulations of the revelatory era are mutable and ought to be subjected to periodic appraisals.

By analysing the relevant verses of the Qur'an, it becomes clear that the notion of *qiwāma* (governorship) was a status (*ʿunwān/iʿtibār sharʿī*) assigned to men (a) to acknowledge the legitimacy of societal positions that were male specific in that context, and (b) to designate men as responsible for 'providing for the spouse' (*infāq*), whereby they became eligible for certain rights exclusively within the familial domain. Thus, if the notion of 'God's bestowal of *faḍl* (existential merit)' upon one individual, collectivity, or gender at the exclusion of others is subject to change in accordance with the growth of the existential aptitudes of these groups, it follows that assigning 'the status of *qiwāma*' and consigning the responsibility of 'providing for the spouse and dependants (*infāq*)' to men exclusively is mutable and subject to change. The implications of this are that societal gender roles and spousal relations, rights, and responsibilities are also mutable and subject to change.

In traditional Islamic scholarship, the discourse on marriage and its related notions of (a) 'men being a degree (*daraja*) above women', (b) 'God's bestowal of *faḍl* (existential merit) upon men', (c) 'the assignment of the status of *qiwāma* (governorship) to men', and (d) 'men's provision of the spouse (*infāq*)' is not one in which Muslim scholars differ sectarianly. Accordingly, there is no reason to differentiate the analyses of such issues in terms of whether scholars are Sunnī or Shīʿī. Thus, this paper presents the views of Muslim scholars on marriage and its related notions without distinguishing Shīʿī scholars from Sunnī and vice versa.

THE TRADITIONAL UNDERSTANDING

As a Muslim theologian or jurist, it is important to understand Q. 4:34 and 2:228, which use the concepts of 'men being a degree (*daraja*) above women', 'God's bestowal of *faḍl* (existential merit) upon men', 'the assignment of the status of *qiwāma* (governorship) to men', and 'men's *infāq* (provision) of the spouse' in the context of spousal relations, rights, and responsibilities. These concepts are fundamental to the understanding of spousal relations and gender roles in traditional Islamic jurisprudence (*fiqh*).

While there is a time gap between the revelations of these verses, they are examined together because Q. 2:228 uses the concept of 'men being a degree (*daraja*) above women' in the sense of 'the assignment of the status of *qiwāma* to men', and Q. 4:34 employs this concept along with the others more clearly. The exact relationship between the concepts of 'the assignment of the status of *qiwāma* (governorship) to men', 'God's bestowal of *faḍl* (existential merit) upon men', and 'men's *infāq* (provision) of the spouse' is unclear, and traditional scholarship offers different views on the nature of this connection.[7]

Q. 4:34 uses a verbal derivative of the adjectival noun *qiwāma* and the verbal nouns *faḍl* and *infāq* as follows:

> Men are the governors (*qawwāmūna*) of women because of God granting merit (*faḍḍala*) to some over others and because of what they expend (*anfaqū*) of their wealth. Righteous women are devotedly obedient and protective of the unseen because of what God has entrusted them with. But those [of your women that] you sense ill-conduct from, counsel them, and [if they persist] do not share their beds, and [if they persist still] beat/discipline them.

The immediate cause of the revelation of this verse is that a man had beaten his wife on account of her disobedience. There are slight variations in the exegetical works regarding the names of the people concerned. According to some narrations,

7 This can be gleaned from the discussions in the chapters on marriage in works of 'discursive jurisprudence' (*fiqh istidlālī*). See also Amina Wadud, *Qur'an and Woman: Rereading the Sacred Text from a Woman's Perspective* (New York: Oxford University Press, 1999), 68–74; Asma Barlas, *"Believing Women" in Islam: Unreading Patriarchal Interpretations of the Qur'an* (Austin: University of Texas Press, 2004), 184–87; Najila Hamadeh, 'Islamic Family Legislation: The Authoritarian Discourse of Silence', in Yamani, *Feminism and Islam*, 342–43.

the woman is said to have been Ḥabība bt. Zayd b. Kharija b. Abī Zuhayr, the wife of Saʿd b. Rabīʿ. Her father, Zayd, took her to the Prophet and lodged a complaint against Saʿd. The Prophet said that Ḥabība ought to invoke her right of retaliation (*qiṣāṣ*) against Saʿd. As they were leaving, the Prophet called them back and explained that the archangel Gabriel had just revealed the aforementioned verse (Q. 4:34). After citing the verse, he stated, 'We intended an affair but God intended otherwise.'[8] Therefore, in light of this context (which is its immediate cause), this verse instructs that men have the right to discipline their wives without any consequence on account of their being 'assigned the status of *qiwāma* (governorship)'.

Although the notions of 'the assignment of the status of *qiwāma* (governorship) to men', 'God's bestowal of *faḍl* (existential merit) upon men', and 'men's *infāq* (provision) of the spouse' in this verse appear to be interconnected, the exact relationship between them is unclear. Hence, traditional scholarship offers several views on the nature of the connection between them. For instance, (a) al-Ṭabarī states that 'men's *infāq* of the spouse' is due to 'God's bestowal of *faḍl* upon men' and not women;[9] (b) al-Ṭanṭāwī maintains that 'men's *infāq* of the spouse', defending them, governing their affairs, and disciplining them, is due to 'the assignment of the status of *qiwāma* to men';[10] (c) al-Ṭabāṭabā'ī states that 'the assignment of the status of *qiwāma* to men' is due to 'God's bestowal of *faḍl* upon men' and not women, but omits to mention the relationship of the notion of 'men's *infāq* of the spouse' to the notions of 'assigning the

8 For reference to the narrations, see the exegeses of al-Ṭabarsī, *Majmaʿ al-bayān*, 3:79; Muḥammad Sayyid al-Ṭanṭāwī, *al-Tafsīr al-wasīṭ li-l-Qur'ān al-karīm* (Cairo: Maṭbaʿat al-Saʿāda, 1983), 3:176; Ismāʿīl Ibn Kathīr, *Tafsīr al-Qur'ān al-ʿaẓīm* (Beirut: Dār wa-Maktabat al-Hilāl, 1990), 2:70. It is worth noting that the Prophet's immediate response prior to the revelation of Q. 4:34 discloses that he regarded Saʿd's physical castigation of his wife, Ḥabība, to be criminal. Hence, he advised her to retaliate or seek assistance in retaliating. Yet, the Qur'an's intervention is indicative of its awareness that instituting such a regulation – albeit fair, just, and egalitarian – would have been premature in and for that context, for it risked mass opposition, ridicule, and ultimately rejection of its essential teachings. See Asma Lamrabet, *Women in the Qur'an: An Emancipatory Reading*, trans. Myriam Francois-Cerrah (Markfield: Square View, 2019), 153–55. In terms of the existential notions of 'form' and 'essence', the Prophet's response is more akin to the 'essence' of the regulation, whereas the Qur'an's intervention is a 'form', that is, a contextual rendering of the 'essence'. For more information on the notions of 'form' and 'essence' in the domains of regulations (*aḥkām*) and jurisprudence (*fiqh*), see Arif Abdul Hussain, 'The Existential Perspective on the Meaning and Implication of the Impure Substances within Shīʿī Jurisprudential Discourse', in *The Regulations of Purity and Impurity in Islam: Proceedings of the 8th AMI Contemporary Fiqhī Issues Workshop, 2–3 July, 2020*, ed. Hashim Bata (Birmingham: AMI Press, 2022), 81–84.

9 See Muḥammad b. Jarīr al-Ṭabarī, *Tafsīr al-Ṭabarī min kitābihi Jāmiʿ al-bayān ʿan ta'wīl āy al-Qur'ān* (Beirut: Mu'assasat al-Risāla, 1994), 2:451.

10 See al-Ṭanṭāwī, *al-Tafsīr al-wasīṭ*, 3:176–78.

status of *qiwāma* to men' and 'God's bestowal of *faḍl* upon men';[11] (d) al-Sa'dī infers that 'the assignment of the status of *qiwāma* to men' is due to 'men's *infāq* of the spouse' and protection, which in turn is due to 'God's bestowal of *faḍl* upon men' and not women;[12] and finally, (e) al-Khū'ī asserts that 'the assignment of the status of *qiwāma* to men' is due to 'God's bestowal of *faḍl* upon men' and 'men's *infāq* of the spouse'.[13]

Traditional scholarship has different ideas about the relationship between 'the assignment of the status of *qiwāma* to men', 'God's bestowal of *faḍl* upon men', and 'men's *infāq* of the spouse'. There are five main views:

1. Men's *infāq* of the spouse depends only on God's bestowal of *faḍl* upon men.
2. Men's *infāq* of the spouse depends only on the assignment of the status of *qiwāma* to men.
3. The assignment of the status of *qiwāma* to men depends only on God's bestowal of *faḍl* upon them.
4. The assignment of the status of *qiwāma* to men depends on men's *infāq* of the spouse, which in turn depends only on God's bestowal of *faḍl* upon them.
5. The assignment of the status of *qiwāma* to men depends on both God's bestowal of *faḍl* upon men and men's *infāq* of the spouse.

The fifth reading (*ẓāhir al-kalām*) of the verse, which is al-Khū'ī's view, is in my opinion the most clear and obvious interpretation of the verse.

THE NOTION OF 'THE ASSIGNMENT OF THE STATUS OF *QIWĀMA* TO MEN'

The superlative verbal adjective *qawwām* (pl. *qawwāmūna*) is derived from the Arabic root letters *qāf-wāw-mīm*. It has several meanings among which are 'manager', 'keeper', 'custodian', and 'guardian'.[14] This is the dictionary meaning of the word *qawwām* agreed upon by both Shī'ī and Sunnī exegetes. For instance, Ibn Kathīr states, 'the qualification *qawwāmūna* implies that a man is her chief, has authority over her, and disciplines her

11 See Muḥammad Ḥusayn al-Ṭabāṭabā'ī, *al-Mīzān fī tafsīr al-Qur'ān* (Qom: Manshūrāt Jamā'at al-Mudarrisīn fī al-Ḥawza al-'Ilmiyya fī Qum, n.d.), 4:343. For a critique of this view, see note 51.

12 See 'Abd al-Raḥmān al-Sa'dī, *Taysīr al-Karīm al-Raḥmān fī tafsīr al-Kalām al-Mannān* (Riyadh: Dār al-Salām li-l-Nashr wa-l-Tawzī', 2002), 190.

13 See Abū al-Qāsim al-Khū'ī, [response to the *fatwā* question] 'What is meant by governorship (*qiwāma*) in the Almighty's words "Men are the governors (*qawwāmūna*) of women", and why is it that men are the governors of women and not vice versa, knowing that sometimes, the woman is the one responsible for the affairs of the house?' [in Arabic], Imam Al-Khoei Benevolent Foundation, www.al-khoei.us/fatawa2/?id=727.

14 See Hans Wehr, *Arabic-English Dictionary*, ed. J. Milton Cowan (Urbana: Spoken Language Services, 1994), 936.

when she strays'; and al-Qurṭubī adds that it entails defending the woman and providing for her (*infāq*).[15] In light of this, the English word 'governorship' – which in Arabic is *qiwāma* – best encapsulates these nuances and variations of the term *qawwām*.[16]

The imperative in Q. 4:34 instructing men to discipline their respective women in a measured manner on account of their ill-conduct (i.e. to reprimand initially, followed by abstention from intimacy, and finally to castigate physically) is based on the notion and understanding that men are the 'governors' (*qawwāmūna*) of women. Thus, the verse affords men the right to discipline their respective women on account of their being 'governors'. It is not a command that has to be carried out; rather, it is akin to the unilateral right to divorce at will accorded to men vis-à-vis their wives in the traditional understanding of the nature of the marriage contract.[17] It should be noted that there is no record of the Imāms castigating their respective spouses physically when the latter had engaged in ill-conduct, but rather they divorced them.[18] That being said, a man can choose to continue to be married to a spouse who has performed such behaviour and in so doing he retains the right to castigate her physically.

Being afforded the right to discipline their spouses in the verse implies that *qiwāma* (governorship) is a status assigned to men deliberately, that is, it is not an arbitrary designation. Furthermore, men are assigned this status because of their roles as protectors and providers of their spouses and other dependants within the existential context of the revelatory era.

Q. 2:228 is situated among verses enunciating the rules of divorce and reconciliation. It states:

> Divorced women must wait for three menstrual cycles [before marrying again]. If they believe in God and the Day of Judgement, it is not lawful for them to hide what God has created in their wombs. During their waiting period, their husbands have the right to resume marital relations if they want reconciliation, and they [i.e. women] have similar [rights] as those [that men have] upon them, in accordance with ethical practice (*bi-l-maʿruf*); but men are a degree (*daraja*) above them [i.e. women, vis-à-vis spousal rights and responsibilities]. God is Mighty and Wise.[19]

15 See Ibn Kathīr, *Tafsīr al-Qur'ān al-ʿaẓīm*, 2:70–71; Muḥammad b. Aḥmad al-Qurṭubī, *al-Jāmiʿ li-aḥkām al-Qur'ān* (Beirut: Mu'assasat al-Risāla, 2006), 6:278–81.

16 See Wehr, *Arabic-English Dictionary*, 936.

17 This is assuming the marriage contract is the standard one, wherein no proviso has been stipulated curtailing men's unilateral right to divorce at will. For rules on additional stipulations in the marriage contract, see ʿAlī Ḥusaynī al-Sīstānī, *Minhāj al-ṣāliḥīn* (Beirut: Dār al-Mu'arrikh al-ʿArabī, 2013), 3:101–2.

18 For instance, see narration no. 1 regarding the divorce of the fifth Imām in the following reference: Muḥammad b. Yaʿqūb al-Kulaynī, *Furūʿ al-Kāfī* (Beirut: Manshūrāt al-Fajr, 2007), 6:36.

19 Note that the phrase *bi-l-maʿrūf* in this verse means 'in accordance with ethical practice'; see

The verse alludes to the rights and responsibilities of women prior to concluding that 'men are a degree (*daraja*) above them'. The exact meaning of the notion of 'men being a degree above women' in the context of this verse is unclear: are men 'a degree above' women in relation to rights and responsibilities only, or are they 'a degree above' them existentially, that is, due to something pertaining to them qua men, whereby they have greater rights and responsibilities? The fact that the pronoun 'them' in the phrase 'a degree above them' refers to 'women' and not 'rights and responsibilities', in spite of the pronoun's position in the verse being posterior to the clause mentioning female rights and responsibilities, suggests that it refers to an existential state by virtue of which men have greater rights and responsibilities. It can be argued that this meaning is corroborated by a previous clause in the verse asserting that men have the *unilateral* right to resume marital relations with their divorced wives during the waiting period of three menstrual cycles (thereby rescinding the divorce).[20]

Exegetical commentaries on the significance of the notion of 'men being a degree (*daraja*) above women' can be categorised as follows:[21]

1. It signifies the superiority of men vis-à-vis elevation and leadership, and having more in terms of 'increase' (*ziyāda*) and rights; examples of 'increase' are the share of inheritance and blood money, and an example of 'more' rights is the unilateral right to divorce.
2. It signifies that men are superior existentially, that is, physically, morally, and rationally.
3. It signifies the superiority of men by virtue of which men have greater and more responsibilities than women, such as defending women and the obligations of participating in *jihād* (warfare), paying the *mahr* (dower), and 'providing for the spouse and dependants (*infāq*)'.

---

al-Ṭabāṭabā'ī, *al-Mīzān*, 2:232. For a detailed discussion on this meaning of the term and its implications, see A. Kevin Reinhart, 'What We Know about *Ma'rūf*', *Journal of Islamic Ethics* 1, no. 1–2 (2017): 51–82.

20 Note that the man has the unilateral right to resume marital relations only if the divorce is revocable. Also, several exegeses of Q. 2:228 quote the following statement attributed to the Prophet to corroborate the notion of 'men being a degree (*daraja*) above women': 'Had prostrating to human beings been permissible, then wives would have been commanded to prostrate before their husbands.' For instance, see al-Qurṭubī, *al-Jāmi' li-aḥkām*, 4:54. For reference to the narration, see Abū Dāwūd Sulaymān al-Sijistānī, *English Translation of Sunan Abī Dāwūd*, trans. Yasir Qadhi (Riyadh: Maktabat Dār al-Salām, 2008), 549–50.

21 For instance, see al-Ṭabarī, *Tafsīr al-Ṭabarī*, 2:32–33; Muḥammad b. Ḥasan al-Ṭūsī, *al-Tibyān fī tafsīr al-Qur'ān* (Qom: Mu'assasat al-Nashr al-Islāmī, 1996), 2:241; al-Ṭabarsī, *Majma' al-bayān*, 2:100–101; Ibn Kathīr, *Tafsīr al-Qur'ān al-'aẓīm*, 1:394; al-Qurṭubī, *al-Jāmi' li-aḥkām*, 4:53–54; al-Ṭabāṭabā'ī, *al-Mīzān*, 2:232–33, 260–77; al-Ṭanṭāwī, *al-Tafsīr al-wasīṭ*, 1:667–69; al-Sa'dī, *Taysīr al-Karīm al-Raḥmān*, 102. Note that the deliberations of exegetes fall into one or more of the categories; often they list all three. For more details of these views on the notion of 'men being a degree (*daraja*) above women', see Ragâ El-Nimr, 'Women in Islamic Law', in Yamani, *Feminism and Islam*, 93–94.

Therefore, the notion of 'men being a degree (*daraja*) above women' in the context of this verse is either (a) equivalent in meaning to the notion of 'God's bestowal of *faḍl* (existential merit) upon men' in Q. 4:34, that is, it refers to an existential feature or state in men lacking in women, or (b) it signifies that 'men' have been assigned as 'being a degree (*daraja*) above women' with respect to rights and responsibilities, and hence is akin to the assignment of a status.

According to al-Ṭabāṭabā'ī, the notion of 'men being a degree (*daraja*) above women' is expressed in the context of rights and responsibilities; it signifies that men have a Sharī'a-assigned status that their spouses do not.[22] For al-Ṭabāṭabā'ī, this assignment is due to 'God's bestowal of *faḍl* (existential merit) upon men' and not women.[23] To reiterate, men are assigned superior societal roles and greater spousal rights and responsibilities because 'men' have been assigned as 'being a degree above women', which in turn is due to 'God's bestowal of *faḍl* upon them'. Al-Ṭanṭāwī concurs with this view in his *al-Tafsīr al-wasīṭ*; he states it is due to the assignment of 'men being a degree above women' that men are given greater and more rights and responsibilities.[24] Undoubtedly, this view is a legitimate and compelling interpretation. This is because the notion of 'men being a degree above women' in this verse can be read as an assignment of a status granting greater rights and responsibilities, especially in light of the context of the clause prior to it, which is the reciprocity of rights and responsibilities between men and women. In view of this, then, the notion of 'men being a degree above women' is not equivalent to the notion of 'God's bestowal of existential merit (*faḍl*) upon men' and not women.

Neither al-Ṭabāṭabā'ī nor al-Ṭanṭāwī mentions the correspondence between the notions of 'the assignment of the status of *qiwāma* (governorship) to men' and 'men being a degree (*daraja*) above women' in Q. 4:34 and 2:228, respectively.[25] Nevertheless, both are akin to one another. This is because neither notion denotes any single right or responsibility, or a specific set of rights or responsibilities; rather, each signifies the assignment of a status to men on account of 'God's bestowal of *faḍl* upon men' whereupon they are afforded additional rights and responsibilities. Therefore, the notion of 'men being a degree (*daraja*) above women' in Q. 2:228 assigns 'men' the status of 'being a degree above women' in relation to rights and responsibilities.[26]

22 See al-Ṭabāṭabā'ī, *al-Mīzān*, 2:232, 268–77.

23 Ibid., 268–77, 4:343. Note that al-Ṭabāṭabā'ī mentions the word *fiṭra* (existential nature) instead of *faḍl* (existential merit) in his exegesis of Q. 2:228, but it amounts to the same, for the existential nature of things is bestowed by God.

24 See al-Ṭanṭāwī, *al-Tafsīr al-wasīṭ*, 1:667–69.

25 Refer to the references in the previous three notes.

26 Note that equating the notion of 'men being a degree (*daraja*) above women' to the notion of 'God's bestowal of *faḍl* (existential merit) upon men' results in the following absurdities: either

THE FUNCTIONALITY OF THE NOTION OF 'THE ASSIGNMENT OF THE STATUS OF *QIWĀMA* TO MEN'

Based on the exegetical literature of Q. 4:34 and 2:228 and the jurisprudential delineation of gender roles, there are two domains in which the notion of 'the assignment of the status of *qiwāma* (governorship) to men' is pivotal in determining gender roles:

1. Gender roles in society generally.
2. Gender roles in marriage, that is, spousal relations, rights, and responsibilities.

In the societal domain, prophethood, kingship, and leadership generally are considered male prerogatives exclusively.[27] This is because 'men are a degree (*daraja*) above women', and hence have 'increase' (*ziyāda*) and the ability to lead.[28] In jurisprudence (*fiqh*), it is argued (on the basis of Q. 4:34 and 2:228, and other textual evidences from the Qur'an and *ḥadīth* literature) that men are best suited to govern (*ḥukūma*), rule (*riyāsa*), and hold positions of leadership and authority in any given society, and hence men alone should occupy all such societal positions and offices. This includes the office of the supreme religious authority who is to be emulated and referred to (*marjaʿ*), judgeship (*qāḍī*), and the leader of prayers (*imām*).[29] Women are considered homemakers, and hence are expected to attend to household affairs.[30]

In the marital domain, men are afforded more rights and responsibilities than women (based on Q. 4:34 and 2:228, and other textual evidences from the Qur'an and *ḥadīth* literature), such as the unilateral right to coitus at will, the right to castigate

(i) that the notion of 'God's bestowal of *faḍl* upon men' signifies the assignment of a status, like the notion of 'men being a degree above women', whereby men are to be afforded greater rights and responsibilities; this would mean it is simultaneously the cause of and equivalent to the notion of 'the assignment of the status of *qiwāma* (governorship) to men', and hence it is the cause of itself; or (ii) it would prompt a more fundamental question of what confers men with the status of 'God's bestowal of *faḍl*'.

27 See Ibn Kathīr, *Tafsīr al-Qur'ān al-ʿaẓīm*, 2:70.

28 Ibid. Ibn Kathīr references the notion of 'men being a degree (*daraja*) above women' in Q. 2:228 in his exposition of Q. 4:34. See also al-Ṭabarsī, *Majmaʿ al-bayān*, 3:79.

29 See al-Khū'ī, 'What is meant by governorship (*qiwāma*)?'. For al-Khū'ī's views on societal gender roles vis-à-vis women, see his *Book of Juristic Reasoning and Emulation* [in Arabic], Shia Online Library, 226, https://tinyurl.com/2p8udx3a; and *Path of Salvation* [in Arabic], Shia Online Library, 2:370, https://tinyurl.com/yp3nyvw3. Note that a few traditional scholars have issued verdicts permitting women to assume societal and religious roles of leadership either explicitly or implicitly. For instance, see Muḥammad Ḥusayn Faḍlallāh, 'Islam's Position on Women Assuming Judgeship' [in Arabic], Bayyināt, 20 January 2021, http://arabic.bayynat.org.lb/ArticlePage.aspx?id=30543; and the opinion of Yūsuf al-Sāniʿī in which he does not mention 'maleness' as a condition for being a legist (*mujtahid*): Yūsuf al-Sāniʿī, *Miṣbāḥ al-muqallidīn* (Qom: Manshūrāt Fiqh al-Thaqalayn, n.d.), 20. For a critique of the universality of the notions in Q. 4:34, see note 51.

30 See al-Khū'ī, 'What is meant by governorship (*qiwāma*)?'.

their spouses physically on account of ill-conduct, and the right to prevent their spouses leaving the house for non-essential matters. Juxtaposed to the extra rights and responsibilities afforded to men is the right of women to be fed, clothed, and maintained in general within reason, that is, in accordance with the economic status of their husbands.[31]

THE NATURE OF 'GOD'S BESTOWAL OF *FAḌL* UPON MEN'

The word *faḍl* is the verbal noun of the verb *faḍala*. Its meanings include 'excellence', 'superiority', 'better', 'merit', and 'increase'.[32] Scholars agree that God has bestowed some additional merit upon men that he has not to women.[33] The following questions arise: What is this 'merit' (*faḍl* – intrinsic in the verb *faḍḍala* in Q. 4:34)? What does the word 'merit' refer to? Is it something that men are bestowed with arbitrarily by God, that is, has God ordained the bestowal of additional merit upon men without any existential basis? Or does the word 'merit' refer to the existential aptitudes and capacities of men that are greater than those of women? Aside from the exegetical commentary of al-Saʿdī, exegetes concur that the notion of 'God's bestowal of *faḍl* upon men' refers to an existential feature or state of men lacking in women. Based on the utility of the word *maʿrūf* in the clause of Q. 2:228 (immediately preceding the clause 'men are a degree (*daraja*) above them') – 'and they [i.e. women] have similar [rights] as those [that men have] upon them in accordance with ethical practice (*bi-l-maʿrūf*)' – al-Saʿdī asserts that the reciprocal rights of men and women are determined in accordance with the moral conventions of the time. He then explains the notion of 'men being a degree (*daraja*) above women' as denoting 'elevation', 'leadership', and 'increase' (*ziyāda*) with respect to rights and responsibilities, and cites Q. 4:34 implying that the notions of 'the assignment of the status of *qiwāma* (governorship) to men' and 'God's bestowal of existential aptitudes (*faḍl*) upon men' are defined as per convention.[34] Yet he also states that 'the assignment of the status of *qiwāma* to men' and 'God's bestowal of *faḍl* upon men' are the reasons why the offices of prophethood, judgeship, and imamate, and other positions of societal leadership and authority,

31 See al-Ṭabarsī, *Majmaʿ al-bayān*, 2:100. See also *masʾala* (issue) no. 420 in al-Sīstānī, *Minhāj al-ṣāliḥīn*, 3:125.

32 See Wehr, *Arabic-English Dictionary*, 840.

33 See al-Ṭabarī, *Tafsīr al-Ṭabarī*, 2:451; Ibn Kathīr, *Tafsīr al-Qurʾān al-ʿaẓīm*, 2:70–71; al-Ṭabāṭabāʾī, *al-Mīzān*, 4:343–44; al-Ṭabarsī, *Majmaʿ al-bayān*, 3:79; al-Ṭanṭāwī, *al-Tafsīr al-wasīṭ*, 3:176–78; al-Saʿdī, *Taysīr al-Karīm al-Raḥmān*, 190.

34 See al-Saʿdī, *Taysīr al-Karīm al-Raḥmān*, 102. Pages 2–3 explain why the term *faḍl* in the notion of 'God's bestowal of *faḍl* upon men' can be translated as 'existential aptitudes'.

are restricted to men.[35] Hence, his exegetical work is unclear as to whether confining such offices and positions to men is because of their superior existential aptitudes or the conventions of the time.[36]

As stated above, traditional scholarship generally considers the notion of 'God's bestowal of *faḍl* upon men' to be referring to the superior physical and mental capacities that men are endowed with existentially. Scholars have expressed this in their discussions on the meaning of the notion of 'men being a *daraja* (degree) above women' vis-à-vis rights and responsibilities, often citing verse of the Qur'an employing the notion of 'God's bestowal of *faḍl* upon men'. For instance, Ibn Kathīr comments that the notion of 'men being a degree above women' signifies the superiority and excellence of men over women in how they have been created both in this world and the hereafter, citing Q. 4:34 (in which the notions of 'the assignment of the status of *qiwāma* to men' and 'God's bestowal of *faḍl* upon men' are employed) to supplement his claim;[37] al-Baghawī asserts that the distinguishing feature in men rendering them 'a degree above women' is the faculty of reason (*ʿaql*), for it is deficient in the latter;[38] al-Ṭanṭāwī states that the notion of 'men being a degree above women' refers to the fact that 'ability' generally is greater in the former than the latter as evinced by Q. 4:34 (in which the notions of 'the assignment of the status of *qiwāma* to men' and 'God's bestowal of *faḍl* upon men' are employed);[39] and al-Ṭabāṭabā'ī interprets the notion of 'God's bestowal of *faḍl* upon men' directly asserting that it denotes 'extra merit' bestowed upon men at the exclusion of women by virtue of the former's nature; this 'extra merit' is the faculty of reason (which is deficient in women) and everything contingent upon it, such as 'understanding' and 'physical strength' – both of which are necessary to undertake difficult tasks; in contrast, the life of women is marked by emotions and sentiments on account of their tender disposition.[40]

In conclusion, the notion of 'God's bestowal of *faḍl* (existential merit) upon men' is analysed in traditional scholarship either directly or as part of the deliberations on

35 Ibid.

36 The question of 'the foundations of human societal conventions' is pertinent here. According to the existential framework, societal conventions are appreciations of existence albeit locally, and hence rational at the point of the formulation of the conventions. For more information, see n63 in Arif Abdul Hussain, 'The Primacy of the Freedoms of Thought and Expression within the Existential Framework: Implications of Sharīʿa Regulations, Rights and Freedom', Shaykh Arif (blog), 10 January 2023, www.shaykharif.com/blog/freedom-of-thought?categoryId=24615. See also al-Ṭabāṭabā'ī, *al-Mīzān*, 2:232, 268–77.

37 Ibn Kathīr, *Tafsīr al-Qur'ān al-ʿaẓīm*, 1:394.

38 See Ḥusayn b. Masʿūd al-Baghawī, *Tafsīr al-Baghawī: maʿālim al-tanzīl* (Riyadh: Dār Ṭayba, 1989), 1:269.

39 See al-Ṭanṭāwī, *al-Tafsīr al-wasīṭ*, 1:668–69.

40 See al-Ṭabāṭabā'ī, *al-Mīzān*, 4:343.

the notion of 'men being a degree (*daraja*) above women', and it refers to the rational, moral, and physical merit bestowed upon men and not women. The next section discusses the remit of the notion of 'God's bestowal of *faḍl* upon men' exclusively and its impact on gender rights.

THE REMIT OF 'GOD'S BESTOWAL OF *FAḌL* UPON MEN' AND IMPLICATIONS ON GENDER RIGHTS

The traditional view is that the disparity between the genders is existential, that is, it is part of the existential make-up of the man and woman intended by the Creator. Hence, the disparity is rooted in maleness and femaleness fundamentally, manifesting as the different physical and psychological constitutions of men and women.[41] One consequence of His decision is that it has allayed the possibility of gender competition with respect to societal, familial, and spousal roles, rights, and responsibilities.[42]

Traditional scholars delineate gender differences in their analyses of verse 3:36 of the Qur'an in which the mother of Lady Mary implores God thus: '"My Lord, I have given birth to her, a daughter." And Allah knew best of what she has given birth to. "And the male is unlike the female."' They include (a) physical difference, where the superior physique of the man enables him to engage in *jihād* and 'provide for the spouse and dependants (*infāq*)'; (b) procreative difference, where the body of the woman is endowed with the ability to gestate and give birth; and (c) dispositional difference, where the existential state of the woman is softness, emotionality, impulsiveness, interacting impetuously at times in a childlike manner without proper assessment of the situation, and the existential state of the man is hardness, rationality, measuredness, interacting in situations with due diligence after thinking and understanding.[43] Scholars also offer such deliberations in their interpretations of the notions of (i) 'men being a *daraja* (degree) above women'(vis-à-vis rights and responsibilities) in Q. 2:228, (ii) 'the assignment of the status of *qiwāma* (governorship) to men', and (iii) 'God's bestowal of *faḍl* (existential merit) upon men' in Q. 4:34.[44] It should be noted that al-Ṭabāṭabā'ī concurs with the traditional view of the physical, procreative, and dispositional differences between the genders; however, he considers the source of the differences to be the notion of 'God's bestowal of *faḍl* upon men' and not God's assignment of 'men' as being 'a degree (*daraja*) above women'. As stated previously,

41 See *The Container of the Interpretation of the Noble Qur'an* [in Arabic], The Call of Faith: The Site of All Muslims, 1850, https://tinyurl.com/36n2urth.

42 Ibid.

43 Ibid.

44 See the references of exegeses of Q. 2:228 and 4:34 mentioned in notes 22–24 and 34.

he asserts that the notion of 'God's bestowal of *faḍl* upon men' signifies additional merit and excellence with respect to physique, morality, and rationality.[45]

Irrespective of which notion is the metaphysical reason for these physical, procreative, and dispositional differences between the genders, both the notions of 'men being a degree (*daraja*) above women' and 'God's bestowal of *faḍl* (existential merit) upon men' are fundamental in the formulation of societal gender roles, spousal relations, rights, and responsibilities, and the differences therein, in all Muslim collectivities since the revelatory era.[46] For instance, al-Ṭabāṭabā'ī states in his commentary of the following clauses of Q. 2:228, 'and they [i.e. women] have similar [rights] as those [that men have] upon them, in accordance with ethical practice (*bi-l-ma'ruf*); but men are a degree (*daraja*) above them [i.e. women, vis-à-vis spousal rights and responsibilities]', that rights and responsibilities are not accorded to each gender equally; rather, they are conferred to each in accordance with their respective aptitudes. Hence, rights and responsibilities are afforded to each gender equitably.[47]

It should be noted that scholars such as al-Ṭanṭāwī contend that although '*faḍl* (existential merit) is bestowed upon men' with regards to physique, morality, and rationality, there can be exceptions, such as occasions or relationships in which the women concerned are rationally more astute than men.[48] This presupposes that 'God's bestowal of *faḍl* upon men' is existential, and hence subject to flux and growth. Interestingly, the contemporary thinker Muhammad Shahrur asserts that the causality between the notions in Q. 4:34 qualifies the unrestrictedness (*iṭlāq*) of the terms *al-rijāl* and *al-nisā'*, which means that 'the status of *qiwāma* (governorship)' is assigned to either men or women on a case-by-case basis effectively.[49] Thus, not only was the notion of 'God's bestowal of *faḍl* upon men' not universal, but 'God's bestowal of *faḍl*' in itself was never an existential feature or state conferred to men qua 'men'; it was an existential feature or state conferred to men qua 'individuals', and hence to women qua 'individuals' too theoretically.

In conclusion, despite admitting to the possibility of occasions and instances in which the notion of 'God's bestowal of *faḍl* (existential merit) upon men' exclusively is contravened and hence the contrary is true (i.e. occasions and instances in which 'God has bestowed *faḍl* upon women' and not men), traditional scholarship gen-

45 See al-Ṭabāṭabā'ī, *al-Mīzān*, 2:275, 4:343.

46 See *The Container of the Interpretation of the Noble Qur'an*, 1850; and the references of exegeses of Q. 2:228 and 4:34 mentioned in notes 22–24 and 34.

47 See al-Ṭabāṭabā'ī, *al-Mīzān*, 2:274.

48 See al-Ṭanṭāwī, *al-Tafsīr al-wasīṭ*, 3:177.

49 See Muḥammad Shaḥrūr, *al-Kitāb wa-l-Qur'ān: qirā'a mu'āṣira* (Damascus: al-Ahālī li-l-Ṭibā'a, 1990), 619–21. For a very brief overview of Shahruh's academic project, see Fakhro, 'Gulf Women and Islamic Law', 253–54.

erally upholds the position that societal gender roles and spousal relations, rights, and responsibilities delineated by the Sharīʿa of the revelatory era are formulated on the basis of universally generalisable differences between men and women, and not individual aptitudes and diversity. In other words, traditional scholarship maintains that 'God's bestowal of *faḍl* upon men' is an existential state or feature of men qua 'men', resulting in differences between the genders, and hence such roles and responsibilities as delineated and assigned by the Sharīʿa are universal.[50] There are a few scholars, such as Shahrur, who do not consider 'God's bestowal of *faḍl* upon men' to be an existential state or feature of men qua 'men', but of men qua 'individuals', and hence of women qua 'individuals' too potentially. For Shahrur, then, Muslim scholarship must interpret societal gender roles and spousal relations, rights, and responsibilities for every context.

THE IMPACT OF THE UNQUALIFIED NOTIONS OF 'GOD'S BESTOWAL OF *FAḌL* UPON MEN' AND 'THE ASSIGNMENT OF THE STATUS OF *QIWĀMA* TO MEN' ON SOCIETAL GENDER ROLES

According to al-Ṭabāṭabāʾī, since Q. 4:34 employs the notion of 'God's bestowal of *faḍl* (existential merit) upon men' in an unrestricted sense, and since 'the assignment of the status of *qiwāma* (governorship) to men' is contingent upon it, then it too is unrestricted. This means that men's status of being governors (*qawwāmūna*) over women is universal. Thus, 'the assignment of the status of *qiwāma* to men', and hence its functionality, is not restricted to the familial or marital domains, but is absolute, embracing all aspects of life; it is an unrestricted, universal, and a generalisable feature of men qua 'men'.[51] Consequently, prophets and rulers have always been men.[52]

---

50 Note that a minority of scholars in traditional Islamic scholarship reject the universality of the notions in Q. 4:34. See note 51 and also the views of Ḥusayn ʿAlī al-Muntaẓirī and ʿAbd al-Hādī al-Faḍlī, 'On Women's Guardianship' [in Arabic], Islam4u, https://tinyurl.com/5e2j6vzx.

51 See al-Ṭabāṭabāʾī, *al-Mīzān*, 4:343–44. Note that Ḥusayn ʿAlī al-Muntaẓirī rejects the unrestrictedness of the notion of 'the assignment of the status of *qiwāma* (governorship) to men' in Q. 4:34. He argues that the context of the verse is the marital relationship, and hence its application is restricted to the marital domain. In view of this, he distinguishes the notion of *qiwāma* in Q. 4:34 from the notion of *qaymūma* (societal governance and administration) – the former notion being restricted to the marital domain and signifying the assignment of the responsibility of (a) attending to the welfare of women and (b) organising their affairs to men. See al-Muntaẓirī and al-Faḍlī, 'On Women's Guardianship'. For information on the implications of an unrestricted understanding of the notions in Q. 4:34, see Hamadeh, 'Islamic Family Legislation', 342–43.

52 See Ibn Kathīr, *Tafsīr al-Qurʾān al-ʿaẓīm*, 2:70; al-Ṭanṭāwī, *al-Tafsīr al-wasīṭ*, 3:177; al-Saʿdī, *Taysīr al-Karīm al-Raḥmān*, 102, 190. It should be noted that the vast majority of the prophets of God are unknown, hence the possibility that female prophetesses of God were sent to some col-

In the domain of jurisprudence (*fiqh*), al-Khū'ī states that the male half of the human species is more capable than the female both physically and rationally. Jurisprudentially, the basis for his assertion is the unrestricted (*iṭlāq*) usage of the term *qawwāmūna* (governors) in Q. 4:34. He speculates that such unrestricted usage may be the reason why women are prevented from occupying positions in the judiciary (*qaḍā'*) specifically or positions of societal authority (*wilāya*) and governance generally.[53] In his deliberations, al-Khū'ī does not cite the connection between the notions of 'the assignment of the status of *qiwāma* to men' and 'God's bestowal of *faḍl* upon men' explicitly;[54] however, traditional scholarship generally regards regulations specific to men, and norms privileging them over women, as being premised on 'the assignment of the status of *qiwāma* to men' on account of 'God's bestowal of *faḍl* upon men'. Examples include (a) obligations specific to men, such as the obligation to participate in *jihād* and 'provide for the spouse and dependants (*infāq*)', (b) the suitability of men to occupy offices of societal governance and positions of leadership only, and (c) regulations and stipulations allocating 'more' or 'increase' (*ziyāda*) to men in comparison to women, such as regulations granting men the unilateral right to divorce and stipulating greater shares of inheritance and higher blood ransom for men.[55]

With regards to spousal relations, rights, and responsibilities privileging men qua 'husbands', the unrestrictedness (*iṭlāq*) of the notion of 'the assignment of the status of *qiwāma* to men' qua 'husbands' is presupposed; however, it seems to be contingent upon the notion of 'men's *infāq* (provision) of the spouse': 'Men are the governors (*qawwāmūna*) of women because of God granting merit (*faḍḍala*) to some over others and because of what they expend (*anfaqū*) of their wealth' (Q. 4:34).

However, this prompts the question of what impels men to 'provide for their spouses (*infāq*)' if men's responsibility of '*infāq* of their spouses' is not the effect of 'the assignment of the status of *qiwāma* to men', which itself is caused by 'God's bestowal of *faḍl* upon them'.

---

lectivities cannot be ruled out. Furthermore, some of the women mentioned in the Qur'an received revelation, inspiration, and conversed with angels, hence they qualify as prophetesses depending on how the notion of 'a prophet of God' is defined. In fact, the Old Testament, or the Hebrew Bible, affirms that prophetesses of God were sent to some collectivities. See Jonathan Stökl, 'Female Prophets in the Ancient Near East', in *Prophecy and Prophets in Ancient Israel: Proceedings of the Oxford Old Testament Seminar*, ed. John Day (New York: T & T Clark, 2010), 47–61.

53 See notes 29 and 30 for references.

54 Ibid.

55 For instance, see al-Ṭabarī, *Tafsīr al-Ṭabarī*, 2:32–33; al-Baghawī, *Tafsīr al-Baghawī*; 1:269, 2:207; al-Ṭanṭāwī, *Aa-Tafsīr al-wasīṭ*, 1:668–69, 3:176–78; al-Sa'dī, *Taysīr al-Karīm al-Raḥmān*, 102, 190.

The word *infāq* is a verbal noun of the verb *anfaqa*. Its meanings include 'providing' and 'expending'.[56] These are the senses in which Q. 4:34 employs the notion. In jurisprudence (*fiqh*), the notion of *infāq* signifies 'providing maintenance to dependants', which includes the wife for she is assumed to be the man's dependant upon ratification of the marriage contract. From the jurisprudential literature, it can be extrapolated that the notion of 'the assignment of the status of *qiwāma* to men' is essential in determining the nature of the marriage contract in the Sharīʿa, and that upon ratification of the marriage contract, a man becomes responsible for 'the *infāq* (provision) of his spouse'.[57] Thus, the notion of 'men's *infāq* of the spouse' is the effect of the notion of 'the assignment of the status of *qiwāma* to men' within the marital set-up. This means it is employed in Q. 4:34 to merely justify 'the assignment of the status of *qiwāma* to men' from the viewpoint of the effect – 'men's *infāq* of the spouse'. In other words, since the verse wants to justify designating men as the governors (*qawwāmūna*) of women, it offers (a) the metaphysical reason or cause (which is 'God's bestowal of *faḍl* upon men') for the designation and (b) something that men already do for their spouses indicating that they are already playing the role that the verse formally wants to designate to them.

Thus, 'the assignment of the status of *qiwāma* to men' is a retroactive assignment, and hence 'men's *infāq* of the spouse' is neither an independent factor alongside the notion of 'God's bestowal of *faḍl* upon men', nor a cause of 'the assignment of the status of *qiwāma* to men'. Rather, it is 'God's bestowal of *faḍl* upon men' that is the cause for designating men as the governors (*qawwāmūna*) of women in the marital domain, which in turn is the reason why they 'provide for their spouses (*infāq*)' and are obligated to do so. That being said, it is appropriate to introduce here that essentially and existentially the notion of 'the *ability* to provide for dependants' is fundamental in 'the assignment of the status of *qiwāma* to men' and hence in determining the degree of rights and responsibilities afforded to each spouse. Thus, the notion of 'the *ability* to provide for dependants' must be connected to 'God's bestowal of *faḍl* upon men'.

---

56 See Wehr, *Arabic-English Dictionary*, 1158.

57 The issue of the nature of the marriage contract, that is, the definition of the marriage contract, was clearly understood in the pre-modern era. This is because spousal relations, rights, and responsibilities were premised on the view that women were subordinate to men. In the contemporary world, the division of the genders on the basis of the superiority/inferiority dichotomy has gradually dissolved. Hence, there is a need for traditional Islamic scholarship to revisit the old definition of the marriage contract, identify its assumptions, discern whether they are congruent with existential aptitudes of people today, and reformulate it if necessary.

THE EXISTENTIAL READING OF THE NOTION OF 'GOD'S BESTOWAL OF *FAḌL* UPON MEN' AND ITS IMPLICATIONS ON THE NOTION OF 'THE ASSIGNMENT OF THE STATUS OF *QIWĀMA* TO MEN'

According to the existential framework, all things are dynamic and in a state of growth as per Ṣadrā's notion of substantive motion. This dynamism means that all things are in a constant state of flux actualising their inherent potential in an evolutionary manner, for all things are imbued with the *telos* of growth. This includes the human soul – it actualises its innate rational, moral, and spiritual potentialities gradually in an evolutionary manner.[58] Hence, the purpose of the societal regulative formulations of the Sharīʿa of the revelatory era was to assist the growth of the existential aptitudes of the people of that time and place, and as such, they are merely rational, contextual, and optimal rules or interpretations formulated in light of the existential aptitudes of the people of that time and place.[59] This means the Sharīʿa regulative system of the revelatory era has a foundation and is not arbitrary. *ʿAdliyya* jurists (*uṣūliyyūn*) agree with the non-arbitrariness of Sharīʿa regulative formulations inasmuch as the relations of things to humans have inherent values that are rationally discernible.[60] However, they have failed to fully appreciate the functionality of the faculty of reason in the domain of norms and regulations. This includes its capacity to (i) assent to norms and regulations that are growth-promoting and optimal in facilitating the growth of the existential aptitudes of the individual and collectivity of a particular existential context, (ii) critique those that are not growth-promoting or suboptimal in facilitating the growth of the existential aptitudes of a given collectivity and its individuals, and (iii) reformulate them so that they are growth-promoting and optimal in facilitating the growth of the existential aptitudes of the people of a given existential context.[61]

58 See Abdul Hussain, 'The Primacy of the Freedoms of Thought and Expression', 14–16.

59 See ibid., 23–24; and Abdul Hussain, 'The Existential Perspective', 81–84. For the notion of 'Sharīʿa regulations being evolutionary', see El-Nimr, 'Women in Islamic Law', 88.

60 See Abdul Hussain, 'The Primacy of the Freedoms of Thought and Expression', 23; Arif Abdul Hussain, 'The Conflict between the Actual and Apparent Regulations – Part 1: The Theoretical Foundations of Uṣūl al-Fiqh and the Uṣūlī Resolutions', Shaykh Arif (blog), www.shaykharif.com/blog/the-conflict-between-the-actual-and-apparent-regulations?categoryId=24615, 1–4. The term *ʿadliyya* refers to the Shīʿī Imāmī school of theology and jurisprudence (*uṣūl al-fiqh*) due to the tenet of 'the justice of God' being the defining feature distinguishing it from other schools.

61 For information on the faculty of reason, its functions, and its interplay with the faculty of intuition, see Abdul Hussain, 'The Primacy of the Freedoms of Thought and Expression', 26–33; and Arif Abdul Hussain, *Islam and God-Centricity: Plurality and Mutability of Religion* (Birmingham: Sajjadiyya Press, 2022), 139–46.

Although it is accepted in the science of the principles of jurisprudence (*ʿilm uṣūl al-fiqh*) that Sharīʿa regulations are rational and the faculty of reason can formulate societal regulations in principle, its remit of operation is restricted largely to the extrapolation of supplementary regulations of text-based Sharīʿa regulations.[62] The general attitude of jurists (*uṣūliyyūn*) and legists (*fuqahāʾ*) regarding Sharīʿa regulations is one of finality and universality.[63] Occasionally, legists do challenge these regulations by appealing to the principle of justice and contextual change; but generally, it is only in extenuating circumstances that text-based Sharīʿa regulations, termed 'primary regulations' (*aḥkām awwaliyya*), can be superseded by other regulations, termed 'secondary regulations' (*aḥkām thānawiyya*).[64]

If it can be acknowledged that the role of the faculty of reason is to constantly assess existential aptitudes which are dynamic, in a constant state of growth and hence subject to change, it is easier to comprehend that Sharīʿa regulations are essentially rational, contextual, and optimal rules or interpretations formulated on the basis, and for the growth, of the existential aptitudes of the people of a particular existential context. Based on this understanding, it becomes clear that existing Sharīʿa regulations do not need to be reinterpreted at all, but rather the existential aptitudes of the people in any given context today need to be appreciated directly and then regulations that are just and growth-promoting need to be formulated accordingly. *ʿAdliyya* jurists obviously concur that Sharīʿa regulations by definition must be congruent with the principle of justice, which postulates that everything ought to be given its rightful place. However, they have not factored that both things and humans are in a constant state of flux, which means the relations between things and humans are not stable and fixed, and hence regulations formulated and issued on the basis of those relations are subject to change. In view of this, the existential understanding of justice is to give everything its rightful due in accordance with its existential aptitude – which is subject to growth – in any given time and place.[65] This means that all regulative systems, irrespective of whether they are religious or secular, are fallible in essence. Thus, regulations are to be (a) formulated and (b) constantly scrutinised, in terms of optimality and efficacy in facilitating the growth of the existential aptitudes of the people in any given time and place.

---

62 See Muḥammad Ṣanqūr ʿAlī, *al-Muʿjam al-uṣūlī* (Qom: Dār al-Mujtabā, 2001), 785, 865–68; Muḥammad Riḍā Muẓaffar, *Uṣūl al-fiqh* (Qom: Intishārāt Ismāʿīliyyāt, 2004), 2:206–10, 3:105–12.

63 The aim of the legist (*faqīh*) is to procure regulations as they are in 'the mind of God', that is, the actual regulations (*al-aḥkām al-wāqiʿiyya*); hence, they are assumed to be universal and immutable. See Abdul Hussain, 'The Conflict between the Actual and Apparent Regulations – Part 1', 1–9.

64 See Ṣanqūr ʿAlī, *al-Muʿjam al-uṣūlī*, 529–30, 531–32.

65 See Abdul Hussain, 'The Primacy of the Freedoms of Thought and Expression', 20; Abdul Hussain, *Islam and God-Centricity*, xi, 60, 120, 143–44.

The principle of justice is fundamental in the formulation of societal regulations generally, which is to give all things their rightful due in accordance with the existential aptitudes of the people of a particular time and place. This means the Sharīʿa regulations and stipulations of the revelatory era regarding societal gender roles and spousal relations, rights, and responsibilities were formulated in accordance with the principle of justice – that is, in accordance with the existential aptitudes of the people of the revelatory era – with the aim of creating a moral society conducive to the rational and spiritual growth of people. However, since Sharīʿa regulations and stipulations vis-à-vis societal gender roles and spousal relations, rights, and responsibilities are not congruent with the existential aptitudes of men and women today, they have lost their optimality in facilitating growth and hence are viewed as being unjust. Consequently, the formulation of new regulations and stipulations is necessary. Note that it is no longer sufficient in many instances to tweak existing Sharīʿa regulations and stipulations of the revelatory era apropos societal gender roles and spousal relations, rights, and responsibilities; rather, it is necessary to discern the status of existential aptitudes afresh via the faculty of reason and then to afford rights and responsibilities to members of the collectivity justly.

Therefore, the notion of 'God's bestowal of existential aptitudes (*faḍl*) to men' and not women in Q. 4:34 is not absolutely and universally true, but it denotes a relative (or contextual) and a local truth. This means it is not proclaiming an unchangeable existential feature and state of men whereby only they qualify for 'the assignment of the status of *qiwāma*', and hence only they can occupy the offices of societal governance and positions of leadership, and only they are to be afforded more rights and responsibilities in marriage – examples include judgeship, rulership, religious leadership, double share of inheritance, greater testimonial credibility, responsibility of *'infāq* (provision) of the spouse and dependants and paying the *mahr* (dower), the unilateral right to divorce at will, the unilateral right to coitus at will, and the right to castigate their wives physically.

The notion of 'God's bestowal of existential aptitudes (*faḍl*) to men' and not women is neither absolute nor universal existentially, that is, it is not true of all people, collectivities, and contexts outside of the revelatory era. In many collectivities and contexts today, it is patently inaccurate to assert that men are innately endowed with superior physique and faculties of reason, and hence are more capable of 'providing for the family (*infāq*)' and leading the collectivity than women. There is not a single field of human intellectual endeavour in which women are not on par with men. Contemporary commerce is not contingent upon hard manual labour but mental skills. Indeed, female heads of states have been as effective as men in governing their countries, if not better in some instances.

In view of these deliberations and this understanding of the notion of 'God's bestowal of existential aptitudes (*faḍl*) to men' in Q. 4:34, the following is the existential understanding of Q. 2:228: both husbands and wives have rights and responsibilities according to their respective roles in marriage; this is because the verse states that men 'are a degree (*daraja*) above' women with respect to rights and responsibilities, and assumes that the disparity in the allocation of rights and responsibilities to each is equitable and just – based on the fact that the clause 'men are a degree (*daraja*) above them (women)' is preceded immediately by the phrase 'in accordance with ethical practice' (*bi-l-maʿruf*); this 'justness' assumed *vis-à-vis* the disparity in the allocation of rights and responsibilities means that the rights and responsibilities allocated to each gender must be appropriate for each gender as per that time and place, or in other words, they are allocated to each in accordance with their existential aptitudes; and this in turn means that Sharīʿa rights and responsibilities are contingent upon existential states and not vice versa.

Similarly (that is, in light of the aforementioned deliberations and understanding of the notion of 'God's bestowal of existential aptitudes (*faḍl*) to men'), the following is the existential understanding of Q. 4:34: 'the assignment of the status of *qiwāma* (governorship) to men' is contingent upon 'God's bestowal of *faḍl* (existential merit) upon men' and has ramifications on both societal gender roles and spousal relations, rights, and responsibilities; the notion of 'God's bestowal of *faḍl* upon men' refers to the superior existential state of men in comparison to women generally in seventh-century Arabia insofar as they were rationally and physically more accomplished than the latter; as discussed above, the notion of 'God's bestowal of *faḍl* upon men' pertains to existential aptitudes, hence the verse's 'assignment of the status of *qiwāma* to men' is based on its assessment of the degree of existential merit (*faḍl*) of each gender; its assessment was accurate, pragmatic, and straightforward, and 'the assignment of the status of *qiwāma* to men' was fair and catered for the needs of its initial audience. In essence, however, the notion of 'God's bestowal of *faḍl*' can refer to either (a) individual or single existential aptitudes of individuals and/or collectivities or (b) the notion of existential aptitudes as a whole apropos individuals and/or collectivities. Thus, the notion of 'God's bestowal of *faḍl*' is relative and its bestowal differs from individual to individual and group to group as alluded to in the following clause of the verse, 'because of God granting merit (*faḍḍala*) to some over others'. The implications of this existential understanding are as follows:

1. In any given time, individuals may excel one another with respect to different aptitudes. Thus, it cannot be asserted that one gender has superior faculties of reason than the other *absolutely*; rather, individuals can excel one another in differing fields of human intellectual thought at any given point. Similarly, 'God's bestowal of *faḍl*' in terms of physique cannot be confined to just physical strength qua physical strength, but rather it needs to be understood as physical strength qua 'physical abilities required to complete the activity under question'. Hence, women work on cotton farms and rice plantations, and are accomplished in crafts, such as pottery and weaving, in countries where the opportunities to

pursue education are lacking. Often, such women are breadwinners and contribute significantly to the upkeep of the family, and in many cases, they are the main or even the sole providers for their families. In such cases, God has 'bestowed *faḍl* (existential merit)' upon them and not their menfolk.

2. As per the existential property and *telos* of growth, human beings are constantly actualising their inherent existential potential by engaging with the opportunities available to them. Thus, over time and the steady progress of humankind, the notion of 'God's bestowal of *faḍl* upon men', and hence not women, does not apply in collectivities in which both genders have equal opportunities to actualise their abilities.

CONCLUSION

The universality and immutability that is ascribed by traditional Islamic scholarship to societal gender roles and spousal relations, rights, and responsibilities espoused in the Sharīʿa regulations and stipulations of the revelatory era assumes an ontology that is fixed and static. This paper asserts that this assumption is false, and the opposite is true – 'apparent' existence is dynamic and in a constant state of flux. In view of this, the purpose of Sharīʿa regulations and stipulations is to facilitate the existential growth of the individual and collectivity. Hence, as people grow rationally, morally, and spiritually, and/or time and place change, societal regulations and stipulations that are suboptimal in facilitating such growth must be reformulated.

The initial assignment of 'men being a degree (*daraja*) above women' vis-à-vis rights and responsibilities in Q. 2:228, and the subsequent 'assignment of the status of *qiwāma* to men' in Q. 4:34, were based on an accurate appreciation of the existential aptitudes of men and women during the revelatory era generally. The menfolk of its existential contexts were more accomplished than their women generally both rationally and physically. They were more suited to the environment and culture of that time, which entailed hard labour and warfare often.[66] Over time, both individuals and collectivities have become more sophisticated. The means of earning have changed dramatically and the operationality of the rational faculties of both genders are on par with each other in most collectivities in the world. Thus, the notion of 'God's bestowal of *faḍl* (existential merit)' has to be representative of the existential aptitudes of men and women today and hence more nuanced.

66 See El-Nimr, 'Women in Islamic Law', 97; Shaikh Inayatullah, 'Pre-Islamic Arabian Thought', in *A History of Muslim Philosophy: With Short Accounts of Other Disciplines and the Modern Renaissance in the Muslim Lands*, vol. 1, ed. Mian Mohammad Sharif (Delhi: Low Price Publications, 2004), 132–34.

Today, individual men and women excel each other in a variety of ways and domains. Thus, there is no sense in generalising 'God's bestowal of *faḍl* (existential merit)' to just one gender and not the other in existential contexts in which both men and women have equal opportunities to actualise their innate potentialities. Consequently, it is also meaningless to generalise the notion of 'the assignment of the status of *qiwāma* (governorship)' to just one gender in such existential contexts due to the causality between it and the notion of 'God's bestowal of *faḍl*'. To do so would be factually inaccurate and hence inconsistent with the spirit of the verse.

From an existential perspective, therefore, each collectivity must assign rights and responsibilities to its individuals in accordance with their aptitudes and the principle of justice (which is to give everything its rightful due). In collectivities such as the UK, it is right that societal roles – for instance, prime ministership, judgeship, teaching, and principalship of educational establishments – are allocated to individuals based on merit and ability. Thus, the view of Shahrur holds true for such existential contexts and collectivities. In other words, 'the assignment of the status of *qiwāma* (governorship)' to individuals of such collectivities and existential contexts must be based on merit and ability. However, in collectivities in which there is a strict demarcation between male and female roles, such as when women are expected to raise children and be housewives, then the notion of 'the assignment of the status of *qiwāma* (governorship) to men' generally is valid, and hence men would be charged with the responsibility of '*infāq* (provision) of the spouse and dependants'. In such cases, societal gender roles and spousal relations, rights, and responsibilities will be defined and assigned in accordance with the context of such collectivities and not on the basis of individual merit and ability.[67]

Therefore, 'the status of *qiwāma*' (governorship) must be assigned to men generally with respect to societal gender roles and spousal relations, rights, and responsibilities in collectivities and existential contexts in which women have not been given the opportunity to actualise their innate potentialities; however, they are not to be assigned 'the status of *qiwāma*' in contexts in which equality between the sexes is presumed. In turn, the nature of the marriage contract must also be congruent with the different degrees of *faḍl* (existential merit) bestowed upon individuals and their collectivities. These different degrees of *faḍl* will then give rise to corresponding notions of *qiwāma* (governorship), which will be assigned to either one or both spouses. Hence, in collec-

67 This does not mean that men in such collectivities today (i.e. in those in which they are assigned the status of *qiwāma*) have absolute *qiwāma* as they did during the revelatory era; rather, they are to be assigned it only to the extent that, or in areas in which, women have not actualised their potential. Thus, men in such collectivities today may have the unilateral right to divorce on account of being responsible for *infāq*, and yet women in those same collectivities who have actualised their potential can hold societal positions, such as judgeship and religious authority.

tivities and existential contexts – such as the UK – in which *faḍl* (existential merit), and its corollary *qiwāma* (governorship), is ascertained on an individual basis, the onus of paying *mahr* (dower), the unilateral right to coitus at will, the unilateral right to divorce, and other such rights conferred upon men exclusively upon ratification of the marriage contract are meaningless. In fact, the husband's unilateral right to coitus at will is problematic even in Islamic countries, for all such countries are signatories of the Universal Declaration of Human Rights (UDHR).[68]

In conclusion, this paper demonstrates that (i) the Sharīʿa regulations and stipulations of the revelatory era governing societal gender roles and spousal relations, rights, and responsibilities were formulated in accordance with 'God's bestowal of *faḍl* (existential merit)' upon the men and women of the revelatory era; (ii) the notion of 'God's bestowal of *faḍl*' refers to the existential aptitudes he bestows upon individuals, collectivities, or genders in any given time and place; (iii) the existential aptitudes of individuals, collectivities, or genders are subject to change with the growth of humankind; (iv) thus, the Sharīʿa regulations and stipulations of the revelatory era governing societal gender roles and spousal relations, rights, and responsibilities, which were formulated in accordance with the existential aptitudes of the people of that era, are neither universal nor eternal; and (v) therefore, societal gender roles and spousal relations, rights, and responsibilities enshrined in the Sharīʿa regulations and stipulations of the revelatory era are mutable and ought to be subjected to periodic appraisals.

BIBLIOGRAPHY

Abdul Hussain, Arif. 'The Existential Perspective on the Meaning and Implication of the Impure Substances within Shīʿī Jurisprudential Discourse'. In *The Regulations of Purity and Impurity in Islam: Proceedings of the 8th AMI Contemporary Fiqhī Issues Workshop, 2–3 July, 2020*, edited by Hashim Bata, 79–110. Birmingham: AMI Press, 2022.

Abdul Hussain, Arif. *Islam and God-Centricity: Plurality and Mutability of Religion*. Birmingham: Sajjadiyya Press, 2022.

Al-Azami, M. Mustafa. *On Schacht's Origins of Muhammadan Jurisprudence*. Cambridge: Islamic Texts Society, 1996.

al-Baghawī, Ḥusayn b. Masʿūd. *Tafsīr al-Baghawī: maʿālim al-tanzīl*. Riyadh: Dār Ṭayba, 1989.

68 See Clinton Bennett, *Muslims and Modernity: An Introduction to the Issues and Debates* (London: Continuum, 2005), 63.

Barlas, Asma. *"Believing Women" in Islam: Unreading Patriarchal Interpretations of the Qur'an*. Austin: University of Texas Press, 2004.

Bennett, Clinton. *Muslims and Modernity: An Introduction to the Issues and Debates*. London: Continuum, 2005.

Coulson, Noel J. *A History of Islamic Law*. Edinburgh: Edinburgh University Press, 2004.

El-Nimr, Ragȧ. 'Women in Islamic Law'. In *Feminism and Islam: Legal and Literary Perspectives*, edited by Mai Yamani, 87–102. Berkshire: Ithaca Press, 1997.

Fakhro, Munira. 'Gulf Women and Islamic Law'. In *Feminism and Islam: Legal and Literary Perspectives*, edited by Mai Yamani, 251–62. Berkshire: Ithaca Press, 1997.

Hamadeh, Najila. 'Islamic Family Legislation: The Authoritarian Discourse of Silence'. In *Feminism and Islam: Legal and Literary Perspectives*, edited by Mai Yamani, 331–46. Berkshire: Ithaca Press, 1997.

Ibn Kathīr, Ismāʿīl. *Tafsīr al-Qurʾān al-ʿaẓīm*. Beirut: Dār wa-Maktabat al-Hilāl, 1990.

Inayatullah, Shaikh. 'Pre-Islamic Arabian Thought'. In *A History of Muslim Philosophy: With Short Accounts of Other Disciplines and the Modern Renaissance in the Muslim Lands*, vol. 1, edited by Mian Mohammad Sharif, 126–35. Delhi: Low Price Publications, 2004.

al-Kulaynī, Muḥammad b. Yaʿqūb. *Furūʿ al-Kāfī*. Beirut: Manshūrāt al-Fajr, 2007.

Lamrabet, Asma. *Women in the Qur'an: An Emancipatory Reading*. Translated by Myriam Francois-Cerrah. Markfield: Square View, 2019.

Lings, Martin. *Muhammad: His Life Based on the Earliest Sources*. Cambridge: Islamic Texts Society, 2019.

Muẓaffar, Muḥammad Riḍā. *Uṣūl al-fiqh*. Qom: Intishārāt Ismāʿīliyyāt, 2004.

al-Qurṭubī, Muḥammad b. Aḥmad. *al-Jāmiʿ li-aḥkām al-Qurʾān*. Beirut: Muʾassasat al-Risāla, 2006.

Rahman, Fazlur. *Islam*. Chicago: The University of Chicago Press, 2002.

Reinhart, A. Kevin. 'What We Know about *Maʿrūf*'. *Journal of Islamic Ethics* 1, no. 1–2 (2017): 51–82.

al-Saʿdī, ʿAbd al-Raḥmān. *Taysīr al-Karīm al-Raḥmān fī tafsīr al-Kalām al-Mannān*. Riyadh: Dār al-Salām li-l-Nashr wa-l-Tawzīʿ, 2002.

Saeed, Abdullah. *Interpreting the Qurʾān: Towards a Contemporary Approach*. Abingdon: Routledge, 2006.

al-Sāniʿī, Yūsuf. *Miṣbāḥ al-muqallidīn*. Qom: Manshūrāt Fiqh al-Thaqalayn, n.d.

Ṣanqūr ʿAlī, Muḥammad. *al-Muʿjam al-uṣūlī*. Qom: Dār al-Mujtabā, 2001.

Schact, Joseph. *An Introduction to Islamic Law*. Oxford: Oxford University Press, 1982.

Shaḥrūr, Muḥammad. *al-Kitāb wa-l-Qurʾān: qirāʾa muʿāṣira*. Damascus: al-Ahālī li-l-Ṭibāʿa, 1990.

al-Sijistānī, Abū Dāwūd Sulaymān. *English Translation of Sunan Abī Dāwūd*. Translated by Yasir Qadhi. Riyadh: Maktabat Dār al-Salām, 2008.

al-Sīstānī, ʿAlī Ḥusaynī. *Minhāj al-ṣāliḥīn*. Beirut: Dār al-Muʾarrikh al-ʿArabī, 2013.

Stökl, Jonathan. 'Female Prophets in the Ancient Near East'. In *Prophecy and Prophets in Ancient Israel: Proceedings of the Oxford Old Testament Seminar*, edited by John Day, 47–61. New York: T & T Clark, 2010.

al-Ṭabarī, Muḥammad b. Jarīr. *Tafsīr al-Ṭabarī min kitābihi Jāmiʿ al-bayān ʿan taʾwīl āy al-Qurʾān*. Beirut: Muʾassasat al-Risāla, 1994.

al-Ṭabarsī, Faḍl b. Ḥasan. *Majmaʿ al-bayān fī tafsīr al-Qurʾān*. Beirut: Muʾassasat al-Aʿlamī li-l-Maṭbūʿāt, 1995.

al-Ṭabāṭabāʾī, Muḥammad Ḥusayn. *al-Mīzān fī tafsīr al-Qurʾān*. Qom: Manshūrāt Jamāʿat al-Mudarrisīn fī al-Ḥawza al-ʿIlmiyya fī Qum, n.d.

al-Ṭanṭāwī, Muḥammad Sayyid. *al-Tafsīr al-wasīṭ li-l-Qurʾān al-karīm*. Cairo: Maṭbaʿat al-Saʿāda, 1983.

al-Ṭūsī, Muḥammad b. Ḥasan. *al-Tibyān fī tafsīr al-Qurʾān*. Qom: Muʾassasat al-Nashr al-Islāmī, 1996.

Wadud, Amina. *Qurʾan and Woman: Rereading the Sacred Text from a Woman's Perspective*. New York: Oxford University Press, 1999.

Wehr, Hans. *Arabic-English Dictionary*. Edited by J. Milton Cowan. Urbana: Spoken Language Services, 1994.

Vikør, Knut S. *Between God and the Sultan: A History of Islamic Law*. London: Hurst and Company, 2005.

The Institution of Marriage in Islam: A Case Study of the First Pillar of the Marriage Contract

'The pillar of a *sharʿī* identity (*al-māhiyya al-sharʿiyya*) is what that identity cannot exist without.'[1] Although there is disagreement about the number and identity of the pillars of marriage in Islam across different legal schools and even within schools, they and their jurists do all agree about the first pillar – that is, the verbal formula, or, the offer and acceptance (*al-ījāb wa-l-qabūl*).[2] There are a lot of details concerning the verbal offer and acceptance, such as the necessity of using the Arabic language, the verbs (and their tenses) that may and may not be used, who should utter the offer and acceptance, and the arrangement between the offer and acceptance.

If the verbal formula is a pillar of marriage in Islam, it means that a written contract alone or a contract without a verbal formula or written document (*al-nikāḥ al-muʿāṭātī*) are null and void. The man and woman in such marriage contracts are not recognised as *sharʿī* spouses (*al-zawjayn*) and the correlations of *sharʿī* marriage do not cover these types of marriages. Their sexual intercourse is forbidden and is considered to be fornication, and any children born of such marriages are therefore illegitimate (*walad al-zinā*).

Unmarried cohabitation – referred to as *musākana* in Arabic and *izdiwāj-i safīd* in Persian – is a growing trend even in Muslim-majority contexts. This is a modern alternative to marriage or a substitute for conventional marriage. None of these living arrangements have been formalised with a verbal formula; only some of them rest on a contract. This paper also considers the religious status of those relationships that are based neither on a written nor a verbal contract. Drawing on *uṣūl al-fiqh* and *fiqh*, on the one hand, and historical and critical thinking, on the other, I argue that (i) any relationship based on a contract even without written documentation or a verbal formula could be considered valid marriage, and (ii) unmarried cohabi-

1 Wahba al-Zuḥaylī, *al-Fiqh al-Islāmī wa-adillatuh* (Damascus: Dār al-Fikr, 1996), 7:36.

2 al-Ḥasan b. Yūsuf al-Ḥillī, *Irshād al-adhhān ilā aḥkām al-īmān*, ed. Fāris al-Ḥassūn (Qom: Islamic Publication Institute, 1989), 2:5; al-Ḥasan b. Yūsuf al-Ḥillī, *Qawāʿid al-aḥkām* (Qom: Islamic Publication Institute, 1998), 3:9.

tation should not be considered a valid marriage. Can we call the latter type *al-nikāḥ al-muʿāṭāṭī*? If so, what is the evidence of the invalidity of such a relationship? And is there any reliable evidence to classify the former type as fornication (*al-zinā*)?

Considering the principles of Sharīʿa, what are the pillars of marriage in Islam? Marriage has at least two dimensions: civil and religious. Civil law, including family law, prepares numerous regulations for the former. Legal marriage is the product of this dimension. This, however, is not the subject of this paper, which instead focuses on the religious dimension. By religion, I mean both Sunnī and Shīʿī Islam, though I will discuss the arguments mostly from a Shīʿī perspective – that of the majority Jaʿfarī (or Twelver) school. Although I have examined the fatwas and arguments of early Muslim jurists, the focus of the paper remains on contemporary fatwas and justifications. By marriage, I mean permanent marriage (*al-nikāḥ al-dā'im*).

This paper comprises three sections: presenting fatwas on the first pillar of marriage; examining arguments of the utterance of the verbal formula as the first pillar of a legitimate marriage; and finally revisiting the first pillar based on 'structural *ijtihād*'.

FATWAS ON THE FIRST PILLAR OF MARRIAGE

In general, there is an agreement across all schools of law that the first pillar of a valid marriage in Islam is the utterance of the verbal formula. I discuss three issues in detail in this section: Sunnī fatwas, Shīʿī fatwas, and a comparative study of fatwas on the first pillar of marriage.

SUNNĪ FATWAS

In the Ḥanafī school of law, marriage has only one pillar: offer and acceptance. It has a few necessary conditions but does not have more than one essential element. In the other Sunnī schools, marriage has four pillars: the formula (i.e. offer and acceptance), the wife, the husband, and the guardian; and the two spouses are the contractors. Based on the Ḥanafī school, the marriage contract may be effected by any verbal formula that indicates ownership of the things in general in the present tense (*tamlīk al-aʿyān fī al-ḥāl*), if the spouses intend to marry, or the witnesses recognise this intent. In the Mālikī school, the marriage contract comes into effect via a verbal formula of marriage (*tazwīj*) and ownership (*tamlīk*) and their alternatives, if the dower (*mahr*) is mentioned. And in the Shāfiʿī and Ḥanbalī schools the marriage is contracted by uttering merely two verbal formulas: *tazwīj* (wedlock) and *nikāḥ* (marriage; literally, coitus), and nothing more.

There is agreement among the Sunnī jurists that the marriage contract does not become legally binding by *muʿāṭāṭ* (action without a verbal formula). One reason could be the emphasis placed on protecting the sanctity of the private parts and preventing potential abuse. Therefore, the legitimate marriage contract is not acceptable except by an explicit or implicit (*kināya*) verbal formula in the Ḥanafī and Mālikī schools; and only by an explicit verbal formula in the Shāfiʿī and Ḥanbalī schools. There is agreement among the jurists that for a non-Arab who is not able to speak Arabic, it is permissible to utter the verbal formula of marriage in a language that the parties understand. If the non-Arab can speak Arabic, the contract is not valid except via an Arabic utterance according to the Ḥanbalīs. The other schools allow non-Arabic verbal formulas in this case.[3]

SHĪʿĪ FATWAS

Al-ʿAllāma al-Ḥillī (d. 725/1325) in his *Irshād al-adhhān* wrote that 'the pillars of marriage are two: the verbal formula and the contractors (*al-ṣīgha wa-l-mutaʿāqidayn*)'.[4] Elsewhere, in his *Qawāʿid al-aḥkām*, he mentions, 'the pillars of the marriage contract are three: verbal formula, the lack of obstacles for marriage, and the contractor, that is, the spouses or their guardians'.[5]

The most recent fatwa of the contemporary Shīʿī jurist ʿAlī al-Sīstānī (b. 1930) states: 'The verbal formula (offer and acceptance) is necessary for the marriage contract, permanently or temporally. Therefore, sole internal consent is not sufficient. It should be noted that neither the written formula nor the explicit action that demonstrates marriages (except for the mute) is sufficient. The verbal formula (offer and acceptance) should be uttered in Arabic if the contactors can. For those who cannot speak Arabic it is acceptable to use the verbal formula of marriage in a language that they understand, even if they can get a representative, but they should use the meaning of *nikāḥ* and *tazwīj* (marriage).'[6] He further states that 'it is recommended that the offer be from the woman and the acceptance from the man, but the reverse is also fine'.[7] And finally: 'It is recommended that the verbal formula in a permanent marriage is with the terms *nikāḥ* and *tazwīj*. Using the word *mutʿa* is acceptable if there is evidence of permanent marriage. It is recommended that the offer and acceptance be in the past tense, but the other tenses are permissible too.'[8]

---

3 al-Zuḥaylī, *al-Fiqh al-Islāmī*, 7:36–41.

4 al-Ḥillī, *Irshād al-adhhān*, 2:5.

5 al-Ḥillī, *Qawāʿid al-aḥkām*, 3:9–11.

6 ʿAlī al-Sīstānī, *Minhāj al-ṣāliḥīn* (Najaf: Dār al-Muwarrikh al-ʿArabī, 2021), 3:15, no. 30.

7 Ibid., no. 31.

8 Ibid., no. 32.

A COMPARATIVE STUDY OF FATWAS

A comparative study of the aforementioned Sunnī and Shīʿī fatwas may be summarised as follows: The first or the only pillar of marriage is the verbal formula of offer and acceptance in all Islamic legal schools. It is required or recommended to use Arabic verbal formulas even for non-Arabs who can speak Arabic, but it is acceptable to use the meaning of these Arabic formulas verbally in the language of non-Arab contractors if they cannot speak Arabic. There is an agreement in all legal schools that the verbal formula comprise either of the following terms for the offer: *nikāḥ* or *tazwīj*. The acceptance is termed *qabūl*. The Shāfiʿī and Ḥanbalī legal schools do not accept any other terms here. The Shīʿīs add *mutʿa* with explicit evidence for permanent marriage. The Mālikī and Ḥanafī schools added ownership (*tamlīk*) with evidence of marriage. It is recommended that the past tense of the verbal formula be used in all Islamic legal schools, with the offer being from the woman and the acceptance from the man, and the offer preceding the acceptance; however, the reverse in all cases is acceptable. The following three marriages without verbal formulas are not valid in all legal schools: (1) the sole internal consent to marriage, but without any contract; (2) the *written* documented marriage contract without uttering any verbal formula, except for mutes; and (3) the explicit *action* that demonstrates marriages, except for mutes. There is agreement among all Sunnī and Shīʿī jurists that the marriage contract is not bound by *muʿāṭāt* (action without a verbal formula), and thus *al-nikāḥ al-muʿāṭātī* is null and void.

I will examine the arguments of the first and last two points of this summary in the next section, since they appear to be the most important elements of the marriage contract in conventional *fiqh*.

The second pillar of the marriage is the contractors who are the spouses or their guardians or their representatives/agents (*wakīl*). Their conditions include juridic-moral responsibility (*taklīf*), namely, puberty; reason (*ʿaql*); choice (*ikhtiyār*), and freedom or (for slaves) their owner's permission. There are several controversial issues regarding the marriage of minors or underage girls, the silence of the girl as her consent, and the requirement of the guardian's permission for virgins. I have discussed these elsewhere,[9] so will focus on the first pillar here.

9 See Mohsen Kadivar, 'Rethinking Muslim Marriage Rulings through Structural Ijtihad', in *Justice and Beauty in Muslim Marriage: Towards Egalitarian Ethics and Laws*, ed. Ziba Mir-Hosseini, Mulki Al-Sharmani, Jana Rumminger, and Sarah Marsso (London: Oneworld, 2022), 229–47.

ARGUMENTS OF VERBAL FORMULA AS THE FIRST PILLAR OF A LEGITIMATE MARRIAGE

There is no verse of the Qur'an, explicitly or implicitly, in support of this subject. We can classify the other arguments of the verbal formula as the first pillar of a legitimate marriage into four categories: *ḥadīth* arguments, rational arguments, consensus, and marriage as a *tawqīfī* issue (beyond rationality matters). These are discussed and analysed in turn below.

ḤADĪTH *ARGUMENTS*

Firstly, many *ḥadīth*s revolve around the verbal formula and take it as certain and an undoubtable issue. We can find such *ḥadīth*s in the section of *nikāḥ* in chapters 1 and 2, concerning the *nikāḥ* contract and its guardians, of *Wasā'il al-Shī'a*[10] and *Mustadrak al-Wasā'il*.[11] The jurists, however, did not discuss these *ḥadīth*s in detail, yet they were somehow certain that the *ḥadīth* evidence recognises the verbal formula as the essential pillar of marriage.[12]

Second, in an authentic *ḥadīth*, Burayd b. Mu'āwiya al-'Ijlī asked Imām Muḥammad al-Bāqir about the verse 'They have taken a solemn pledge from you' (Q. 4:21).[13] The Imām responded: 'the pledge is the verbal formula of the marriage contract, and the solemn pledge is a man's semen that leads to his wife.'[14] Many Shī'ī jurists relied on this *ḥadīth* because of its authentic transmitters and explicit indication.[15] It remains the most important *ḥadīth* argument in support of the first pillar of marriage.

- Examining the *ḥadīth* arguments

I have three criticisms here: one of the first *ḥadīth* argument and two major criticisms of the second *ḥadīth* argument.

The title of the first chapter (*bāb*) under the section 'the marriage contract and its guardians' is 'the consideration of the [verbal] formula and how to offer and accept'

10 Muḥammad b. al-Ḥasan al-Ḥurr al-'Āmilī, *Tafṣīl Wasā'il al-Shī'a ilā taḥṣīl masā'il al-Sharī'a* (Qom: Mu'assasat Āl al-Bayt li-Iḥyā' al-Turāth, 1994), 20:261–67.

11 Ḥusayn al-Nūrī al-Ṭabrisī, *Mustadrak al-Wasā'il wa-mustanbaṭ al-masā'il* (Qom: Mu'assasat Āl al-Bayt li-Iḥyā' al-Turāth, 1991),15–14:311 .

12 Abū al-Qāsim al-Mūsawī al-Khū'ī, *al-Mabānī fī sharḥ al-'Urwa al-wuthqā*, transc. Muḥammad Taqī al-Khū'ī (Qom: Mu'assasat al-Khū'ī al-Islāmiyya, 2009), *Kitāb al-Nikāḥ*, 2:160; Nāṣir Makārim Shīrāzī, *Anwār al-fiqāha fī aḥkām al-'iṭra al-ṭāhira* (Qom: Dār Nashr al-Imām 'Alī b. Abī Ṭālib, 2011), *Kitāb al-Nikāḥ*, 1:166.

13 M. A. S. Abdel Haleem, *The Qur'an: A New Translation* (Oxford: Oxford University Press, 2005).

14 al-Ḥurr al-'Āmilī, *Tafṣīl*, 20:262, *ḥadīth* no. 4.

15 al-Khū'ī, *al-Mabānī*, 2:160; Shīrāzī, *Anwār al-fiqāha*, 1:160.

(*bāb iʿtibār al-ṣīgha wa-kayfiyyat al-ījāb wa-l-qabūl*) in two collections of *ḥadīth* among Shīʿī jurists, namely, *Wasāʾil al-Shīʿa*[16] and *Mustadrak al-Wasāʾil.*[17] The former includes ten *ḥadīth*s, and the latter six. Now, only the first five *ḥadīth*s in *Wasāʾil al-Shīʿa* have authentic chains of transmitters: the first two are from *Man lā yaḥḍuruhu al-faqīh* by al-Ṣadūq,[18] and the other three are from *al-Kāfī* by al-Kulaynī.[19] The first concerns the marriage of Adam and Eve, and the last does not mention any sort of verbal formula. The second and third are ambiguous regarding the verbal formula; nor do they provide any evidence of its necessity. This means that the first *ḥadīth* argument is untenable.

Only the fourth *ḥadīth* includes a clear indication of the verbal formula. This *ḥadīth* is on the authority of Burayd from Imām al-Bāqir: 'The pledge is the formula (*kalima*) of the marriage contract.' The formula (*kalima*), however, may be verbal (*malfūẓ*) or written and signed (*maktūb*). It is not a clear statement (*naṣṣ*) of a verbal formula. Moreover, *kalima*, in the terminology of the Qur'an and *ḥadīth*, is not identical to a pronounced formula or a written/signed document.

Kalima is used twenty-eight times in the Qur'an in twenty-seven verses in the singular form.[20] At least two-thirds of these instances constitute an existential or actional sense (not verbal). For example, 'The Messiah, Jesus, son of Mary, was nothing more than a messenger of God, His *word*, directed to Mary, a spirit from Him' (Q. 4:171); '[God] brought down the disbelievers' *plan*. God's *plan* is higher: God is almighty and wise' (9:40); 'But the *sentence* of punishment will have been passed against those who rejected the truth' (39:71); and 'God sent His tranquility down onto His Messenger and the believers and made binding on them [their] *promise* to obey God' (48:26).

Kalim, as the plural of *kalima*, is used four times,[21] all of which in a verbal sense. Another plural form, *kalimāt*, is used fourteen times,[22] more than three quarters of which is actional or existential, and non-verbal. Overall, more than two-thirds of *kalima*, singular and plural, is used in actional or existential senses (without utterance). Al-Rāghib al-Iṣfahānī (d. 502/1108), in his *al-Mufradāt fī gharīb al-Qurʾān*, described these verses in detail and concluded that *kalima* may be verbal (*maqāl*) or actional

16 al-Ḥurr al-ʿĀmilī, *Tafṣīl*, 20:261–64.

17 al-Ṭabrisī, *Mustadrak*, 14:311–14.

18 Muḥammad b. ʿAlī b. Bābawayh al-Ṣadūq, *Man lā yaḥḍuruh al-faqīh*, ed. ʿAlī Akbar al-Ghaffārī (Tehran: Maktabat al-Ṣadūq, 1972), 3:379–80.

19 Muḥammad b. Yaʿqūb al-Kulaynī, *al-Kāfī*, ed. ʿAlī Akbar al-Ghaffārī (Tehran: Dār al-Kutub al-Isb lāmiyya, 1968), 5:380, 560, 564.

20 Fuʾād ʿAbd al-Bāqī, *al-Muʿjam al-mufahras li-alfāẓ al-Qurʾān al-karīm* (Cairo: Dār al-Kutub al-Miṣriyya, 1945), 620–21.

21 Ibid.

22 Ibid.

(*fiʿāl*).[23] This position is also found in *al-Mīzān* by al-Ṭabāṭabāʾī (d. 1981).[24]

We can conclude therefore that what Imām al-Bāqir said in the *ḥadīth* of Burayd includes all three types of marriage contract: verbal, written/signed, and actional or *muʿāṭāṭī*.

Al-Ṭabrisī (d. 548/1153) wrote in *Majmaʿ al-bayān* in his commentary on the verse 'They have taken a solemn pledge from you' (Q. 4:21): 'There are three possible meanings related for this verse: the first is that a solemn pledge is a covenant taken from the husband that the marriage contract either be kept on in an acceptable manner or released in a good way [Q. 2:229]. [He narrated this from Imām al-Bāqir.] The second is the *kalima* of marriage through which sexual intercourse would be rendered permissible. [He did not attribute the second meaning to Imām al-Bāqir.] The third is the sayings of the Prophet "You took them with the honesty of God (*amānat Allāh*)", and "sexual intercourse with them is permitted by God's permission (*kalimat Allāh*)".'[25]

The first approach is narrated in *Tafsīr al-ʿAyyāshī* on the authority of ʿAbd al-Raḥmān b. Aʿyan from Imām al-Bāqir.[26] The same *ḥadīth*, with a chain of transmitters, is narrated from Imām al-Ṣādiq in *al-Kāfī*.[27] Because of ʿAbd al-Raḥmān b. Aʿyan, the brother of Zurāra, this *ḥadīth* is classified as *ḥasan* or *muwaththaq* (well-authenticated).[28] This approach is not exclusive to verbal formulas. The second approach is close to the *ḥadīth* of Burayd, although al-Ṭabrisī ignored this *ḥadīth* of Imām al-Bāqir. As per my analysis of this *ḥadīth* above, I have proposed that it is not exclusive to the verbal formula either. We can argue in the same way about the third approach. In sum, there is no obstacle in the *ḥadīth*s discussed that restricts the marriage contract to a verbal formula.

RATIONAL ARGUMENTS

The rational argument differentiates marriage from fornication based on whether the people involved uttered the verbal formula indicating the intent to marry. Since mutual consent to sexual intercourse characterises both marriage and fornication, it

23 Abū al-Qāsim Ḥusayn b. Muḥammad al-Rāghib al-Iṣfahānī, *al-Mufradāt fī gharīb al-Qurʾān*, ed. Ṣafwān ʿAdnān Dāwūdī (Damascus: Dār al-Qalam, 2009), 723.

24 Muḥammad Ḥusayn al-Ṭabāṭabāʾī, *al-Mīzān fī tafsīr al-Qurʾān* (Qom: Jamāʿat al-Mudarrisīn, 2009), 7:328–30.

25 Faḍl b. al-Ḥasan al-Ṭabrisī, *Majmaʿ al-bayān fī tafsīr al-Qurʾān* (Beirut: Dār al-Murtaḍā wa-Dār al-ʿUlūm, 2005–6), 3:50.

26 Muḥammad b. Masʿūd al-ʿAyyāshī al-Samarqandī, *Tafsīr al-ʿAyyāshī* (Qom: Muʾassisat al-Biʿtha, 2000), 1:115.

27 al-Kulaynī, *al-Kāfī*, 5:501n5.

28 Muḥammad Bāqir al-Majlisī, *Mirʾāt al-ʿuqūl fī sharḥ Akhbār Āl al-Rasūl* (Tehran: Dār al-Kutub al-Islāmiyya, 1984), 20:312.

is the presence (or absence) of verbal assent to marriage that marks a key difference. There are at least two justifications for this rational argument. The first comes from al-Anṣārī and the second from Nā'īnī.

Murtaḍā al-Anṣārī (d. 1864), in his *Kitāb al-Nikāḥ*, a commentary on *Irshād al-adhhān*, explains the first pillar as follows: 'The *'ulamā'* of Islam unanimously agreed – as stated by numerous scholars – on the consideration of the requirement of the formula in the marriage contract, and that sexual intercourse is not permitted (*al-ibāḥa*) by contract (*al-mu'āṭāt*) without the verbal formula, and thus marriage is distinguished from fornication (*al-zinā*) because it [i.e. the latter] often involves consent.'[29] I will discuss the issue of consensus in the next subsection. Here I highlight al-Anṣārī's comparison and the necessity of the verbal formula to distinguish marriage (i.e. that its requirement is consent) from fornication because the latter is also often based on consent.

Mirzā Muḥammad Ḥusayn Nā'īnī Gharawī (d. 1936) in *Munyat al-ṭālib* describes the argument in this way: 'The action [i.e. marriage without verbal formula] is the particular of its opposite, namely, fornication. The opposite of marriage is nothing other than the action [i.e. sexual intercourse] without the verbalised intent to marry (*al-inshā' al-fi'lī*); and the Lawmaker made the verbal formula the means for rendering marriage permissible (*ḥilliyya*).'[30] For Nā'īnī, the action of sexual intercourse through consent in marriage and fornication is the same – what differentiates them is the verbal formula, which removes intercourse from the realm of prohibition and makes it *ḥalāl* and permissible.

▪ Examining the Rational Arguments

In his rational argument, al-Anṣārī clarified that heartfelt (unexpressed) consent and *mu'āṭāt* are not sufficient, and the verbal formula is required to distinguish between marriage and fornication. Both are based on consent; the distinction is the verbal formula.

Muḥammad Ḥusayn Gharawī Iṣfahānī (d. 1942), the distinguished student of Ākhund Khurāsānī and the author of *Nihāyat al-dirāya fī sharḥ al-Kifāya*, concludes in his commentary on the *al-Makāsib* of al-Anṣārī: 'There is no problem with the validity of *mu'āṭāt* in marriage except consensus. The contract may be bound by verbal formula or written document, or actional creative indication (*al-inshā' al-fi'lī*). Submissiveness (*tamkīn*) of the female and intercourse are examples of actional creative indication, which means illegal intercourse – based on the consent of both parties to be spouses – and could

29 Murtaḍā al-Anṣārī, *Kitāb al-Nikāḥ* (Qom: Turāth al-Shaykh al-A'ẓam, 1994), 77.

30 Muḥammad Ḥusayn Nā'īnī Gharawī, *Munyat al-ṭālib fī ḥāshiyat al-Makāsib*, transc. Mūsā Narjafī Khānsārī (Qom: al-Maktaba al-Muḥammadiyya, 1954) 1:81, see also 48, 285.

be the indication of their legal marriage later. While intercourse even with consent is fornication when the consent is not on being spouses.'[31]

Mu'āṭāṭ is neither pure consent nor only the external action, but the external action with the intention of establishing a contract. The two parties of fornication do not intend by their action to establish a marriage, but they want only lustful pleasure and nothing else, whereas a marriage is established if a woman places herself in relation to a man with the intention of becoming his wife, and the nullification of the marriage by *mu'āṭāṭ* is based on consensus.

The essence of marriage is the acceptance of the position of wifehood by a woman and the position of husbandhood by a man. This essence requires a manifestation, be it verbal, written, or actional. There is no evidence for the nullification of the third, namely, *mu'āṭāṭ*, except through consensus.

Iṣfahānī's argument was adopted by many jurists after him, of whom I shall mention only two. His student Abū al-Qāsim al-Khū'ī (d. 1992) in *Kitāb al-Nikāḥ* mentions that 'the difference between marriage and fornication is not verbal. Marriage is a contractual matter (*i'tibārī*), whereby the man recognises the woman as his wife and the woman recognises the man as her husband, while fornication is intercourse without recognising the spousehood (*i'tibār al-zawjiyya*) between them.'[32] He further states: 'The contract is based on intention, and the verbal formula is its manifestation (*mubriz*).'[33]

Being spouses (*al-zawjiyya*) is in contrast to being an individual (*fardiyya*), and is the joining of the one to the other with the unity of their relationship. Accordingly, each of them has their own creative action (*inshā'*) and recognises the other as his/her spouse. When such an offer is made by one of them and accepted by the other, the contract and the treaty become valid.[34]

Nāṣir Makārim Shīrāzī (b. 1927), a contemporary jurist, analyses al-Anṣārī's position and writes: 'The reason why internal consent or heartfelt satisfaction is insufficient is because it is not a contract, and the woman does not become a wife. It appears that the insufficiency of *mu'āṭāṭ* is due to consensus. We could say that convention among all reasonable people – even those of no faith – is not to be satisfied with *mu'āṭāṭ*, but to require the establishment of a contract verbally, or at least with written documentation. As a result, there is no question among the distinguished *'ulamā'* that the marriage contract must be effected via a verbal formula, and that this is the

31 Muḥammad Ḥusayn Gharawī Iṣfahānī, *Ḥāshiyat Kitāb al-Makāsib*, ed. 'Abbas Muḥammad Āl Saba' al-Qaṭīfī (Qom: 'Abbas Muḥammad Āl Sabá al-Qaṭīfī, 1997), 1:183–84.

32 al-Khū'ī, *al-Mabānī*, 2:159.

33 Ibid., 162.

34 Ibid., 175.

agreement of both Shīʿī and Sunnī jurists. It is necessary to negate the sufficiency of heartfelt consent alone, as well as *muʿāṭāṭ* and written documentation.'[35]

The response of Iṣfahānī and the justifications of his followers have crippled al-Anṣārī's argument. I will examine what they said about consensus and the invalidity of *muʿāṭāṭ* in marriage later.

Nā'īnī's rational argument was that the action (marriage without verbal formula) is the particular of its opposite, that is, fornication. However, it was criticised by contemporary jurists; for example, Ruhollah Khomeini (d. 1982) states in his *Kitāb al-Bayʿ*: 'Conventionally, fornication is different from marriage regardless of a verbal formula or actional indication. Accordingly, if after negotiating the spouses and their intention to marry, the woman manifested (*anshȧa*) her intention by going to the man's house with her property, for instance, and the man accepted it, we can say that *mu'āṭāṭī nikāḥ* occurred if the woman submits (*tamkīn*) to him in his house, and its legal provisions follow, such as the permissibility of seeing her unveiled, sexual intercourse, the necessity of paying her life expenses (*nafaqa*), and so on. Granted, if the woman and man intended their marriage via sexual intercourse, such intercourse is forbidden, but there is no obstacle to the permission of the marriage thereby because the prohibited cause could be effective declaratorily (*waḍʿan*).'[36] Khomeini concedes that intercourse is not among the conventional and reasonable causes of marriage, suggesting that the actions and hints in *muʿāṭāṭ* may be reasonable.[37] After much discussion, he concludes that *muʿāṭāṭī* marriage in such cases is against the understanding of religious people (*irtikāz al-mutasharriʿa*) and the agreement of Shīʿī *ʿulamā'*.[38]

Muḥammad Sādiq al-Rūḥānī (d. 2022) in his *Fiqh al-Ṣādiq* responds to Nā'īnī's rational argument: 'First, this argument is based only on creating (*inshā'*) the marriage by sexual intercourse, but it does not cover the other particulars of *nikāḥ muʿāṭāṭī* such as submission of the wife. Second, the point of contention is the intercourse with the intent of creating the state of being a spouse, not excluded from the intention. Such intercourse is a particular of fornication, but this prohibited action could be the manifestation (*mubriz*) of marriage. There is no inherent problem if a harmful act may be the manifestation of something *ḥalāl*.'[39]

The criticisms of these jurists have seriously undermined the rational argument of Nā'īnī. These arguments accepted, I also have reservations about the consensus against the validity of *muʿāṭāṭī* marriage. We can conclude therefore that there is no valid rational argument in support of the verbal formula as the first pillar of marriage.

35 Makārim Shīrāzī, *Anwār al-fiqāha*, 1:164.

36 Ruhollah Khomeini, *Kitāb al-Bayʿ*, Mawsūʿat al-Imām al-Khomeini, no. 16 (Tehran: Institute for Compilation and Publication of Imam Khomeini's Work, 2013), 1:267.

37 Ibid., 368.

38 Ibid., 269.

39 Muḥammad Ṣādiq Ḥusaynī al-Rūḥānī, *Fiqh al-Ṣādiq* (Qom: Manshūrāt al-Ijtihād, 2008), 22:443–44.

CONSENSUS

Muḥammad b. ʿAlī al-Mūsawī al-ʿĀmilī (d. 1009/1600) in *Nihāyat al-marām fī sharḥ Mukhtaṣar Sharāʾiʿ al-Islām* wrote: 'All *ʿulamāʾ* of Islam agreed [i.e. reached a consensus] that legitimate marriage is dependent on a verbal formula of offer and acceptance.'[40] ʿAlī al-Ṭabāṭabāʾī (d. 1816) in his *Riyāḍ al-masāʾil fī taḥqīq al-aḥkām bi-l-dalāʾil* mentions: 'The verbal formula is undeniable because of the consensus of the *ʿulamāʾ* of Islam that it comprises the verbal offer and the acceptance.'[41] Yūsuf al-Baḥrānī (d. 1772) in his *al-Ḥadāʾiq al-nāḍira* mentions: 'Shīʿī and Sunnī *ʿulamāʾ* are in consensus on the dependence of the marriage on the verbal offer and acceptance.'[42] All the later jurists refer to these claims of consensus and introduce it as the major argument for the necessity of the verbal formula as the first pillar of legitimate marriage in Islam.

▪ Examining the Consensus

Creative action (*al-inshāʾ*) in the heart means establishing the situations of wifehood and husbandhood. This internal situation requires at least one of three types of manifestations (*mubriz*): verbal formula, written documentation, and implied actions (*muʿāṭāt*). The latter (i.e. implied actions) are said to be not valid, rendering *nikāḥ muʿāṭātī* a legally unrecognised form of marriage, because of consensus. Iṣfahānī and his followers conceded that if there was no consensus, *muʿāṭāt* would be acceptable in marriage. Is this consensus valid and reliable? This is a narrative consensus (*al-ijmāʿ al-manqūl*) not gained consensus (*al-ijmāʿ al-muḥaṣṣal*). The earliest claim of such a consensus returned to the late ninth/sixteenth century.[43] That means this is the derivation (*istinbāṭ*) of the late jurists (*mutáakhkhirīn*). The consensus of the jurists in the early centuries (*mutaqaddimīn*) could be based on the sayings of the Imāms that were not received in our time. This probability is very weak in the later centuries.

The second weakness of this consensus is because of *al-ijmāʿ al-madrakī* (consensus based on evidence), which means it is not an independent argument and we should examine the evidence. The evidence offered comprises a few *ḥadīth*s and rational arguments, which I have already examined and proven their invalidity above. The conclusion is that this consensus is not valid and reliable, and cannot be considered as the sayings of Imāms in this case.

---

40 Muḥammad b. ʿAlī al-Mūsawī al-ʿĀmilī, *Nihāyat al-marām fī sharḥ Mukhtaṣar Sharāʾiʿ al-Islām* (Qom: Muʾassasat al-Nashr al-Islāmī, 1992), 1:20.

41 ʿAlī al-Ṭabāṭabāʾī, *Riyāḍ al-masāʾil fī taḥqīq al-aḥkām bi-l-dalāʾil* (Mashhad: Muʾassasat Āl al-Bayt li-Iḥyāʾ al-Turāth, 1997), 11:10.

42 Yūsuf al-Baḥrānī, *al-Ḥadāʾiq al-nāḍira fī aḥkām al-ʿiṭra al-ṭāhira* (Qom: Muʾassasat al-Nashr al-IsN lāmī, 1984), 23:156.

43 al-Mūsawī al-ʿĀmilī, *Nihāyat al-marām*, 1:20.

The consensus here is narrated and documented (*al-manqūl wa-l-madrakī*) and a few jurists cited it based on that document/narration, so its value is the value of that document, which is the *ḥadīth*. I have clarified that we cannot find any *ḥadīth* in support of confining the validity of the marriage contract to the verbal formula. When the *ḥadīth* foundation of such a consensus is destroyed, the consensus becomes unreliable and unacceptable.

Rūḥānī concluded in his *Fiqh al-Ṣādiq* that there is no obstacle to the validity of *muʿāṭāt* in marriage, neither rational nor *sharʿī*. The only concern is the consensus on its invalidity. It is reliable if there would be such a consensus, and it is *tawqīfī* (he mentions *taʿabbudī*), not referring to the previous arguments.[44] If it was a real consensus uncovering the Imām's rejection of *muʿāṭāt* marriage, we should accept it, but the documental consensus is not acceptable.

MARRIAGE BEYOND RATIONAL MATTERS

This argument could be understood as the reason for consensus. There are two references in support of this argument, one implicitly, and the other explicitly. The former belongs to Narāqī and the latter is the statement of al-Najafī.

Mullā Aḥmad Narāqī (d. 1829) went one step further than consensus and wrote in his *Mustnad al-Shīʿa*: 'The verbal formula is required in marriage according to the agreement of the *ʿulamāʿ* of Islam. Moreover, it is one of the essentials of the religion of the Prophet Muḥammad, and the principle of the originality of negating the consequences of spousehood (*aṣālat ʿadam āthār al-zawjiyya*) [cannot function] without it.'[45]

Narāqī introduced two points here: the first is the verbal formula as one of the essentials of Islam, and the second is the principle of the originality of negating the consequences of spousehood, that is, if there is any doubt as to a woman and a man being spouses, we should consider them as unmarried or non-spouses, and do not apply the legal implications of marriage to them. This is a pertinent point taken up by our next jurist.

Muḥammad Ḥasan al-Najafī (d. 1850) in his masterpiece *Jawāhir al-kalām fī sharḥ Sharāʾiʿ al-Islām*, in the beginning of the chapter on the marriage contract, mentioned: 'There is no doubt that precaution should not be left, especially in a marriage that is contaminated with the acts of worship received from the Lawgiver. The primary basis is that sexual intercourse is forbidden until the reason for its permission is established according to Sharīʿa law.'[46]

44 al-Rūḥānī, *Fiqh al-Ṣādiq*, 22:446.

45 Aḥmad Narāqī, *Mustanad al-Shīʿa fī aḥkām al-Sharīʿa* (Qom: Muʾassasat Āl al-Bayt li-Iḥyāʾ al-Turāth, 2008), 16:84.

46 Muḥammad Ḥasan al-Najafī, *Jawāhir al-kalām fī sharḥ Sharāʾiʿ al-Islām*, ed. Ḥaydar al-Dabbāgh (Qom: Muʾassasat al-Nashr al-Islāmī, 2012), 29:133.

There are two points in this expression. I present the summary of analysis of Makārim Shīrāzī on both points:

> Marriage is a *tawqifi* issue, that is, beyond rational matters. It is obvious that worship here does not mean the intention of closeness to God (*qaṣd al-qurba*) as a requirement of validity. Instead, in this context the expression means that a sexual relationship is not a rational matter (*tawqīfiyyāt*), since the Lawgiver needs to clarify its principle in each instance, according to the originality of corruption (*aṣālat al-fasād*) that takes place when the validity of the marriage is doubtful. This is the expansion of what Narāqī wrote.
>
> In other words, marriage and divorce are different from other contracts and unilateral acts. Such human interactions (*muʿāmalāt*) are considered ratified rulings (*al-aḥkām al-imḍāʾī*) and are based on the rationale of reasonable people (*sīrat al-ʿuqalāʾ*), whom the principle of the originality of validity (*aṣālat al-ṣiḥḥa*) works for, except when presented with evidence. In other words, in contrast to marriage and divorce, when we are doubtful about the validity of human interactions (*muʿāmalāt*), practically, we should consider them as valid, except if there is specific evidence [to the contrary].
>
> Although marriage and divorce existed before Islam, the Lawgiver made significant changes to them, assigning them new implications and identities. Accordingly, and as with acts of worship, they became the cases of *tawqīfiyyāt* (beyond rational matters) in which it is not possible to consider the custom or the rationale of the reasonable people, under the rubric that the lack of deterrence therein is sufficient to accept it. Rather, its conditions and prohibitions must be established and expressed from the Sharīʿa, and nothing but the principle of the originality of corruption (*aṣālat al-fasād*) takes place in them.[47]

This is the approach that has dominated among traditionists in Islamic jurisprudence. According to this approach, the institution of marriage in all its details is beyond human reason and the only source for discussing it is the narrative indicated by the Qurʾan and Sunna. There is no role for reason or the rationale of reasonable people in it. It follows therefore that revisiting the institution of marriage in modern times is meaningless. This approach means that at least the pillars of marriage in Islam are the most identical elements of *tawqīfī* issues (beyond rational matters).

47 Makārim Shīrāzī, *Anwār al-fiqāha*, 1:26–27.

▪ Examining the Claim 'Marriage beyond Rational Matters'

After challenging the three aforementioned arguments, the only way for supporting the necessity of the verbal formula for a valid marriage contract is to take it as *tawqīfī* (beyond rational matters). I have reproduced above al-Najafī's statement in *al-Jawāhir*[48] and that of his followers.[49] Such a claim is acceptable in the framework of 'traditional *ijtihād* in derivatives' (*al-ijtihād fī al-furūʿ al-fiqhiyya*). I have discussed elsewhere the shortcoming of this type of *ijtihād*.[50]

My approach, instead, is 'structural *ijtihād*', meaning *ijtihād* in principles and foundations (*al-ijtihād fī al-uṣūl wa-l-mabānī*). In this framework, the domain of *tawqīfiyyāt* (beyond rational matters) is precisely restricted to devotional rituals (acts of worship) and quasi-rituals (non-devotional acts). The former includes only the main acts themselves, namely, ritual prayer (*ṣalāt*), fasting (*ṣawm*), hajj, and zakat, not all their elements. Otherwise, there are new fatwas on the prayer of passengers in modern modes of transportation, the duration of fasting in the long summer days in lands above the 43-degree orbit in the Northern Hemisphere, the possibility of ritual slaughter outside of Mina during hajj, and the requirement of paying zakat on savings beyond the nine traditional categories.[51] In other words, the devotional is not identical to the *tawqīfī* (beyond rational matters).

Quasi-rituals (*tawqīfiyyāt ghayr al-taʿabbudiyya*) are restricted to three subjects: *maʾkūlāt, mashrūbāt,* and *mankūḥat*. An example of the first is the prohibition of eating pork. An example of the second is the prohibition of drinking even one drop of wine that is less than intoxicating. An example of the third is a sexual relationship and its domain for those who restrict legal marriage to opposite sexes. It does not mean that all *sharʿī* rulings in these three subjects are *tawqīfī*; rather, it means at least a few rulings in each of these three subjects are beyond rational matters. There are no cases of *tawqīfī* issues from devotional rituals and quasi-rituals.

The primary principle (*al-aṣl al-awwalī*) in human interactions (*muʿāmalāt*) is the negation of *tawqīfiyyāt*; that is, *tawqīfiyyāt* requires strong evidence such as clear verses of the Qur'an (*muḥkamāt*) or a clear indication of mass-transmitted (*mutawātir*) *ḥadīth* or authentic singular *ḥadīth* with certain evidence. In the case of marriage at least its pillars are not *tawqīfī*. In this framework, almost all elements of marriage are open to being revisited. In reformist Islam, the institution of marriage is not 'beyond rational matters' (*tawqīfiyyāt*).

---

48 al-Najafi, *Jawāhir al-kalām*, 29:133.

49 For example, Shīrāzī, *Anwār al-fiqāha*, 1:26–27.

50 Mohsen Kadivar, '*Ijtihad* in *Usul al-Fiqh*: Reforming Islamic Thought through Structural *Ijtihad*', *Iran Nameh* 30, no. 3 (2015): 20–27.

51 For detailed *fiqhī* arguments on all these subjects, see 'Ārā' fiqhī' [*Fiqhī* opinions], Mohsen Kadivar: Official Website, https://kadivar.com/category/8-vote/.

There is no reason to believe that what the Lawgiver added to or omitted from the institution of marriage in the rationale of reasonable people was permanent rulings, on the one hand, and that there is a hidden interest or harm beyond these rulings except for the protection of the family, on the other. What was said in the justification of *al-Jawāhir*'s claim that the identity of marriage in Islam is different from other traditions and cultures is problematic and needs strong evidence.

REVISITING THE FIRST PILLAR OF MARRIAGE BASED ON STRUCTURAL *IJTIHĀD*

First, the required foundations of a legitimate marriage (*al-zawāj al-sharʿī*) in Islam between an adult man and woman – that is, not any legitimate obstacle (*al-māniʿ al-sharʿī*) for their marriage – are two: (i) explicit consent of the two parties themselves (not their guardians) for marriage, and (ii) effecting an agreement or contract of marriage so that they become husband and wife based on this contract. This explicit consent is a necessary condition for establishing the institution of marriage, but not a sufficient one. The institution of marriage in Islam is not completed except by binding an agreement or contract of marriage so that they become husband and wife based on this explicit contract. Clearly, no legitimate marriage in Islam is meaningful without a contract (*ʿaqd*). The strongest form of this institution is a marriage with a verbal formula in the language of the spouses and is recorded with their signatures and that of a few witnesses, especially their parents, and registration in a legal and civil office for marriage. The verbal formula is recommended religiously and its registration in a legal office is a civil duty. A marriage without any verbal formula but with the signing of a marriage contract intentionally is the same as the verbal formula. As seen, there is no hidden interest in the verbal formula, since its signed written counterpart serves the same function.

In the third scenario described above (*muʿāṭāṭī*), the verbal *sharʿī* formulation of marriage (*al-ṣīgha al-sharʿiyya li-l-zawāj*) is pronounced neither in Arabic nor in any other languages, the two parties do not sign any document, and nor do they register their marriage in any legal or civil office. But they recognise themselves as husband and wife, and agree to live as a couple permanently. This is precisely a *muʿāṭāṭī* marriage. There is an unexpressed, unregistered marriage, without any written documentation, but with an explicit contract. The man recognises himself as a husband and the woman herself as a wife. The manifestation of the marriage contract is an explicit action: living together by consent and recognising themselves as husband and wife. They fulfilled the minimum requirement of a *sharʿī* marriage, although recommended neither religiously nor legally. The verbal formula, signing the written document of the marriage contract, and registration in a legal office are all strongly recommended, because of their benefits in the time of conflict between spouses. Registration in legal offices and providing signed written documents support the right of both spouses, especially women. However, if, for any reason, they bind a *muʿāṭāṭī* marriage contract, can we call their relationship fornication and their child illegitimate (*walad al-zinā*)? According to traditional *ijtihād*, this is fornication because of the lack of verbal formula and the child is therefore illegitimate. Keeping my arguments in mind, however, this is a *sharʿī* marriage and the child is like any other legitimate offspring.

Do not forget that this situation is not imaginary. The phenomenon of *muʿāṭāṭī* marriage is growing in modern times, including in Muslim-majority countries. Of course, we can and should encourage Muslims to the recommended style of marriage, namely, with a verbal formula, a signed written document, and registration in a civil legal office for marriage, but we should not overlook the reality of this phenomenon. Moreover, it is not becoming for the Lawgiver to increase fornication and illegitimate children, which goes against God's tradition (*sunnat Allāh*).

The major point of the second required foundation of legitimate marriage is the contract. The male and the female parties recognise themselves as husband and wife, respectively, as the product of the marriage contract between them. The manifestation of this contract is an explicit action: their coming together. They do not hide this relationship and the community accepts such a union. Therefore, the rationale of reasonable people in our times does not reject *muʿāṭāṭī nikāḥ*.

Conventional marriage based on implied action without any verbal formula or written document, namely, a *nikāḥ muʿāṭāṭī*, is a legitimate marriage because both required foundations of marriage are observed therein. A man and a woman are satisfied with each other's marriage, and a woman is legitimately married to a man. The only difference is that the marriage contract formula is not pronounced, and there is no written document. We should accept the claim of marriage at the time of agreement of both parties to it. They do not need any evidence for proving it except their confession. Those who deny their marriage should prove their claim, not the spouses. This is the content of the principle of originality of the authenticity in the sayings and actions of Muslims (*aṣālat al-ṣiḥḥa fī qawl wa-fiʿl al-Muslim*).

Second, is the Western style of partnership 'cohabitation' equivalent to conventional marriage based on implied action? No. If, and only if, the cohabitation of a man and a woman has taken place with a marriage contract (though it need not be written, registered, or even pronounced), it is permissible to treat it as a conventional *muʿāṭāṭ* marriage based on the implied action to fulfil the same purpose. It is obvious that a written and signed document of a marriage contract and especially its registration in a legal office for marriage is more precautionary in order to pre-empt any future disagreement.

Because different names were given to 'cohabitation' in different cultures and legal systems, and they do not have an agreed meaning and condition, wherever both required fundamentals are observed under any name, such a marriage is permissible; it remains impermissible in the absence of these two.

If cohabitation is not based on any type of marriage contract, even *muʿāṭāṭ*, we cannot justify it as *sharʿī* or an Islamically permissible marriage. But can we call it fornication? Couples outside of wedlock do not refer to themselves as husband and wife but partners; they do not call their relationship marriage, but a partnership or cohabitation; they do not observe the institution of marriage, and they frankly reject having a marriage contract. I do not know of any justification for permitting this type of sexual relationship in Islam. It is fornication based on mutual consent. I have written elsewhere that a worldly punishment for any crime in the name of the Sharīʿa is not acceptable, and have called for the abrogation of criminal *fiqh*.[52] Criminology and criminal law are not part of the immutable Sharīʿa. These two sciences are secular, not religious.

Third, why do some people reject religious marriage that is based on a contract and a few Islamic traditions, or even reject civil marriage that is based on the registration of a marriage contract in a civil and legal office for marriage? There are two objections here: objection to religious regulations, rulings, and values, and objection to civil regulations and values and legal administration for social affairs. There is also a benefit here, namely, freedom from any religious and civil restrictions. Such couples do not accept any responsibility that comes from constituting a family: they can separate and terminate this cohabitation at will, and there is neither inheritance nor order for dividing common properties in some legal systems.

I do not advocate such a relationship and do not justify its objections and benefits but understand that some Muslims as well as followers of other traditions have concluded that the harms of religious and civil marriage are greater than cohabitation, and the benefits of cohabitation outweigh those of religious and civil marriage. This is a worrying conclusion. Although there are Sharīʿa rulings and legal regulations that prevent cohabitation in Muslim-majority countries, such as its criminalisation and much supportive administration of *sharʿī* and legal marriage, some people have turned their backs to these types of marriage and adopted an opposite style of sexual relationship, one that is neither legitimate nor legal. Legal restrictions are not sufficient; rather, we should convince these people that *sharʿī* and civil marriages have several advantages over cohabitation and partnership. The mechanism of encouraging such a policy is beyond the scope of this paper.

52 Mohsen Kadivar, 'Ḥadhf mujāzāt iʿdām' [Abolition of the death penalty], Mohsen Kadivar: Official Website, August 2017, https://kadivar.com/16696/; Mohsen Kadivar, 'Mujāzāt iʿdām dar Islām muʿāṣir' [The death penalty in contemporary Islam], Mohsen Kadivar: Official Website, September 2020, https://kadivar.com/18157/.

BIBLIOGRAPHY

ʿAbd al-Bāqī, Fuʾād. *al-Muʿjam al-mufahras li-alfāẓ al-Qurʾān al-karīm*. Cairo: Dār al-Kutub al-Miṣriyya, 1945.

Abdel Haleem, M. A. S. *The Qur'an: A New Translation*. Oxford: Oxford University Press, 2005.

al-Anṣārī, Murtaḍā. *Kitāb al-Nikāḥ*. Qom: Turāth al-Shaykh al-Aʿẓam, 1994.

al-ʿAyyāshī al-Samarqandī, Muḥammad b. Masʿūd. *Tafsīr al-ʿAyyāshī*. Qom: Muʾassisat al-Biʿtha, 2000.

al-Baḥrānī, Yūsuf. *al-Ḥadāʾiq al-nāḍira fī aḥkām al-ʿiṭra al-ṭāhira*. Qom: Muʾassasat al-Nashr al-Islāmī, 1984.

al-Ḥillī, al-Ḥasan b. Yūsuf. *Irshād al-adhhān ilā aḥkām al-īmān*. Edited by Fāris al-Ḥassūn. Qom: Islamic Publication Institute, 1989.

al-Ḥillī, al-Ḥasan b. Yūsuf. *Qawāʿid al-aḥkām*. Qom: Islamic Publication Institute, 1998.

al-Ḥurr al-ʿĀmilī, Muḥammad b. al-Ḥasan. *Tafṣīl Wasāʾil al-Shīʿa ilā taḥṣīl masāʾil al-Sharīʿa*. Qom: Muʾassasat Āl al-Bayt li-Iḥyāʾ al-Turāth, 1994.

Iṣfahānī, Muḥammad Ḥusayn Gharawī. *Ḥāshiyat Kitāb al-Makāsib*. Edited by ʿAbbas Muḥammad Āl Sabȧ al-Qaṭīfī. Qom: ʿAbbas Muḥammad Āl Sabȧ al-Qaṭīfī, 1997.

Kadivar, Mohsen. '*Ijtihad* in *Usul al-Fiqh*: Reforming Islamic Thought through Structural *Ijtihad*'. *Iran Nameh* 30, no. 3 (2015): 20–27.

Kadivar, Mohsen. 'Rethinking Muslim Marriage Rulings through Structural Ijtihad'. In *Justice and Beauty in Muslim Marriage: Towards Egalitarian Ethics and Laws*, edited by Ziba Mir-Hosseini, Mulki Al-Sharmani, Jana Rumminger, and Sarah Marsso, 229–47. London: Oneworld, 2022.

Khomeini, Ruhollah. *Kitāb al-Bayʿ*. Mawsūʿat al-Imām al-Khomeini, no. 16. Tehran: Institute for Compilation and Publication of Imam Khomeini's Work, 2013.

al-Khūʾī, Abū al-Qāsim al-Mūsawī. *al-Mabānī fī sharḥ al-ʿUrwa al-wuthqā*. Transcribed by Muḥammad Taqī al-Khūʾī. Qom: Muʾassasat al-Khūʾī al-Islāmiyya, 2009.

al-Kulaynī, Muḥammad b. Yaʿqūb. *al-Kāfī*. Edited by ʿAlī Akbar al-Ghaffārī. Tehran: Dār al-Kutub al-Islāmiyya, 1968.

al-Majlisī, Muḥammad Bāqir. *Mirʾāt al-ʿuqūl fī sharḥ Akhbār Āl al-Rasūl*. Tehran: Dār al-Kutub al-Islāmiyya, 1984.

Makārim Shīrāzī, Nāṣir. *Anwār al-fiqāha fī aḥkām al-ʿiṭra al-ṭāhira*. Qom: Dār Nashr al-Imām ʿAlī b. Abī Ṭālib, 2011.

al-Mūsawī al-ʿĀmilī, Muḥammad b. ʿAlī. *Nihāyat al-marām fī sharḥ Mukhtaṣar Sharāʾiʿ al-Islām*. Qom: Muʾassasat al-Nashr al-Islāmī, 1992.

Nāʾīnī Gharawī, Muḥammad Ḥusayn. *Munyat al-ṭālib fī ḥāshiyat al-Makāsib*. Transcribed by Mūsā Najafī Khānsārī. Qom: al-Maktaba al-Muḥammadiyya, 1954.

al-Najafī, Muḥammad Ḥasan. *Jawāhir al-kalām fī sharḥ Sharāʾiʿ al-Islām*. Edited by Ḥaydar al-Dabbāgh. Qom: Muʾassasat al-Nashr al-Islāmī, 2012.

Narāqī, Aḥmad. *Mustanad al-Shīʿa fī aḥkām al-Sharīʿa*. Qom: Muʾassasat Āl al-Bayt li-Iḥyāʾ al-Turāth, 2008.

al-Rāghib al-Iṣfahānī, Abū al-Qāsim Ḥusayn b. Muḥammad. *al-Mufradāt fī gharīb al-Qurʾān*. Edited by Ṣafwān ʿAdnān Dāwūdī. Damascus: Dār al-Qalam, 2009.

al-Rūḥānī, Muḥammad Ṣādiq Ḥusaynī. *Fiqh al-Ṣādiq*. Qom: Manshūrāt al-Ijtihād, 2008.

al-Ṣadūq, Muḥammad b. ʿAlī b. Bābawayh. *Man lā yaḥḍuruh al-faqīh*. Edited by ʿAlī Akbar al-Ghaffārī. Tehran: Maktabat al-Ṣadūq, 1972.

al-Sīstānī, ʿAlī. *Minhāj al-ṣāliḥīn*. Najaf: Dār al-Muwarrikh al-ʿArabī, 2021.

al-Ṭabāṭabāʾī, ʿAlī. *Riyāḍ al-masāʾil fī taḥqīq al-aḥkām bi-l-dalāʾil*. Mashhad: Muʾassasat Āl al-Bayt li-Iḥyāʾ al-Turāth, 1997.

al-Ṭabāṭabāʾī, Muḥammad Ḥusayn. *al-Mīzān fī tafsīr al-Qurʾān*. Qom: Jamāʿat al-Mudarrisīn, 2009.

al-Ṭabrisī, Faḍl b. al-Ḥasan. *Majmaʿ al-bayān fī tafsīr al-Qurʾān*. Beirut: Dār al-Murtaḍā wa-Dār al-ʿUlūm, 2005–6.

al-Ṭabrisī, Ḥusayn al-Nūrī. *Mustadrak al-Wasāʾil wa-mustanbaṭ al-masāʾil*. Qom: Muʾassasat Āl al-Bayt li-Iḥyāʾ al-Turāth, 1991.

al-Zuḥaylī, Wahba. *al-Fiqh al-Islāmī wa-adillatuh*. Damascus: Dār al-Fikr, 1996.

ZIBA MIR-HOSSEINI

Competing Conceptions of Marriage in Islam: Between Tradition and Modernity

Marriage, as constructed in classical fiqh rulings (*aḥkām*),[1] is informed by patriarchal ethics and readings of Islam's sacred texts. Over the course of the twentieth century, these rulings confronted the ideals of universal human rights and gender equality, as well as Muslim women's changed status in society and the rise of feminist voices and scholarship in Islam. Today, there are competing conceptions of marriage in Islamic discourses, from subscribing to a modified version of classical fiqh rulings to striving for gender equality.

In this paper, I explore this contestation as a Muslim woman who aspires to social justice, and as a long-term participant in debates on gender equality in law. I argue that classical fiqh rulings on marriage and divorce are neither divine nor immutable but juristic constructions that need to be rethought from within the tradition in the light of contemporary lived realities and notions of justice that include gender equality. I begin by outlining classical fiqh rulings on marriage and their underpinning assumptions, which continue to be reflected in contemporary Muslim family laws. I proceed to show how twentieth-century developments – notably shifts in the politics of religion, law, and gender in Muslim contexts and the expansion of feminism and human rights discourses – placed the question of women's rights at the centre of Muslim debates and by the end of the century gave rise to a new gender discourse that came to be known as 'Islamic feminism'. This is followed by a discussion of recent reformist and feminist voices and scholarship in Islam, and the political and hermeneutical challenges they face. The focus will be on the work of Musawah, a movement of scholars and activists for justice and equality in the Muslim family.

Three themes run through and link the three parts of my narrative. First, gender rights are neither fixed, given, nor absolute. They are social, cultural, and legal constructs which are asserted, negotiated, and subject to change. They are produced in response to lived realities, in particular, to power relations in the family and society,

1 By 'classical', I mean dating from the formative period, up to the nineteenth century.

by those who want either to retain or to change the present situation. They exist in and through the ways in which we think and talk (both publicly and privately) and study and write about them.[2]

Secondly, gender equality is a modern ideal that did not enter Islam's juristic landscape until the twentieth century, along with the expansion of feminist and human rights discourses. To use an idiom from the Muslim juristic tradition, the idea of equality between men is among the 'newly created issues' (*masāʾil mustaḥdatha*). Simply put, it is an idea foreign to pre-twentieth-century Muslim jurists, as it was not part of their social experience.

Finally, the idea of gender equality has created an 'epistemological crisis' in the Muslim legal tradition that Muslims have been trying to resolve with varying degrees of success, since the late nineteenth century. I borrow this concept from the philosopher Alasdair MacIntyre, who argues that every rational enquiry is embedded in a tradition of learning, and that tradition reaches an epistemological crisis when, by its own standards of rational justification, disagreements can no longer be resolved rationally. This, MacIntyre asserts, gives rise to an internal critique that will eventually transform the tradition.[3] The breakthrough in the Muslim legal tradition, I contend, came with the rise of new reformist and feminist voices and scholarship.

MARRIAGE AS CONCEPTUALISED IN CLASSICAL FIQH[4]

In classical fiqh texts marriage is not a sacrament, but a contract imbued with a strong patriarchal ethos, and crosses the boundary between its two main categories of rulings: those pertaining to *ʿibādāt* (ritual/spiritual acts) and those pertaining to *muʿāmalāt* (social/contractual acts). In spirit, marriage belongs to *ʿibādāt*, in that jurists speak of it as a religious duty ordained by God. In form, however, it comes in the category of *muʿāmalāt*, being defined as a contract that renders sexual relations between a man and a woman licit; any sexual contact outside this contract is defined as *zinā* and is subject to punishment. In its legal structure, marriage is a contract of exchange with defined terms and uniform effect, and is patterned after

2 Ziba Mir-Hosseini, *Islam and Gender: The Religious Debate in Contemporary Iran* (Princeton: Princeton University Press, 1999), 6.

3 Alisdair MacIntyre, *Whose Justice? Which Rationality?* (Notre Dame, IN: University of Notre Dame Press, 1988), 350–52.

4 The discussion here is intended merely to outline the salient features of the marriage contract; for critical analysis of the conception of marriage in classical texts, see Kecia Ali, *Sexual Ethics and Islam: Feminist Reflections on Qur'an, Hadith, and Jurisprudence*, 2nd ed. (London: Oneworld, 2016); and Kecia Ali, *Marriage and Slavery in Early Islam* (Cambridge, MA: Harvard University Press, 2010).

the contract of sale (*bayʿ*). The contract has three essential components: the offer (*ījāb*) by the woman or her guardian, the acceptance (*qabūl*) by the man, and the payment of dower (*mahr*), a sum of money or any valuable that the husband pays or undertakes to pay to the bride before or after consummation, according to their mutual agreement.[5]

The contract places a wife under her husband's *qiwāma*, a mixture of dominion and protection. It also defines a default set of fixed rights and obligations for each party, some supported by legal force, others with moral sanction. Those with legal force revolve around sexual access and compensation, embodied in the two concepts *tamkīn* (obedience; also, *ṭāʿa*) and *nafaqa* (maintenance). *Tamkīn*, defined as sexual submission, is a man's right and thus a woman's duty; whereas *nafaqa*, defined as shelter, food, and clothing, is a woman's right and thus a man's duty. In some schools, a woman becomes entitled to *nafaqa* only after consummation of the marriage; in others, this comes with the contract itself – but in all schools she loses her claim if she is in a state of *nushūz* (disobedience), which the classical jurists defined only in sexual terms. Among the default rights of the husband is his power to control his wife's movements and her 'excess piety'. She needs his permission to leave the house, to take up employment, or to engage in fasting or forms of worship other than what is obligatory (e.g. the fast of Ramadan). Such acts may infringe on the husband's right of 'unhampered sexual access'. There is no matrimonial regime; the husband is the sole owner of the matrimonial resources, and the wife remains the possessor of her dower and whatever she brings to or earns during the marriage.

A man can enter up to four marriages at a time,[6] and can terminate each contract at will. Legally speaking, *ṭalāq*, repudiation of the wife, is a unilateral act (*īqāʿ*), which acquires legal effect by the declaration of the husband. A woman cannot be released without her husband's consent, although she can secure her release through offering him inducements, by means of *khulʿ*, which is often referred to as 'divorce by mutual consent'. As defined by classical jurists, *khulʿ* is a separation claimed by the wife as a result of her extreme 'reluctance' (*karāhiyya*) towards her husband. The essential element is the payment of compensation (*ʿiwaḍ*) to the husband in return for her release. This can be the return of the dower, or any other form of compensation.

5 For a concise discussion of the terms of the marriage contract in classical fiqh texts, see Muḥammad Jawād Maghniyya, *Marriage according to the Five Schools of Islamic Law*, vol. 5 (Tehran: Department of Translation and Publication, Islamic Culture and Relations Organisation, 1997); and Kecia Ali, 'Marriage in Classical Islamic Jurisprudence: A Survey of Doctrines', in *The Islamic Marriage Contract: Case Studies in Islamic Family Law*, ed. Asifa Quraishi and Frank E. Vogel (Cambridge, MA: Harvard University Press, 2008), 11–45.

6 In Shīʿa law, a man may contract as many temporary marriages (*mutʿa*) as he desires or can afford.

Unlike *ṭalāq*, *khulʿ* is not a unilateral but a bilateral act, as it cannot take legal effect without the consent of the husband. If she fails to secure his consent, then her only recourse is the intervention of the court and the judge's power either to compel the husband to pronounce *ṭalāq* or to pronounce it on his behalf if the wife establishes one of the recognised grounds – which again vary from school to school.

These rulings, in brief, embody the classical fiqh construction of marriage, and this construction, of course, must be understood and analysed in its proper social and historical contexts. Classical jurists lived in a world in which patriarchy and slavery were part of the fabric of society; inequality and hierarchy were the natural order of things. Thus, they saw no reason to disguise the patriarchal logic behind these rulings on marriage, which reflected the culture of the time.

For instance, this is how Muḥaqqiq al-Ḥillī, the thirteenth-century Shīʿī jurist, defined marriage:

> Marriage etymologically is uniting one thing with another thing; it is also said to mean sexual intercourse ... it has been said that it is a contract whose object is that of dominion over the vagina (*baḍʿ*), without the right of its possession. It has also been said that it is a verbal contract that first establishes the right to sexual intercourse, that is to say: it is not like buying a female slave when the man acquires the right of intercourse as a consequence of the possession of the slave.[7]

Khalīl b. Isḥāq, the fourteenth-century Mālikī jurist, was more explicit when it came to the dower (*mahr*) and its function in marriage: 'When a woman marries, she sells a part of her person. In the market one buys merchandise, in marriage the husband buys the genital *arvum mulieris*.'[8] Jurjānī, another Mālikī jurist, defined marriage as 'a contract through which the husband acquires exclusive rights over the sexual organs of a woman'.[9]

By saying that in classical fiqh the contracts of marriage and sale share the same legal structure, I do not mean to suggest that jurists considered the marriage contract to be a 'sale'; they showed themselves aware of possible misunderstanding and were careful to stress that marriage resembles sale only in form, not in essence. However, there is no denying that, in their definition of marriage, a woman's sexuality, if not

7 Muḥaqqiq al-Ḥillī, *Sharāyiʿ al-Islām*, vol. 2, Persian trans. 'Abd al-Qāsim b. Aḥmad Yazdī, compiled by Muḥammad Taqī Dānish-Pazhuh (Tehran: Tehran University Press, 1985), 428.

8 F. H. Ruxton, *Maliki Law: A Summary from French Translations of the Mukhtaṣar of Sīdī Khalīl* (London: Luzac & Co., 1916), 106. 'Genital *arvum mulieris*' is Ruxton's Latinisation of the Arabic *badʿ* (vagina).

9 Quoted by Octave Pesle, *Le Mariage chez les Malekites de l'Afrique du Nord* (Rabat: Moncho, 1936), 20.

her person, became an object of exchange, treated as property.[10] It was this logic that lurked behind the classical fiqh conception of marriage and defined its parameters in laws. This in turn was bolstered by a set of philosophical, metaphysical, social, and legal assumptions and beliefs about gender roles that shaped the jurists' readings of the sacred texts. Salient among them were: 'women are created of and for men', 'God made men superior to women', 'women are defective in reason and faith', and women's sexuality was a source of corruption in society that served as a rationale for excluding them from public life and subjugating them in marriage.[11]

UPHOLDING CLASSICAL FIQH RULINGS ON MARRIAGE IN THE TWENTIETH CENTURY

Classical fiqh rulings on marriage continue to be the source of family law in Muslim contexts, though they have been the subject of intense contestation and debate. For some, these laws embody the ideal model of family and gender relations; for others, they encapsulate the patriarchal logic of pre-modern interpretations of Islam's sacred sources. The debate began in the late nineteenth century, and it remains entangled with the politics of Muslim encounters with modernity and with Western colonial powers, during which women and Islamic law became symbols and carriers of cultural tradition, a battleground between the forces of traditionalism and modernity.[12]

In much of the Muslim world the first part of the twentieth century saw the expansion of secular education, the retreat of religion from politics, and the secularisation of laws and legal systems. With the end of colonial rule, new nation-states founded in Muslim-majority countries in most cases put aside classical fiqh rulings in all legal areas except family and personal status law. In family law, they selectively reformed, codified, and grafted the rulings of classical fiqh onto unified legal systems inspired by Western models. In codifying these rulings, the modernisers left the substance of

10 This is an old patriarchal idea that predates the emergence of Abrahamic religions, including Islam. 'The establishment of patriarchy was not a single "event" but a process developing over a period of nearly 2,500 years from approximately 3100 to 600 BC.' Gerda Lerner, *The Creation of Patriarchy* (Oxford: Oxford University Press, 1986), 8.

11 All have been challenged by feminist scholarship in Islam, as discussed below.

12 Whether these rulings corresponded to actual marriage practices and gender relations is, of course, another area of enquiry. Indeed recent scholarship tells us of discrepancies between juristic discourse and judicial and marriage practices; see, for instance, Yossef Rapoport, *Marriage, Money and Divorce in Medieval Islamic Society* (Cambridge: Cambridge University Press, 2005); Amira El Azhary Sonbol, ed., *Women, the Family and Divorce Laws in Islamic History* (Syracuse: Syracuse University Press, 1996); Judith E. Tucker, *In the House of Law: Gender and Islamic Law in Ottoman Syria and Palestine* (Berkeley: University of California Press, 1998).

the marriage contract, as defined by classical jurists, intact, and instituted reforms through procedural rules, such as requiring the registration of marriage and divorce, and limiting men's rights to unilateral divorce and polygamy.[13]

Codification of fiqh provisions led to the creation of hybrid family laws that were neither classical fiqh nor modern. Codes and statute books took the place of classical fiqh manuals, and laws regulating marriage and divorce were no longer solely a matter for Muslim scholars, the ulema, operating within their respective fiqh schools, but became the concern of the legislative assembly of a particular nation-state. Deprived of the power to define and administer family law, fiqh and its practitioners lost touch with changing political realities and were unable to meet the epistemological challenges of modernity, including the idea of gender equality.

These developments led to the emergence of both a modified version of classical fiqh gender discourse, and a genre of literature under the rubric of 'the status of women in Islam', which promoted this discourse by smoothing the harsh edges of classical fiqh language. Published by religious houses in both Muslim and Western countries, this literature is now available (much of it on the internet) in a variety of languages, including English.[14]

Written for the public and, at least until recently, by men, these texts are punctuated by general and abstract statements such as 'Islamic law grants women all their rights', 'Islamic law honours and protects women'. Aware of and sensitive to criticisms of the patriarchal bias of Muslim family law, the authors' objectives are to clarify 'misunderstandings' about Islamic family laws and to explain the 'high status of women in Islam'. They quote Qur'anic verses and *aḥādīth* that affirm the essential equality of the sexes in marriage, which they define using the terms 'equity' and 'complementarity'. But they keep silent on the logic that underlies the whole edifice of marriage in classical fiqh texts: women's sexuality as property, and marriage as a form of sale.

13 For codification and reforms, see Norman Anderson, *Law Reforms in the Muslim World* (London: Athlone Press, 1976); and Fazlur Rahman, 'A Survey of Modernization of Muslim Family Law', *International Journal of Middle East Studies* 11, no. 4 (1980): 451–65.

14 This literature is too vast to be listed here. For discussion of such writings in the Arab world, see Yvonne Yazbeck Haddad, 'Islam and Gender: Dilemmas in the Changing Arab World', in *Islam, Gender, and Social Change*, ed. Yvonne Yazbeck Haddad and John L. Esposito (New York: Oxford University Press, 1988), 1–29; Barbara F. Stowasser, 'Women's Issues in Modern Islamic Thought', in *Arab Women: Old Boundaries, New Frontiers*, ed. Judith E. Tucker (Bloomington: Indiana University Press, 1993), 3–28. For Iran, see Mir-Hosseini, *Islam and Gender*. For Muslims living in Europe and North America, see Anne Sofie Roald, 'Feminist Reinterpretation of Islamic Sources: Muslim Feminist Theology in the Light of the Christian Tradition of Feminist Thought', in *Women and Islamization: Contemporary Dimensions of Discourse on Gender Relations*, ed. Karin Ask and Marit Tjomsland (Oxford: Berg, 1998), 17–44. For a critical engagement with them, see Lamia Rustum Shehadeh, *The Idea of Women in Fundamentalist Islam* (Gainesville: University Press of Florida, 2003).

Likewise, they enumerate the ethical and moral rules that govern marriage for both spouses, and show concern about the protection of women, but overlook the fact that these rules, in effect, carry no legal sanction, nor do they offer comprehensive and viable arguments for translating them into imperatives. In doing so, they reproduce an obscured version of the classical fiqh discourse on marriage.

Not all these texts contain arguments in their defence of classical fiqh rulings, and those that do tend to follow a similar line: Men and women are created equal and are equal in the eyes of God, but the roles assigned to them in creation are different. The laws of Islam are in line with 'human nature' (*fiṭra*) and take into consideration the biological and psychological differences between the sexes. Differences in rights and duties, and inequality in law, do not mean injustice; if correctly understood, they are the very essence of justice. This line of argument continues to form the theoretical backbone of opposition to reform in family law in contemporary Muslim contexts.

The underlying patriarchal assumptions concealed in the arguments of the proponents of 'complementarily of rights and duties', and their notion of justice in marriage, come to the surface, for example, in Abul A'la Maudoodi's *Laws of Marriage and Divorce in Islam,*[15] and in Murtaḍā Muṭahharī's *Rights of Women in Islam.*[16] Both authors were Islamic ideologues, and their writings, rooted in anti-colonial and anti-Western discourses, have become seminal texts for Islamist groups and movements. For both, equality between men and women is an imported Western concept, alien to Islam, that must be resisted.[17] They differ in their language and style of argument, but they share the classical jurists' conception of marriage, as evident in the following passages in which they oppose women's demand for an equal right to divorce.

Maudoodi:

> If she were to be given this right, she would grow over-bold and easily violate the man's rights. It is evident that if a person buys something with money, he tries to keep it as long as he can. He parts with it only when he cannot help it. But when a thing is purchased by one individual, and the right to cast it away is given to another, there is little hope that the latter will protect the interest of the buyer, who invested the money. Investing man with the right to divorce

15 Maulana Abul A'ala Maudoodi, *The Laws of Marriage and Divorce in Islam*, trans. Fazl Ahmed (Kuwait: Islamic Book Publishers, 1983); the translation gives no date for the Urdu original, but includes two appendices dated 1940 and 1941.

16 Murtaḍā Muṭahharī, *The Rights of Women in Islam*, 4th ed. (Tehran: World Organisation for Islamic Services, 1991).

17 Writing in Urdu in the context of pre-partition India, Maudoodi was inflexible in rejecting and condemning modernity and liberal values; Muṭahharī, writing in Persian in 1960s Iran as part of the religious opposition to the Pahlavi regime's secularising policies, was less adamant in his opposition to modernity and less overtly patriarchal in his language.

> amounts to the protection of his legitimate rights. This also checks the growth of the divorce rate.[18]

Muṭahharī:

> Sometimes these people ask: 'Why does divorce take the form of a release, an emancipation? Surely it should have a judicial form.' To answer these people, it should be said: 'Divorce is a release in the same way that marriage is a state of dominance.' If you can possibly do so, change the natural law of seeking a mate in its absoluteness with regard to the male and the female, remove the natural state of marriage from the condition of dominance; if you can, make the role of the male and female sexes in all human beings and animals identical in their relations, and change the law of nature. Then you will be able to rid divorce of its aspect of release and emancipation.[19]

The mode of language in these two passages may differ from that of classical jurists, but there is no denying that they share the notion of marriage as domination and the legal logic of sale. By not engaging critically with the classical fiqh rulings on marriage and divorce, much of twentieth-century literature on 'the status of women in Islam' resorted to notions such as 'nature' and 'essential differences' to provide new rationales for these rulings. In this way, the 'equity/complementarity' discourse perpetuates gender stereotypes that both stem from and reinforce unequal power relations in marriage.

CONTESTING CLASSICAL FIQH RULINGS ON MARRIAGE: THE EMERGENCE OF ISLAMIC FEMINISM

Towards the end of the twentieth century, two parallel developments brought an open critique of the classical fiqh notion of marriage. One was the success of political Islam and its slogan of 'return to Sharī'a', which in practice amounted to little more than attempts to translate into state law and policy classical fiqh rulings on gender relations and family. In late colonial times and the immediately postcolonial decades of the twentieth century, many advocates of women's rights in Muslim contexts had increasingly come to identify Islam with patriarchy and to fear that the removal of the latter could not be achieved under a polity and a legal regime dominated by Islam. Wherever political Islam gained power or influence – as in Iran, Pakistan, and Sudan – such policies proved the validity of these fears. Arguing for patriarchal rulings as 'God's law', as the authentic 'Islamic' way of life, Islamists in power tried to reverse

18 Maudoodi, *Laws of Marriage and Divorce*, 27.

19 Muṭahharī, *Rights of Women in Islam*, 247.

some of the legal gains that women had made earlier in the century. They dismantled elements of earlier family law reforms and introduced morality laws, such as those prescribing gender segregation and dress codes.[20]

These measures had some unintended consequences; the most important was that they brought classical fiqh texts out of the closet and exposed them to unprecedented critical scrutiny and public debate. A new wave of Muslim reform thinkers started to respond to the Islamist challenge and to take Islamic legal thought onto new ground. Building on the earlier reformers, these new thinkers contended that the human understanding of Islam is flexible, that Islam's tenets can be interpreted to encourage both pluralism and democracy, and that Islam allows change in the face of time, place, and experience. Unlike the earlier trend of reform thinkers, instead of searching Islamic textual sources for a genealogy for modern concepts like gender equality, human rights, and democracy, they placed the emphasis on how religion is understood and how religious knowledge is produced.[21]

The other development was the expansion of transnational feminism and women's groups, and the emergence of women's NGOs, which led to the opening of a new phase in the politics of gender and Islamic law. Women were largely absent from earlier processes of reforming and codifying Muslim family law and the associated debates, but by the end of the century, Muslim women were refusing to be merely objects of the law; rather, they claimed the right to speak and to be active participants in the debates and the process of law-making. The changed status of women in Muslim societies, and other socio-economic imperatives, meant that many more women than before were educated and in employment. Women's rights were by now part of human rights discourse, and human rights treaties and documents, in particular the Convention on the Elimination of All Forms of Discrimination Against Women (CEDAW), gave women a new language in which to frame their demands.

The confluence of these two developments opened new space for activism and debate. Not only recognised religious authorities and those with other interpretations and agendas, not least women scholars, but also laypeople, started engaging in debate and in criticism of interpretations old and new. There were, of course, Muslim women who argued for an egalitarian interpretation of the Sharīʿa, but there now emerged critical feminist voices and scholarship from within the Muslim legal

20 For this development in several countries, see Norani Othman, ed., *Muslim Women and the Challenge of Islamic Fundamentalism* (Kuala Lumpur: Sisters in Islam, 2005).

21 For an introduction to and samples of the work of Muslim reform thinkers, see Charles Kurzman, ed., *Modernist Islam, 1840–1940: A Sourcebook* (Oxford: Oxford University Press, 2002); and Katajun Amirpur, *New Thinking in Islam: The Jihad for Freedom, Democracy and Women's Rights* (London: Gingko Library, 2015). For a critical historical analysis, see Nasr Abu Zayd, *Reformation of Islamic Thought: A Critical Historical Analysis* (Amsterdam: Amsterdam University Press, 2006).

tradition, in the form of a new literature that deserves the label 'feminist', in that it is sustained and informed by an analysis that inserts gender as a category of analysis into religious knowledge.[22] Taking Islam as the source of legitimacy, Islamic feminists began to question both the hegemony of patriarchal interpretations of the Sharīʿa and the authority of those who speak in the name of Islam. They have produced an impressive body of scholarship to tackle patriarchal interpretations and text-based sources of gender inequalities and to reclaim Islam's egalitarian message.[23]

This literature is extensive and diverse in approach;[24] here I can merely outline the argument as to how and why male dominance came to be embedded in the Muslim legal tradition. This was done through two sets of related processes. The first is ideological and political and has to do with the strong patriarchal ethos that informed readings of the sacred texts, the exclusion of women from the production of religious knowledge, and their consequent inability to have their voices heard and their interests reflected in law. Women had been among the main transmitters of the *ḥadīth* traditions and remained active in transmitting religious knowledge, but their activities were limited to the informal arena of homes and mosques and their status as jurists was not officially recognised.[25] By the time the fiqh schools were consolidated, over a century after the Prophet's death, their critical faculties were so far denigrated as to make their concerns irrelevant to law-making processes.

22 See Ziba Mir-Hosseini, 'Justice, Equality and Muslim Family Laws: New Ideas, New Prospects', in *Gender and Equality in Muslim Family Law: Justice and Ethics in the Islamic Legal Tradition*, ed. Ziba Mir-Hosseini, Kari Vogt, Lena Larsen, and Christian Moe (London: I.B. Tauris, 2013), 7–34.

23 See, for instance, Azizah al-Hibri, 'A Study of Islamic Herstory: How Did We Ever Get into This Mess', in 'Islam and Women', special issue, *Women's Studies International Forum* 5, no.2 (1982): 207–19; Riffat Hassan, 'Equal before Allah? Woman-Man Equality in the Islamic Tradition', *Harvard Divinity Bulletin* 7, no. 2 (1987): 2–4; Fatima Mernissi, *Women and Islam: An Historical and Theological Enquiry*, trans. Mary Jo Lakeland (Oxford: Blackwell, 1991); Amina Wadud, *Qur'an and Woman: Rereading the Sacred Text from a Woman's Perspective* (New York: Oxford University Press, 1999); Kecia Ali, 'Progressive Muslims and Islamic Jurisprudence: The Necessity for Critical Engagement with Marriage and Divorce Law', in *Progressive Muslims: On Justice, Gender and Pluralism*, ed. Omid Safi (Oxford: Oneworld, 2003), 163–89; Asma Barlas, *'Believing Women' in Islam: Unreading Patriarchal Interpretations of the Qur'an* (Austin: University of Texas Press, 2002); Sa'diyya Shaikh, 'Knowledge, Women, and Gender in the Ḥadīth: A Feminist Interpretation', *Islam and Christian–Muslim Relations* 15, no. 1 (2004): 99–108.

24 For recent assessments of this literature, see Omaima Abou-Bakr, ed., *Feminist and Islamic Perspectives: New Horizons of Knowledge and Reform* (Cairo: The Women and Memory Forum, 2013); Fatima Seedat, 'When Islam and Feminism Converge', *The Muslim World* 103, no. 3 (2013): 404–20; Marcia Hermansen, 'New Voices of Women Theologians', in *Muslima Theology: The Voices of Muslim Women Theologians*, ed. Ednan Aslan, Marcia Hermansen, and Elif Medeni (Frankfurt am Main: Peter Lang, 2013), 11–34; Adis Duderija, 'Toward a Scriptural Hermeneutics of Islamic Feminism', *Journal of Feminist Studies in Religion* 31, no. 2 (2015): 45–64.

25 Asma Sayeed, *Women and the Transmission of Religious Knowledge in Islam* (New York: Cambridge University Press, 2013).

The second set of processes is more epistemological and involves the ways in which seventh-century social norms, marriage practices, and gender ideologies were sanctified, and then turned into fixed entities and legal concepts. That is, rather than being considered as social, thus temporal, institutions, and phenomena, they were treated as 'divinely ordained', thus immutable.[26]

Muslim feminists have also been engaging critically with the main argument of the gender 'equity/complementary' discourse, whose advocates, as we have seen, adhere to a modified version of classical fiqh rulings, according to which gender equality goes against both the laws of nature and the requirements of justice. Because of their nature, women need protection by men, and treating them as equal with men amounts to the denial of 'natural' differences between them, and constitutes thereby an injustice.[27]

Drawing on feminist legal studies and notions of justice, Muslim feminists argue for going beyond the binary of 'equality' versus 'difference'. Instead of opposites, we need to see them as interdependent: equality is not the elimination of difference, and difference does not preclude equality. We need equality as a principle of justice in society, in law, for regulating human relations, including gender relations, precisely because all humans are different in their capacities, access to resources, and so on. Creating a binary opposition between the two produces a false choice when it comes to gender relations: between endorsing either 'equality' or its presumed antithesis, 'difference'.[28]

This way of thinking about equality and difference is embodied in what came to be known as 'substantive equality', which takes into account differences between the sexes as well as offering a critique of the gender-neutral laws that underpinned the earlier approach to equality. Known as 'formal equality', this model does not necessarily enable women to enjoy their rights on the same basis as men, because the starting point is not the same for men and women, and the playing field is not level. Not only do women *not* have the same access as men to socio-economic resources and political opportunities, but women are not a homogeneous group; they do not all experience discrimination in the same way; class, age, ethnicity, socio-economic situation are all determinants of disadvantages faced by women.[29] A *substantive* approach to equality,

26 Abdulaziz Sachedina, 'Women, Half-the-Man? Crisis of Male Epistemology in Islamic Jurisprudence', in *Perspectives on Islamic Law, Justice, and Society*, ed. R. S. Khare (Lanham: Rowman & Littlefield, 1999), 15–31.

27 For a critique of pre-modern notions of justice, see Mohsen Kadivar, 'Revisiting Women's Rights in Islam: "Egalitarian Justice" in Lieu of "Deserts-Based Justice"', in Mir-Hosseini et al., *Gender and Equality in Muslim Family Law*, 213–34.

28 Joan Scott, 'Deconstructing Equality-versus-Difference: Or, the Uses of Poststructuralist Theory for Feminism', *Feminist Studies* 14, no. 1 (1998): 33–50.

29 For instance, see Sandra Fredman, 'Providing Equality: Substantive Equality and the Positive Duty to Provide', *South African Journal of Human Rights* 21 (2005): 163–90; and Ratna Kapur,

by contrast, takes these factors into account. Instead of striving for gender-neutral laws, the objective is the kinds of laws and legal reforms that can ensure equality of opportunity and result, and that regulate power relations between men and women in such a way that women are able to enjoy dignity, security, and respect in the family, and full participation in society.

Inspired by the Qur'anic vision of justice, Muslim feminists contend that justice can be achieved with laws that transform power relations in marriage and in society in the direction of just outcomes. The protectionist approach, on the other hand, which underlies both the classical fiqh notion of marriage and gender relations and its current version of 'equity/complementarity', keeps unequal power relations in marriage and society intact, and in effect leads to injustice. This is so because, in order to 'protect' women from harm and wrongdoing, it curtails their freedom and sphere of activities. It treats women as perpetual minors, undermines their human dignity (*karāma*), and prevents them from fulfilling their potential in both spiritual and social realms.

To give a concrete example, let me introduce Musawah and its research activities. Launched in 2009 in Kuala Lumpur, Musawah is a global movement that brings together scholars and activists advocating equality and justice in the Muslim family. Our aim (I am a founding member) is to encourage new perspectives on Islamic teachings by reinserting women's lived realities and voices into the processes of law-making and the production of religious knowledge. We build our arguments for reform and our claim to gender equality using a holistic approach that combines Islamic teachings, international human rights standards, national laws and constitutional guarantees of equality and non-discrimination, and the lived realities of Muslim families. We understand 'equality' to mean substantive and transformative equality that aims at the long-term transformation of institutions and systems to ensure that women have equal and full decision-making powers in family, society, and the state.[30]

Two questions are at the centre of our work: If justice and equality are values central to Islam, as we believe they are, why have women been treated as inferior to men in the Muslim legal tradition and in Muslim societies? And if equality has become inherent to conceptions of justice in modern times, as many Muslims now recognise, how can it be reflected in Muslim laws?

In 2011, as part of its knowledge-building area of work, Musawah initiated a long-term, multifaceted project to rethink the notion of authority in the Muslim family,

---

'Un-veiling Equality: Disciplining the "Other" Woman through the Human Rights Discourse', in *Islamic Law and International Human Rights Law: Searching for Common Ground?*, ed. Anver M. Emon, Mark Ellis, and Benjamin Glahn (Oxford: Oxford University Press, 2012), 265–90.

30 This approach is outlined in Musawah's 'Framework for Action', available in five languages: www.musawah.org/resources/musawah-framework-for-action/.

as encapsulated in the twin concepts of *qiwāma* and *wilāya*, which place women under male guardianship. For the project, we commissioned background papers that expound and interrogate the construction of these two concepts in classical fiqh texts and their underlying religious and legal doctrines, as well as their place and workings in contemporary laws and practices.[31] This naturally took us to Q. 4:34:

> Men are Un (protectors/maintainers) in relation to women, according to what God has favored some over others and according to what they spend from their wealth. Righteous women are *qanitat* (obedient) guarding the unseen according to what God has guarded. Those [women] whose *nushuz* (rebellion) you fear, admonish them, and abandon them in bed, and *adribuhunna* (strike them). If they obey you, do not pursue a strategy against them. Indeed, God is Exalted, Great.[32]

This verse has been the focus of intense contestation and debate among Muslims for over a century. It constitutes the main textual evidence in support of men's authority over women, and from it the classical jurists derived the concept of *qiwāma* or male guardianship over women. It is often the only verse that ordinary Muslims know in relation to family law. There is now a substantial body of literature that contests and reconstructs the meanings and connotations of the four terms that I have highlighted. In her translation of the verse, Kecia Ali has left these four terms in their original Arabic, rightly saying that any translation of them amounts to an interpretation. The translations that I have given in parentheses approximate the consensus of classical jurists, as reflected in the rulings that they devised to define marriage and gender relations.

It is no exaggeration to say that the edifice of family law in the Muslim legal tradition is built on the ways in which classical jurists understood this verse and translated it into legal rulings. As already noted, they defined marriage as a contract that automatically places a wife under her husband's *qiwāma* and presumes an exchange: the wife's obedience and submission (*tamkīn*) in return for maintenance (*nafaqa*) by the husband.

This conception of marriage, which continues, in modified form, to be the backbone of Muslim family law, is premised on a single postulate: that God made men *qawwāmūn* of women and placed them under male authority and protection. This postulate, our research shows, is a juristic construction that has no basis in the Qur'an; it represents a

31 For this project and its objectives, see www.musawah.org/knowledge-building/qiwamah-wilayah. Its first publication appeared as a collected volume, Ziba Mir-Hosseini, Mulki Al-Sharmani, and Jana Rumminger, eds., *Men in Charge? Rethinking Male Authority in Muslim Legal Tradition* (London: Oneworld, 2015).

32 Translation by Kecia Ali, 'Muslim Sexual Ethics: Understanding a Difficult Verse, Qur'an 4:34', Brandeis University, revised 11 February 2003, www.brandeis.edu/projects/fse/muslim/diff-verse.html.

reading of Q. 4:34 that is no longer in line with either contemporary notions of justice or the exigencies of lived realities among contemporary Muslims.

In one of our studies, Omaima Abou-Bakr shows how and through what processes the first sentence of the verse – *al-rijāl qawwāmūn ʿalā al-nisāʾ bi-mā faḍḍal Allāh baʿḍahum ʿalā baʿḍ wa-bi-mā anfaqū min amwālihim* (men are *qawwāmūn* in relation to women according to what God has favoured some over others and according to what they spend from their wealth) – was continually reinterpreted until it became a patriarchal construct.[33] She identifies four stages in this construction. In the first, the sentence was isolated from the rest of the Qur'an and turned into 'an independent and separate (trans-contextual) patriarchal construct'. This, she shows, was done by taking the term *qawwāmūn* out of its immediate context and transforming it into a grammatical *maṣdar* (a verbal noun or infinitive) of *qiwāma*. In the second stage, when the concept was consolidated, rational arguments and justifications were provided for hierarchal relations between men and women. In the third stage, *qiwāma* was expanded by linking it to the idea that men have an advantage over women, from the last phrase in Q. 2:22, 'but men have a *daraja* (degree) over them (women)'. This phrase, part of a long passage on the theme of divorce, was again taken out of its immediate context and interpreted as further support for male superiority; and a selection of *aḥādīth* was also invoked to establish women's duty of obedience. The final stage came in the twentieth century with the modernist thinkers, who linked *qiwāma* with the theory of the 'naturalness' of Islamic law and the ideology of domesticity, using pseudo-psychological knowledge to argue for men's and women's different natures (*fiṭra*).[34]

In another of our studies, Asma Lamrabet argues that *qiwāma* and *wilāya*, in the sense of placing women under male guardianship, are not Qur'anic concepts, but juristic. The term *qiwāma* does not appear at all in the Qur'an; the classical jurists derived the concept from the term *qawwāmūn* in Q. 4:34. *Qawwāmūn* appears in two other Qur'anic verses (Q. 4:135, 5:8), where it has a very different, positive, and gender-inclusive meaning; it exhorts believers – both men and women – to *stand firmly* for God, and uphold the core values of justice, fairness, and impartiality in their actions and judgements. The term *wilāya* does occur in the Qur'an, but never as endorsing male authority over women; yet this is the interpretation of the term enshrined in juristic rulings on marriage. Words related to *wilāya* such as *walī* and its plural *awliyāʾ* appear in many verses as an attribute of God or to describe human beings in particular contexts and stories in the Qur'an. But none of the verses on which the jurists based the doctrine of *wilāya* in regard to marriage guardianship (Q. 2:221,

33 Omaima Abou-Bakr, 'The Interpretive Legacy of *Qiwamah* as an Exegetical Construct', in Mir-Hosseini et al., *Men in Charge?*, 44–64.

34 Ibid.

2:232, 2:234, 2:237, 4:2, 4:3, 4:6, 4:25, 24:32, 60:10, 65:4) uses the term *walī* or *wilāya*. In relation to marriage and marital relations, two other terms appear numerous times: *maʿrūf* (common good) and *mawwada wa-raḥma* (love and compassion, Q. 2:235, 4:19, 30:21, 65:2).[35]

One of the objectives of the research was to bring insights from feminist theory and gender studies into the debates around Muslim family law, and to ask new questions. Why and how did Q. 4:34 become the foundation for the legal construction of marriage? How, and through what juristic processes, was men's authority over women legitimated and translated into law? Why is *qiwāma* still the basis of gender relations in the imagination of modern-day jurists and Muslims who resist and denounce the idea of equality in marriage as alien to Islam? What does male guardianship, derived from the concepts *qiwāma* and *wilāya*, entail in practice? How can Muslim women rethink and reconstruct these concepts in ways that reflect their own notions of justice? What kind of family do Sharīʿa-based laws aim to protect? What do equality and justice mean for women and the family?

The key insight from this project is that the pre-modern construction of male authority, which continues to be the source of contemporary family law, is not only based on theologically unfounded constructions of the two concepts but also poses a crisis for contemporary Muslims on multiple levels. The solution to this crisis does not simply lie in reforming individual juristic rulings and/or their modern-day manifestations in state laws, but rather requires a substantive transformation, entailing the production of an egalitarian jurisprudence of marriage. This necessitates a systematic hermeneutical engagement with different areas of Islamic interpretive tradition, including mapping the central ethical principles of the Qur'an and examining their relevance to contemporary times in order to envision a jurisprudence of marriage that regards spouses as equal partners.

It is towards this objective that in 2019 Musawah initiated its second research project, to build and promote an understanding of marriage as a partnership of equals in a way that is rooted within the Muslim legal tradition. Entitled 'Reclaiming *ʿAdl* and *Iḥsān* in Muslim Marriages: Between Ethics and Law', the project starts from the premise that the ethical worldview and message of Islam affirm the equal worth of all humans and call for social relations (including gender relations) to reflect core Qur'anic ethical principles such as justice (*ʿadl*), goodness and beauty (*iḥsān*), and doing what is commonly known to be good (*maʿrūf*). While these values have multiple meanings that evolve according to different contexts and circumstances, the research project is based on an understanding of *ʿadl* as encompassing values of transformative

35 Asma Lamrabet, 'An Egalitarian Reading of the Concepts of *Khalifah*, *Wilayah* and *Qiwamah*', in Mir-Hosseini et al., *Men in Charge?*, 65–87.

justice and equality; and *iḥsān* as a call to pursue beauty and goodness and care in individual and broader social relations.[36]

The first product of this project is an edited volume published in 2022.[37] It comprises twelve chapters written by seventeen international scholars from different disciplines, who engage with various theological, historical, and legal sources in the Islamic tradition as well as contemporary trajectories of Muslim family law reforms. Collectively, these chapters provide a wealth of ideas as to why and how the dominant conception of Muslim marriage can be shifted from a contract of exchange that requires a woman's obedience in exchange for a man's protection and maintenance, to a partnership of equals, grounded in justice and the mutual well-being of the spouses.

Musawah is one among several movements around the Muslim world now active in meetings as well as through lively online and social media debates, challenging from within the authoritarian and patriarchal ethics of established interpretations of the Sharīʿa, which have become irrelevant to the ethical values of many Muslims.

CONCLUSION

I conclude by summarising my argument and considering the potential of Muslim feminist voices in transforming the patriarchal ethics in the Muslim legal tradition to bring about egalitarian gender relations.

As equality has become inherent to widely accepted conceptions of justice, in the course of the twentieth century, the resultant 'epistemological crisis' in the Muslim legal tradition has opened a space for contestations and negotiations. Reformist and feminist voices and scholarship in Islam offer an internal critique of pre-modern interpretations of the Sharīʿa that cannot be ignored. The old rationale and logic for laws that deny equality to women, previously undisputed, have lost their power to convince and cannot be defended on ethical grounds. The new internal critique is giving increasing legitimacy, among Muslims too, to the idea of gender equality – an idea that until recently was considered alien.

New interpretations of Islam's sacred texts have emerged that are slowly but surely changing the terms of reference of gender discourses from within. Nurtured by new trends of reformist thought, they start from the premise that the textual sources of Islam are not inherently patriarchal, nor do they set out an exhaustive set of eternal laws. What they give us is ethical guidance and principles for the creation of just laws. The Qur'an upholds justice and exhorts Muslims to stand for justice; but it does not

36 See www.musawah.org/knowledge-building/reclaiming-adl-and-ihsan/.

37 Ziba Mir-Hosseini, Mulki Al-Sharmani, Jana Rumminger, and Sarah Marsso, eds., *Justice and Beauty in Muslim Marriages: Towards Egalitarian Ethics and Law* (London: Oneworld, 2022).

give us a definition of justice; rather, it gives direction, the path to follow towards justice, which is always bound by time and context. To understand the Qur'an's direction, they contend, we need a critical reassessment of the entire Islamic intellectual tradition: theology, ethics, philosophy, and jurisprudence.

However, this fresh approach faces a major obstacle: entrenched patriarchal and authoritarian structures in Muslim contexts that conspire to silence the voices of reform and change. The proponents of traditionalist ideas and practices will not easily relinquish established interpretations of the Sharīʿa, as reflected in classical fiqh rulings that allowed discrimination on the basis of gender, and continue to be the source of contemporary family law and practices in many Muslim contexts.

In other words, the problem is not – and never was – with the text, but with the context, and with the ways of knowing the text, as well as the ways in which the text has been used to sustain patriarchal and authoritarian structures. The strategy cannot be just logical argument and informed reinterpretations from within the tradition; there must also be challenges on the political front. What are the motives and interests of those who claim the authority to speak in the name of religion, who manipulate interpretations of the texts for authoritarian purposes?

Feminist voices and scholarship in Islam take up these challenges. They are opening the way for a meaningful and constructive conversation between feminism and the Muslim legal tradition. This conversation, I argue, has important epistemological and political implications. On the epistemological side, feminist critical theory enables us to see how unreflective assumptions and 'common-sense' arguments limit and deform our knowledge; and gives us tools for analysing relations between the production of knowledge and the practices of power. It also provides us with a research methodology for giving voice to women and inserting their concerns and interests in the process of law-making.

On the political front, bringing current Muslim legal thought into conversation with feminism can pave the way for transcending ideological dichotomies such as 'secular' versus 'religious' feminism, or 'Islam' versus 'human rights', to which Muslim women's quest for equality and dignity has remained hostage since the early twentieth century. These dichotomies have masked the real site of battle, which is between patriarchal and authoritarian structures, on the one hand, and egalitarian, pluralist, and democratic ideologies and forces, on the other.[38]

Unmasking this reality entails two linked processes: recovering and reclaiming the ethical and egalitarian ethos in Islam's sacred texts, and decoding and exposing the relation between the production of knowledge and the practices of power. Here lies

38 Ziba Mir-Hosseini, 'Muslim Legal Tradition and the Challenge of Equality', in Mir-Hosseini et al., *Men in Charge?*, 13–43.

the potential and promise of the new feminist voices and scholarship in Islam: they are part of the larger struggle for the democratisation of knowledge in Islam and for the authority to interpret its sacred texts.

BIBLIOGRAPHY

Abou-Bakr, Omaima, ed. *Feminist and Islamic Perspectives: New Horizons of Knowledge and Reform*. Cairo: The Women and Memory Forum, 2013.

Abou-Bakr, Omaima. 'The Interpretive Legacy of *Qiwamah* as an Exegetical Construct'. In *Men in Charge? Rethinking Male Authority in Muslim Legal Tradition*, edited by Ziba Mir-Hosseini, Mulki Al-Sharmani, and Jana Rumminger, 44–64. London: Oneworld, 2015.

Abu Zayd, Nasr. *Reformation of Islamic Thought: A Critical Historical Analysis*. Amsterdam: Amsterdam University Press, 2006.

Ali, Kecia. *Marriage and Slavery in Early Islam*. Cambridge, MA: Harvard University Press, 2010.

Ali, Kecia. 'Marriage in Classical Islamic Jurisprudence: A Survey of Doctrines'. In *The Islamic Marriage Contract: Case Studies in Islamic Family Law*, edited by Asifa Quraishi and Frank E. Vogel, 11–45. Cambridge, MA: Harvard University Press, 2008.

Ali, Kecia. 'Progressive Muslims and Islamic Jurisprudence: The Necessity for Critical Engagement with Marriage and Divorce Law'. In *Progressive Muslims: On Justice, Gender and Pluralism*, edited by Omid Safi, 163–89. Oxford: Oneworld, 2003.

Ali, Kecia. *Sexual Ethics and Islam: Feminist Reflections on Qur'an, Hadith, and Jurisprudence*. 2nd ed. London: Oneworld, 2016.

Amirpur, Katajun. *New Thinking in Islam: The Jihad for Freedom, Democracy and Women's Rights*. London: Gingko Library, 2015.

Anderson, Norman. *Law Reforms in the Muslim World*. London: Athlone Press, 1976.

Barlas, Asma. *'Believing Women' in Islam: Unreading Patriarchal Interpretations of the Qur'an*. Austin: University of Texas Press, 2002.

Duderija, Adis. 'Toward a Scriptural Hermeneutics of Islamic Feminism'. *Journal of Feminist Studies in Religion* 31, no. 2 (2015): 45–64.

Fredman, Sandra. 'Providing Equality: Substantive Equality and the Positive Duty to Provide'. *South African Journal of Human Rights* 21 (2005): 163–90.

Haddad, Yvonne Yazbeck. 'Islam and Gender: Dilemmas in the Changing Arab World'. In *Islam, Gender, and Social Change*, edited by Yvonne Yazbeck Haddad and John L. Esposito, 1–29. New York: Oxford University Press, 1988.

Hassan, Riffat. 'Equal before Allah? Woman-Man Equality in the Islamic Tradition'. *Harvard Divinity Bulletin* 7, no. 2 (1987): 2–4.

Hermansen, Marcia. 'New Voices of Women Theologians'. In *Muslima Theology: The*

Voices of Muslim Women Theologians, edited by Ednan Aslan, Marcia Hermansen, and Elif Medeni, 11–34. Frankfurt am Main: Peter Lang, 2013.

al-Hibri, Azizah. 'A Study of Islamic Herstory: How Did We Ever Get into This Mess'. In 'Islam and Women', special issue, *Women's Studies International Forum* 5, no.2 (1982): 207–19.

al-Ḥillī, Muḥaqqiq. *Sharāyiʿ al-Islām*. Vol. 2. Persian translation by 'Abd al-Qāsim Aḥmad b. Yazdī, compiled by Muḥammad Taqī Dānish-Pazhuh. Tehran: Tehran University Press, 1985.

Kadivar, Mohsen. 'Revisiting Women's Rights in Islam: "Egalitarian Justice" in Lieu of "Deserts-Based Justice"'. In *Gender and Equality in Muslim Family Law: Justice and Ethics in the Islamic Legal Tradition*, edited by Ziba Mir-Hosseini, Kari Vogt, Lena Larsen, and Christian Moe, 213–34. London: I.B. Tauris, 2013.

Kapur, Ratna. 'Un-veiling Equality: Disciplining the "Other" Woman through the Human Rights Discourse'. In *Islamic Law and International Human Rights Law: Searching for Common Ground?*, edited by Anver M. Emon, Mark Ellis, and Benjamin Glahn, 265–90. Oxford: Oxford University Press, 2012.

Kurzman, Charles, ed. *Modernist Islam, 1840–1940: A Sourcebook*. Oxford: Oxford University Press, 2002.

Lamrabet, Asma. 'An Egalitarian Reading of the Concepts of *Khalifah*, *Wilayah* and *Qiwamah*'. In *Men in Charge? Rethinking Male Authority in Muslim Legal Tradition*, edited by Ziba Mir-Hosseini, Mulki Al-Sharmani, and Jana Rumminger, 65–87. London: Oneworld, 2015.

Lerner, Gerda. *The Creation of Patriarchy*. Oxford: Oxford University Press, 1986.

MacIntyre, Alisdair. *Whose Justice? Which Rationality?* Notre Dame, IN: University of Notre Dame Press, 1988.

Maghniyya, Muḥammad Jawād. *Marriage according to the Five Schools of Islamic Law*. Vol. 5. Tehran: Department of Translation and Publication, Islamic Culture and Relations Organisation, 1997.

Maudoodi, Maulana Abul A'ala. *The Laws of Marriage and Divorce in Islam*. Translated by Fazl Ahmed. Kuwait: Islamic Book Publishers, 1983.

Mernissi, Fatima. *Women and Islam: An Historical and Theological Enquiry*. Translated by Mary Jo Lakeland. Oxford: Blackwell, 1991.

Mir-Hosseini, Ziba. *Islam and Gender: The Religious Debate in Contemporary Iran*. Princeton: Princeton University Press, 1999.

Mir-Hosseini, Ziba. 'Justice, Equality and Muslim Family Laws: New Ideas, New Prospects'. In *Gender and Equality in Muslim Family Law: Justice and Ethics in the Islamic Legal Tradition*, edited by Ziba Mir-Hosseini, Kari Vogt, Lena Larsen, and Christian Moe, 7–34. London: I.B. Tauris, 2013.

Mir-Hosseini, Ziba. 'Muslim Legal Tradition and the Challenge of Equality'. In *Men in Charge? Rethinking Male Authority in Muslim Legal Tradition*, edited by Ziba Mir-Hosseini, Mulki Al-Sharmani, and Jana Rumminger, 13–43. London: Oneworld, 2015.

Mir-Hosseini, Ziba, Mulki Al-Sharmani, and Jana Rumminger, eds. *Men in Charge? Rethinking Male Authority in Muslim Legal Tradition.* London: Oneworld, 2015.

Mir-Hosseini, Ziba, Mulki Al-Sharmani, Jana Rumminger, and Sarah Marsso, eds. *Justice and Beauty in Muslim Marriages: Towards Egalitarian Ethics and Law.* London: Oneworld, 2022.

Muṭahharī, Murtaḍā. *The Rights of Women in Islam.* 4th ed. Tehran: World Organisation for Islamic Services, 1991.

Othman, Norani, ed. *Muslim Women and the Challenge of Islamic Fundamentalism.* Kuala Lumpur: Sisters in Islam, 2005.

Pesle, Octave. *Le Mariage chez les Malekites de l'Afrique du Nord.* Rabat: Moncho, 1936.

Rapoport, Yossef. *Marriage, Money and Divorce in Medieval Islamic Society.* Cambridge: Cambridge University Press, 2005.

Roald, Anne Sofie. 'Feminist Reinterpretation of Islamic Sources: Muslim Feminist Theology in the Light of the Christian Tradition of Feminist Thought'. In *Women and Islamization: Contemporary Dimensions of Discourse on Gender Relations*, edited by Karin Ask and Marit Tjomsland, 17–44. Oxford: Berg, 1998.

Ruxton, F. H. *Maliki Law: A Summary from French Translations of the Mukhtaṣar of Sīdī Khalīl.* London: Luzac & Co., 1916.

Sachedina, Abdulaziz. 'Women, Half-the-Man? Crisis of Male Epistemology in Islamic Jurisprudence'. In *Perspectives on Islamic Law, Justice, and Society*, edited by R. S. Khare, 15–31. Lanham: Rowman & Littlefield, 1999.

Sayeed, Asma. *Women and the Transmission of Religious Knowledge in Islam.* New York: Cambridge University Press, 2013.

Scott, Joan. 'Deconstructing Equality-versus-Difference: Or, the Uses of Poststructuralist Theory for Feminism'. *Feminist Studies* 14, no. 1 (1998): 33–50.

Seedat, Fatima. 'When Islam and Feminism Converge'. *The Muslim World* 103, no. 3 (2013): 404–20.

Shaikh, Sa'diyya. 'Knowledge, Women, and Gender in the Ḥadīth: A Feminist Interpretation'. *Islam and Christian–Muslim Relations* 15, no. 1 (2004): 99–108.

Shehadeh, Lamia Rustum. *The Idea of Women in Fundamentalist Islam.* Gainesville: University Press of Florida, 2003.

Sonbol, Amira El Azhary, ed. *Women, the Family and Divorce Laws in Islamic History.* Syracuse: Syracuse University Press, 1996.

Stowasser, Barbara F. 'Women's Issues in Modern Islamic Thought'. In *Arab Women: Old Boundaries, New Frontiers*, edited by Judith E. Tucker, 3–28. Bloomington: Indiana University Press, 1993.

Tucker, Judith E. *In the House of Law: Gender and Islamic Law in Ottoman Syria and Palestine.* Berkeley: University of California Press, 1998.

SAYED MUSTAFA MUHAQQIQ DAMAD &
SYED WAJEE UL-HASAN SHAH

Juristic Principles Governing Family Life

Muslim legal jurists (*mujtahids*) believe that the function of Islamic law (Sharīʿa law)[1] is to govern and regulate the lives of Muslims and answer questions related to their daily practice. This became all the more relevant with the finality of the Prophet Muḥammad, and therefore whatever the Prophet had declared permissible and impermissible remains as such indefinitely. As such, Muslim jurists in the present day must reinterpret the Qur'an and Sunna to help answer questions posed by the challenges of living in a modern society, where the latter two scriptural sources remain silent. Many Muslim jurists believed that through the process of *ijtihād*,[2] the scope of Sharīʿa can be extended to tackle new issues. Over the years, this task was performed (by *mujtahids*) through the reinterpretation of the Qur'an and Sunna, as well as the use of reason (*ʿaql*), in order to help maintain an Islamic identity in an ever-changing society and provide legal rulings on what God's law would entail in any given society.

The central focus of this paper is on sexual intercourse within marriage and subsequently an argument against marital rape. This is a major issue within the current Shīʿī jurisprudential (*fiqhī*) discourse today, due to the overarching influence of the clerical authority (*marjaʿiyya* system),[3] and its discriminatory edicts issued against

1 Islamic (Sharīʿa) law includes legal doctrine and the judiciary. Hallaq describes the Sharīʿa as the 'religious law of Islam ... [and it is] the reaffirmation of Islamic identity [and forms] the foundation of a cultural uniqueness'. He believes that for Muslims 'to live by Islamic law is not merely a legal issue, but one that is distinctly psychological'. Wael B. Hallaq, *The Origins and Evolution of Islamic Law* (Cambridge: Cambridge University Press, 2005), 1. For a further in-depth study of the development of Sharīʿa law and its implications in modern society and law, see Wael B. Hallaq, 'The Quest for Origins or Doctrine? Islamic Legal Studies as Colonialist Discourse', *UCLA Journal of Islamic and Near Eastern Law* 2, no. 1 (2002–3): 1–31. See also Wael B. Hallaq, ed., *The Formation of Islamic Law*, The Formation of the Classical Islamic World, ed. Lawrence I. Conrad, vol. 27 (Aldershot: Routledge, 2003); and Joseph Schacht, *The Origins of Muhammadan Jurisprudence* (Oxford: Clarendon Press, 1950).

2 A process of legal reasoning and hermeneutics whereby a legal jurist (*mujtahid*) exerts his utmost effort to extrapolate Islamic legal rulings from the Qur'an and Sunna.

3 Millions of Shīʿī Muslims depend on this system for religious guidance and as a source of emulation (*taqlīd*).

women, whereby issues such as marital rape and a woman's autonomy in marriage are predominantly patriarchal and thus ignored. The edicts range from the absolute obligation of a wife's obedience of her husband in many aspects of her life, including asking permission to leave the house and remaining sexually available whenever the husband desires.[4] Also, in many cases the wife does not have the right to oppose her husband in such matters – such as the refusal of sexual intercourse.

However, we will argue here that the Qur'an dictates that respect and honour must be maintained by both spouses and any sexual contact must be out of freedom of choice rather than enforced. Thus, if the wife does not give consent to engage in sexual relations, this would be classed as sexual harassment and/or marital rape[5] and she has a legal right (under both state and Islamic law) to take legal action against her husband. This is based on a Qur'anic understanding in line with women's rights in modern society, whereby a woman has sexual autonomy and sexual intercourse is not an unrestricted right provided for the husband by Islam.

Therefore, in order to address conditions of modern life, jurists must attend to the general ethical Qur'anic guidelines and only accept those reported traditions which align with the ethos of the Qur'an and those which do not must be abandoned.

In dealing with the issues at hand, we will adopt a Qur'an-centric jurisprudential (*ijtihādī*) framework in order to critically analyse the reported traditions (*aḥadīth*) which many illustrious Shīʿī jurists have based their juristic edicts upon. This will allow scope for a new fatwa to be issued based on today's context. First, we will critique the methodology of the classical and contemporary scholars and demonstrate the flaws in adopting a *ḥadīth*-centric approach to issuing edicts based on women's issues. Secondly, we will examine certain classical opinions regarding women and the application of *tamkīn*[6] and prove how and why they are incompatible with modern society and are discriminatory. We will also discuss the implications of such views and provide an alternate opinion based on our own *ijtihād* where the Qur'anic message is at the forefront and through which many problems in family law can be resolved.[7] This alternative opinion will be presented in the following manner: firstly, we will provide a Qur'anic hermeneutical discussion on the word *maʿrūf* and demonstrate the way in which this word is interpreted to allow for a fluid and flexible understand-

4 al-Sayyid ʿAlī al-Ḥusaynī al-Sistānī, *Minhāj al-ṣāliḥīn: muʿāmalāt* (Qom: Saʿīd b. Jubayr, 2000), 103; Ḥusayn al-Waḥīd al-Khurāsānī, *Islamic Rulings* (*Islamic Laws*) (Qom: Madrasat al-Imām Bāqir al-ʿUlūm, 2015), 524; Zayn al-Dīn b. ʿAlī al-ʿĀmilī, *al-Rawḍa al-bahiyya fī sharḥ al-Lumʿa al-dimishqiyya*, 7th ed. (Qom: Dār al-Tafsīr, 2006), 2:365–66.

5 Notably, in both the classical and contemporary jurisprudential framework the concept of marital rape/sexual harassment between spouses does not exist.

6 Loosely translated as sexual willingness. This term is discussed further in the next section.

7 Specifically focusing on the jurisprudence of marriage (*fiqh al-nikāḥ*).

ing of spousal roles and how marital life should be conducted in different contexts. Secondly, we will highlight the Qur'anic conception of marriage and its core values, and in doing so, provide a sound basis for our reasoning. With our Qur'an-centric framework established, we will then apply it when analysing the evidences, that is, the *aḥādīth* some scholars have utilised in their own *ijtihād* when forming legal opinions regarding women.

DISCRIMINATORY EDICTS AGAINST WOMEN AND THEIR EVIDENCES

Within the jurisprudential writings of many great Shīʿī jurists of the past and present, we find several discriminatory juristic edicts (*fatāwā*) against women. Arguably, one of the most controversial edicts stipulates that it is forbidden for a wife to leave the house without the permission of her husband.[8] This ruling has been made absolute (*muṭlaq*) and thus applies to all times. According to al-Muḥaqqiq al-Ḥillī's (d. 676/1277) *ijtihād*, 'the husband can prohibit his wife from visiting her parents when they are sick, and from leaving the house, except in situations where it is necessary.'[9] In addition, Muḥammad Ḥasan al-Najafī (Sāḥib al-Jawāhir) (d. 1849) states that 'if the wife travels without the permission of her husband, he does not have to provide her [financial] maintenance (*nafaqa*)'.[10] There are major implications of this view, one being that if the wife leaves the house without the permission of her husband, even if the husband is not at home, this is an example of disobedience (*nushūz*). The wife would be deemed disobedient (*nāshiza*), the legal repercussions of this being that the husband is not legally obliged to pay his wife's maintenance (*nafaqa*) for any of her daily needs.

Al-Ḥillī is in line with this view, as he is of the opinion that the obligation of maintenance for the wife is conditional on the wife's obedience to the husband in regard to satisfying all his sexual desires. Al-Ḥillī defines this disobedience as the unwillingness of the wife to offer herself to satisfy her husband's sexual desires whenever he so wishes – this is termed *tamkīn* in jurisprudence. On this point al-Ḥillī states that disobedience of the wife 'is to relieve herself from [having intercourse with] the husband irrespective of a particular place and time. If she offers herself [for intercourse] at one [specific] time and not another, or one [specific] place and not another, she

---

8 Muḥammad b. Ḥasan al-Ḥurr al-ʿĀmilī, *Tafṣīl Wasāʾil al-Shīʿa* (Beirut: Muʾassasat Āl al-Bayt, 2008), 20:157–58, *ḥadīth* no. 25300.

9 Abū Qāsim Najm al-Dīn Jaʿfar b. al-Ḥasan al-Muḥaqqiq al-Ḥillī, *Sharāʾiʿ al-Islām fī masāʾil al-ḥalāl wa-l-ḥarām*, 3rd ed. (Qom: al-Fiqāha, 2009), 2:558.

10 Muḥammad Ḥasan al-Najafī, *Jawāhir al-kalām fī sharḥ Sharāʾiʿ al-Islām* (Beirut: Dār al-Iḥyāʾ, n.d.), 31:314.

is [considered] disobedient.'[11]

Al-Shahīd al-Thānī comments on this opinion that the word 'place' refers to the body parts of the wife. Therefore, the wife cannot prevent her husband from acquiring sexual pleasure from any part of her body.[12] According to these views, while there is no legal impediment, the wife should be ready to offer herself to satisfy her husband's sexual desires, even if she has no sexual need or desire at the time. Thus, for al-Ḥillī and al-Shahīd al-Thānī, *tamkīn* is absolute (*muṭlaq*) and entirely dependent upon the wishes of the husband.

However, the reverse is not true: the wife cannot make such demands of her husband, even if she has the sexual desire to do so and he does not. As a bare minimum she has a right to sexual intercourse once every four months. Sayyid Muḥammad Kāẓim al-Yazdī states:

> It is impermissible to abstain from intercourse with one's wife for more than four months; there is no difference [in this matter] between the permanent, temporary, young, or the old [wife]. This is based on the absoluteness of the narration (*ḥadīth*).[13]

Sayyid Abū al-Qāsim al-Khū'ī in his commentary of al-Yazdī's text states that 'this idea is a matter of consensus, and no one has opposed it'.[14]

Among the contemporary grand Shīʿī jurists who also hold such a view are the likes of Sayyid ʿAlī al-Sistānī and Waḥīd al-Khurāsānī.[15] Al-Sistānī states in this regard: 'the right of a husband over his wife is that she should offer herself to him whenever he requires for her to satisfy his sexual desires unless there is a legal impediment … and that she should not leave the house without the husband's permission if it coincides with him wanting intercourse.'[16]

11 al-Muḥaqqiq al-Ḥillī, *Sharāʾiʿ al-Islām*, 2:585–86.

12 Zayn al-Dīn b. ʿAlī al-ʿĀmilī, *Masālik al-afhām ilā tanqīḥ Sharāʾiʿ al-Islām* (Qom: Mu'assasat al-Maʿārif al-Islāmiyya, 1995), 8:439–40.

13 al-Sayyid Muḥammad Kāẓim al-Ṭabāṭabā'ī al-Yazdī, *al-ʿUrwa al-wuthqā* (Qom: Jamāʿat al-Mudarrisīn, n.d.), 5:499.

14 al-Sayyid Abū al-Qāsim al-Mūsawī al-Khū'ī, *Mabānī fī sharḥ al-ʿUrwa al-wuthqā* (Iraq: Mu'assasat al-Khū'ī al-Islāmiyya, 2016), 32:1115. Al-Khū'ī reports that Ṣāḥib al-Jawāhir also believes this is a matter of consensus between the Shīʿī scholars.

15 Ḥusayn al-Waḥīd al-Khurāsānī, *Minhāj al-ṣāliḥīn: al-muʿāmalāt li-Samāḥat Āyat Allāh al-ʿUẓmā al-Sayyid Abī al-Qāsim al-Khū'ī maʿ fatwā Samāḥat Āyat Allāh al-ʿUẓmā al-Shaykh Ḥusayn al-Waḥīd al-Khurāsānī* (Qom: Madrasat al-Imām al-Bāqir al-ʿUlūm, n.d.), 3:294, 321–22; al-Khurāsānī, *Islamic Rulings*, 524. However, it must be noted that al-Khurāsānī's view is slightly more nuanced as he states, 'A man cannot refrain from intercourse for more than four months with a young permanent wife unless the wife consents to it.' Ibid., 525. But this seems to be an exception to his general rule that she must make herself sexually available (*tamkīn*) whenever the husband desires; otherwise, he does not have to pay her financial maintenance.

16 al-Sistānī, *Minhāj al-ṣāliḥīn*, 103.

ḤADĪTH ANALYSIS

These juristic edicts are based on a specific type of interpretation of the reported traditions of the Prophet and Imāms. For instance, the following tradition indicates that the woman is forbidden to leave the house without her husband's permission: Muḥammad b. Muslim reports a lengthy tradition from Imām al-Bāqir which states that a wife is forbidden to leave her home without the permission of her husband.[17]

However, upon further analysis of the content of this narration we find that this is not an absolute (*muṭlaq*) ruling issued from the Imām; rather, this narration is referring to the fact that the wife cannot leave the house indefinitely (forever) without the permission of her husband. Therefore, we disagree with those edicts which categorically state that the wife is unable to leave the house without her husband's permission. Indeed, she is able to leave to do her daily tasks such as shopping, school runs, or to visit her parents. These are ordinary tasks which spouses/parents carry out daily that do not usually require prior consent in the modern age.

Furthermore, regarding al-Yazdī's opinion on the necessity to have intercourse once every four months as a minimum, this can be deduced from the following tradition:

> Ṣafwān b. Yaḥyā asked Imām al-Riḍā about a man who is married to a young woman. He abstained from sexual intercourse with her for one year ... Ṣafwān asked whether this man was a sinner. The Imām answered: 'If he abstained from sexual intercourse for four months, he is a sinner.'[18]

The content of these narrations, which state that the wife is a sinner if she does not have intercourse with her husband at least once every forty days, not only opposes the Qur'anic ethos that mentions the principle of equality of the rights and duties of spouses but also opposes the principles of general human rights. Irrespective of the fact that it has been deemed as authentic by scholars of *ʿilm al-rijāl* (biographical studies or the study of narrators), we believe that any rules pertaining to human rights of an individual cannot be deduced by solitary narrations (*akhbār al-āḥād*, sing. *khabar al-wāḥid*). Therefore, the narrations that stipulate that the wife must have intercourse every forty days irrespective of her contentment become problematic, especially considering the Qur'anic notion of *maʿrūf* (discussed below). In the present day, narrations such as these can be seen to promote marital rape among other human

---

17 al-ʿĀmilī, *Tafṣīl*, 20:157–58, *ḥadīth* no. 25300.

18 Ibid., 140, *ḥadīth* no. 25246. Al-Khūʾī believes that views such as al-Yazdī's and other jurists, that sexual intercourse should be performed once every four months as a minimum requirement, are based upon this reported tradition. al-Khūʾī, *Mabānī*, 32:115–17.

rights violations and thus cannot be accepted, neither according to the Qur'an nor in line with modern society.[19]

Another such reported tradition indicates the absolute obedience of the wife to the husband:

> It is reported that 'Abd Allāh b. Sinān narrated from Imām Ja'far al-Ṣādiq that during the time of the Prophet a man from among the Anṣār was assigned a task by the Prophet. So, the man left his house to fulfil some of his needs and told his wife that she cannot leave the house until he returns. The woman wrote to the Prophet asking permission to leave the house because her father became unwell. The Prophet told her to remain in her house and obey her husband. This became burdensome to her, so she wrote to the Prophet a second time. The Prophet replied 'remain in your house and obey your husband'. Then her father passed away, so she wrote to the Prophet and told him her father had died and if he would permit her to attend the funeral. The Prophet replied 'remain in your house and obey your husband'. When her father was buried, the Prophet wrote to the wife and told her, 'God has forgiven you and your father due to your obedience of your husband.'[20]

We find the content of this narration highly problematic,[21] as the order of the husband to his wife to not leave the house could have only meant that she was not allowed to leave for unimportant matters. Even if she did leave the house to visit her terminally ill father, she could have said that she interpreted the command of the husband to mean not going out for leisurely pursuits. Therefore, she did not need to ask the Prophet. Also, beseeching the Prophet for permission while her father was on the verge of death is an unusual occurrence.

Overall, regarding *āḥādīth*, it must be emphasised that they are context bound. They were revealed in a particular time and place, hence during these times such narrations were the norm and were acceptable to that society. However, in light of the Qur'an, Islamic ethics, and spousal and gender roles in modern society, *ḥadīth* literature and

---

19 Qur'anic guidance (based on love, mutual understanding, and respect between all people) should be used to make edicts in reference to modern human rights conventions, and any legislation that contravenes this guidance must be rejected or re-examined. Thus, the Qur'an is epistemically more authoritative than modern-day human rights legislation and as such should govern such rulings.

20 al-'Āmilī, *Tafṣīl*, 20:174–75, *ḥadīth* no. 25350.

21 For a more in-depth discussion regarding this narration and its veracity, see Ḥaydar Ḥubb Allāh, *Dirāsāt fī al-fiqh al-Islāmī al-mu'āṣir* (Beirut: Dār al-Fiqh al-Islāmī al-Mu'āṣir, 2011), 2:286–92; al-Sayyid Abū al-Qāsim al-Mūsawī al-Khū'ī, *Mu'jam rijāl al-ḥadīth* (Najaf: Madīnat al-'Ilm, 1978), 10:284; Aḥmad b. 'Alī al-Najāshī, *Rijāl al-Najāshī* (Beirut: Sharikat al-A'lamī li-l-Maṭbū'āt, 2010), 217.

juristic edicts which are discriminatory against women must be either reinterpreted or deemed anachronistic in the deduction of Islamic rulings for contemporary society.

A QUR'ANIC APPROACH

The Qur'an is the greatest source of guidance for all Muslims, although many jurists have, in error, overemphasised the *ḥadīth* literature. When placing the Qur'an at the centre of such a jurisprudential topic as family law, we can focus on the general guidelines it provides when discussing marriage and its different elements and build a framework based on these guidelines.

When discussing the intricacies of family life and gender roles in Islam in the twenty-first century, we find that the Qur'an places great emphasis on respecting womenfolk and living with them in a kind and honourable manner. We have selected three verses where the Qur'an uses the word *maʿrūf* (regarding spouses) which can be interpreted in many ways according to different contexts. For instance, the following verse speaks about how women (i.e. wives) should be treated:

> O believers! It is not permissible for you to inherit women against their will or mistreat them ... Treat them fairly [in an honourable manner] (*bi-l-maʿrūf*). If you happen to dislike them, you may hate something which God turns into a great blessing.[22]

The generality of this verse allows for many different interpretations. As the Qur'an does not designate a specific meaning for the word *maʿrūf* (here translated as fairly/honourably), it appears that it allows for Muslims from different societies and eras to interpret it according to their respective contexts. As the application of this word can change due to the passage of time, it can be reasonably assumed that it can also differ from one culture to another. The Qur'an here provides a fluid and flexible framework, so whatever is considered *maʿrūf* in reference to spousal rights in a particular society will be endorsed by the Qur'an and Sharīʿa as long as the essence of the Qur'an is preserved. Hence, if wives are being treated unfairly this would be Islamically unethical and impermissible.

Accordingly, we have extrapolated the following principles from the Qur'an which will form the foundation of how family law can be understood and how such verses can explain the role and position of the husband and wife in marriage. The principles we shall explore are those of equal rights with regards to marital duties; either

22 Q. 4:19. All Qur'anic translations are from Mustafa Khattab, trans., *The Clear Quran: A Thematic Translation of the Message of the Final Revelation* (Lombard: Book of Signs Foundation, 2016), though occasionally modified where the authors have deemed it necessary.

living on reasonable terms or separating with kindness; and finally, mutual love and marriage being the source of tranquillity.

THE PRINCIPLE OF EQUAL RIGHTS REGARDING MARITAL DUTIES

The following Qur'anic verse indicates the rights and norms of wives within a marriage. The Qur'an states, regarding rights and obligations of both the husband and wife, that 'Women [i.e. wives] have rights similar to those of men equitably [in accordance with honourable norms] (*bi-l-maʿrūf*).'[23] In our opinion, this verse is clear and explicit in emphasising equality between the duties and rights in family relations. It is important to consider that in the context of the revelation of the Qur'an, the way women live today is drastically different. Studies show that more women today are career focused, and many are attending colleges and universities to further their education. Therefore, it is important to bear this fact in mind in relation to this verse, whereby marital duties must take into consideration the work commitments, career goals, and family life of both spouses.[24]

THE PRINCIPLE OF EITHER LIVING ON REASONABLE TERMS OR SEPARATING WITH KINDNESS

The Qur'an also deals with the topic of divorce and how it should be performed with respectable conduct between all parties involved. For instance, 'the divorce [shall be lawful] only twice. Then you [the husband], should either keep the wife on reasonable terms or release her with kindness (*bi-l-maʿrūf*).'[25] This verse highlights that a marriage should be based on terms which promote mutual consent and living in harmony with one another. Furthermore, it stipulates two conditions for the husband: either he must live honourably with his spouse or, if he cannot do this, he must divorce or separate with her in a respectable and merciful manner. One may conclude, then, that if the husband does not divorce his wife when/if the condition of living on reasonable terms is not fulfilled, when it is mandatory, the government or responsible authorities can intervene by asking the wife to separate from her partner amicably.

We have highlighted how in all three of the aforementioned Qur'anic verses, the word *maʿrūf* has been used to signify fairness and justice in whatever context it is mentioned. Linguistically, this term in the Arabic language can denote many different

23 Q. 2:228.

24 Katharine Sanderson, 'More Women than Ever Are Starting Careers in Science', *Nature*, 5 August 2021, www.nature.com/articles/d41586-021-02147-9; Kim Parker, 'Women More than Men Adjust Their Careers for Family Life', Pew Research Center, 1 October 2015, www.pewresearch.org/fact-tank/2015/10/01/women-more-than-men-adjust-their-careers-for-family-life/.

25 Q. 2:229.

meanings depending on the context of the verse and the specific target audience. We believe that God has left the word *maʿrūf* open to varying interpretations, and that because no definitive definition has been provided for it, this is an advantage for the many different audiences who wish to apply these Qur'anic principles in their lives. This term can be defined or interpreted appropriately according to human reason or wisdom (*ḥikma*) in line with the relevant context(s). Therefore, we believe that the Qur'anic conception of family life, more specifically, marital life, should be based on honour, companionship, mutual respect, love, and kindness.

THE PRINCIPLE OF MUTUAL LOVE AND MARRIAGE BEING THE SOURCE OF TRANQUILLITY

The Qur'an places emphasis on universal principles such as love, tranquillity, and amicability, with all three being the fundamental foundations of any marriage. This is evident according to the following verse, 'And one of His signs is that He created for you spouses from among yourselves so that you may find comfort in them. And He has placed between you compassion and mercy.'[26] This oft-mentioned verse regarding marriage highlights the core function of the institution of marriage, which is that it promotes love, tranquillity, and kindness. According to Islam, this is what should be sought and the primary motivation when seeking a partner or looking to get married, that is, a partner with whom one can live with in tranquillity and peace, ultimately leading to love and mercy in the relationship.

Such a Qur'anic-centric approach unveils a two-tiered hermeneutical process, whereby fixed and static values of love, tranquillity, and mercy form the foundation and basis of any marriage. On such a basis, and in response to the many changing tides in culture and gender roles, there applies the principle of *maʿrūf* – that is, dealing with fairness, equity, and justice in all situations between spouses.

REVISITING *IJTIHĀD*: A CONTEMPORARY APPROACH

Although the Qur'an provides such guidance, we find the opinions of many classical and contemporary scholars in conflict with the Qur'anic ethos and how people live in modern society. Firstly, these types of *fatāwā* are in contrast with the above-mentioned Qur'anic guidelines such as consorting in an honourable manner. For instance, if a wife's parents are unwell, she may feel (morally) obliged to visit them to take care of them even if her husband is not at home or is away for a certain period. Therefore, if the husband prohibits his wife from leaving the house in order to care for her sick parents, this is a direct violation of the Qur'anic verse of dealing with people in a respectable manner.

26 Q. 30:21.

Importantly, other contemporary jurists have also critiqued many jurisprudential rulings which are discriminatory against women. One such jurist is Nāṣir Makārim al-Shirāzī who opposes the orthodox edict (*fatwā*) concerning the preference of keeping women at home and says: 'This edict causes many problems as it isolates women and can be a prevention of knowledge and growth.'[27]

Moreover, there is an Islamic principle which emphasises maintaining relations with the family, known as *ṣilat al-raḥim*. One of the most important principles in Islamic ethics regarding family is devotion towards relatives. The Qur'an has emphasised this in many verses; for example:

> And those who violate God's covenant after it has been affirmed, break whatever ties [kinship] God has ordered to be maintained, and spread corruption in the land – it is they who will be condemned and will have the worst abode.[28]

In reference to this verse, Imām Ja'far al-Ṣādiq was once asked, 'Who are the relatives?' The Imām replied: 'Your family.'[29] Due to this, within Islamic family law, every person is expected to maintain respectful relations with their immediate and extended family members. Therefore, if a husband prohibits his wife from visiting her family, this can lead to an instance of her cutting off her family relations, which is among the great sins (*al-muḥarramāt al-kabīra*). The husband does not have the authority to do this, but even if he does make such a demand, the wife should not comply.

In addition, the view that the wife does not have to comply with such a demand regarding the welfare of her parents has precedent in the Qur'an. The Qur'an clearly emphasises one's duties towards one's parents. For instance, we read in the following verse: 'And be humble with them [i.e. your parents] out of mercy, and pray, "My Lord! Be merciful to them as they raised me when I was young."'[30] This verse highlights the respect parents deserve on account of how they looked after their own children. The same message is also explicated here, 'Worship God and associate nothing with Him, and do good to your parents [and] relatives.'[31] These verses are not conditional upon the husband's permission, but they are absolute (*muṭlaq*), meaning they are general rules that always apply to everyone. The only exception the Qur'an provides regarding obeying and respecting one's parents is if they call towards polytheism (*shirk*): 'But if they pressure you to associate with Me what you have no knowledge of, do not obey

27 Nāṣir Makārim al-Shīrāzī, *al-'Urwa al-wuthqā ma' ta'līqāt al-Shaykh Nāṣir Makārim al-Shīrāzī* (Qom: Intishārāt Madrasat al-Imām 'Alī b. Abī Ṭālib, 2007), 2:755.

28 Q. 13:25.

29 Muḥammad b. Ya'qūb al-Kulaynī, *Uṣūl al-Kāfī* (Beirut: Dār al-Ta'āruf li-l-Maṭbū'āt, n.d.), 2:163.

30 Q. 17:24.

31 Q. 4:36.

them. Still keep their company in this world courteously.'[32] In sum, it is evident that one must always strive to maintain respectful relations with one's parents and the husband cannot force his wife to not visit her parents as this is a direct violation of the Qur'anic injunction to behave in an honourable manner. Also, his prohibition may even lead to a hostile relationship within the marriage.

CONCLUSION

In modern society Muslims are faced with new and challenging issues which were arguably not present in previous eras. This is demonstrated in family life where gender roles are not as fixed as they once were, and thus, spousal roles have also shifted in modern times. Consequently, the discriminatory edicts issued by certain religious authorities must either be re-examined with modern society in mind, or they must be rejected. As such, the classical jurisprudential framework needs re-evaluating and further development with the Qur'an as the basis and the modern context in mind, or an entirely new jurisprudential framework must be constructed. Moreover, we believe that Muslim jurists of today must re-examine their conception of family law and consider the different contexts in which Muslims live before issuing a 'one-size-fits-all' opinion for their followers to abide by.

We want to highlight that although in both the traditional and majority of the current jurisprudential rulings, the concept of marital rape does not exist and *tamkīn* is still valid, in our framework marital rape is a serious issue, whereby the woman has both the freedom and legal authority to refuse sexual intercourse and expect mutual consent in any sexual activity. The result of a general, one-size-fits-all approach by Muslim jurists is that it renders Islam and its Sharīʿa, as viewed in the modern context, both primitive and discriminatory. Hence why the flexible and dynamic framework of *ijtihād* is crucial in today's world as it can help jurists answer such questions relating to family life as well as other issues which Muslims need guidance on. However, scholarly *ijtihād* must be Qur'an centred, with it primarily relying upon the Qur'an and secondarily on the reported traditions of the Prophet and Imāms. Therefore, if any reported traditions or rulings – both secular and juristic – oppose the Qur'anic guidance, they should not be considered. The Qur'an will always have legitimacy and supremacy in this area due to its flexible and fluid nature, especially in relation to the interpretation of what is considered *maʿrūf* in the present day from the aforementioned Qur'anic verses.

32 Q. 31:15.

BIBLIOGRAPHY

al-ʿĀmilī, Muḥammad b. Ḥasan al-Ḥurr. *Tafṣīl Wasāʾil al-Shīʿa*. Beirut: Muʾassasat Āl al-Bayt, 2008.

al-ʿĀmilī, Zayn al-Dīn b. ʿAlī. *Masālik al-afhām ilā tanqīḥ Sharāʾiʿ al-Islām*. Qom: Muʾassasat al-Maʿārif al-Islāmiyya, 1995.

al-ʿĀmilī, Zayn al-Dīn b. ʿAlī. *al-Rawḍa al-bahiyya fī sharḥ al-Lumʿa al-dimishqiyya*. 7th ed. Qom: Dār al-Tafsīr, 2006.

Hallaq, Wael B., ed. *The Formation of Islamic Law*. The Formation of the Classical Islamic World, edited by Lawrence I. Conrad, vol. 27. Aldershot: Routledge, 2003.

Hallaq, Wael B. *The Origins and Evolution of Islamic Law*. Cambridge: Cambridge University Press, 2005.

Hallaq, Wael B. 'The Quest for Origins or Doctrine? Islamic Legal Studies as Colonialist Discourse'. *UCLA Journal of Islamic and Near Eastern Law* 2, no. 1 (2002–3): 1–31.

Ḥubb Allāh, Ḥaydar. *Dirāsāt fī al-fiqh al-Islāmī al-muʿāṣir*. Beirut: Dār al-Fiqh al-Islāmī al-Muʿāṣir, 2011.

Khattab, Mustafa, trans. *The Clear Quran: A Thematic Translation of the Message of the Final Revelation*. Lombard: Book of Signs Foundation, 2016.

al-Khūʾī, al-Sayyid Abū al-Qāsim al-Mūsawī. *Mabānī fī sharḥ al-ʿUrwa al-wuthqā*. Iraq: Muʾassasat al-Khūʾī al-Islāmiyya, 2016.

al-Khūʾī, al-Sayyid Abū al-Qāsim al-Mūsawī. *Muʿjam rijāl al-ḥadīth*. Najaf: Madīnat al-ʿIlm, 1978.

al-Khurāsānī, Ḥusayn al-Waḥīd. *Islamic Rulings (Islamic Laws)*. Qom: Madrasat al-Imām Bāqir al-ʿUlūm, 2015.

al-Khurāsānī, Ḥusayn al-Waḥīd. *Minhāj al-ṣāliḥīn: al-muʿāmalāt li-Samāḥat Āyat Allāh al-ʿUẓmā al-Sayyid Abī al-Qāsim al-Khūʾī maʿ fatwā Samāḥat Āyat Allāh al-ʿUẓmā al-Shaykh Ḥusayn al-Waḥīd al-Khurāsānī*. Qom: Madrasat al-Imām al-Bāqir al-ʿUlūm, n.d.

al-Kulaynī, Muḥammad b. Yaʿqūb. *Uṣūl al-Kāfī*. Beirut: Dār al-Taʿāruf li-l-Maṭbūʿāt, n.d.

al-Muḥaqqiq al-Ḥillī, Abū Qāsim Najm al-Dīn Jaʿfar b. al-Ḥasan. *Sharāʾiʿ al-Islām fī masāʾil al-ḥalāl wa-l-ḥarām*. 3rd ed. Qom: al-Fiqāha, 2009.

al-Najafī, Muḥammad Ḥasan. *Jawāhir al-kalām fī sharḥ Sharāʾiʿ al-Islām*. Beirut: Dār al-Iḥyāʾ, n.d.

al-Najāshī, Aḥmad b. ʿAlī. *Rijāl al-Najāshī*. Beirut: Sharikat al-Aʿlamī li-l-Maṭbūʿāt, 2010.

Schacht, Joseph. *The Origins of Muhammadan Jurisprudence*. Oxford: Clarendon Press, 1950.

al-Shīrāzī, Nāṣir Makārim. *al-ʿUrwa al-wuthqā maʿ taʿlīqāt al-Shaykh Nāṣir Makārim al-Shīrāzī*. Qom: Intishārāt Madrasat al-Imām ʿAlī b. Abī Ṭālib, 2007.

al-Sistānī, al-Sayyid ʿAlī al-Ḥusaynī. *Minhāj al-ṣāliḥīn: muʿāmalāt*. Qom: Saʿīd b. Jubayr, 2000.

al-Yazdī, al-Sayyid Muḥammad Kāẓim al-Ṭabāṭabāʾī. *al-ʿUrwa al-wuthqā*. Qom: Jamāʿat al-Mudarrisīn, n.d.

PART II

Sociological Analyses

FOUZIA AZZOUZ

Unregistered Muslim Marriages in Britain: Avenues for Regulation

Unregistered Muslim marriages have existed for decades in Britain, and for the most part had been neglected or simply tolerated.[1] Increasingly, however, public attention has focused on the 'problem' of unregistered Muslim marriages. This focus has been fuelled in part by studies of Sharīʿa councils, many of whose users are Muslim women in *nikāḥ*-only marriages. In addition to scholarly attention, there have been calls to reform marriage law in England and to address registered marriages by registering mosques to solemnise marriage, introducing cohabitation rights, and raising awareness on the consequences of non-registration.

Despite many important insights offered by the existing literature, there is little consensus regarding proposals for regulating Muslim marriage practices that would accommodate the diverse needs and circumstances of Muslim couples. This is why the task of appraising the above proposals remains necessary if the debate is to move forward. This paper is based on empirical research that sought to fill this gap by exploring avenues for reform which are grounded in the experiences and narratives of British Muslims.

In the present study and elsewhere, I argue that it is not enough to merely reflect on British Muslims' experiences in drawing up proposals or recommendations. It is essential that we continue to test out views on the potential solutions that different stakeholders are proposing for regulating Muslim marriage practices. This was the task that I undertook in my research, the findings of which are explored in detail in the following sections.

In what follows, I highlight the various problems and concerns about unregistered Muslim marriages which underpin various proposals and recommendations for change. I then assess the proposals themselves, exploring their aims and entailments. Drawing on my own sociological research, I clarify the variety of reasons that Muslim men and women do not register their marriages and the range of clerical views on the matter.

1 Rajnaara C. Akhtar, Rebecca Probert, and Annelies Moors, 'Informal Muslim Marriages: Regulations and Contestations', *Oxford Journal of Law and Religion* 7, no. 3 (2018): 367–75.

Finally, the proposals for change are appraised and re-evaluated in light of my findings to decide which course of action is best suitable to address the challenges associated with the practice of unregistered *nikāḥ* marriage in Britain.

PROBLEMS WITH UNREGISTERED MUSLIM MARRIAGES

Entry into marriage in England and Wales is governed by the Marriage Act 1949 (and subsequent amendments). At present, if a Muslim couple wishes to have a legally binding marriage, they can do so in two ways. The first is to undertake a civil marriage that is independent of the religious *nikāḥ* marriage ceremony. The second is to have a religious *nikāḥ* ceremony performed inside a mosque that is registered to conduct legal marriages and with the presence of an authorised person or a superintendent registrar to register the marriage.[2] With this in mind, we can largely delineate four forms of marriage arrangements within Muslim communities in Britain. The first is where a couple have the *nikāḥ* and civil marriage at two separate events, where one precedes the other. The second is where the couple have their *nikāḥ* at a place of worship that is authorised to conduct and register such ceremonies leading to a legally recognised marriage in the eyes of the state. The third is where a *nikāḥ* is conducted abroad in a jurisdiction where such ceremonies are registered and legally recognised; this marriage is then recognised as legally valid according to English law. The fourth form, discussed further below, is where state recognition is forgone and the couple, for various reasons or circumstances, have a *nikāḥ*-only marriage outside of the jurisdiction of the state.

It has often been cited, both in academic works[3] and the media,[4] that up to two-thirds of Muslim marriages in Britain may be unregistered.[5] Regardless of its significance to the parties involved, the marriage falls outside the grasp of civil law and is thus not considered legally binding. Muslim couples who, for whatever reasons, fail to register their marriages are regarded as cohabitants. The law does not provide a clear definition of who a cohabitant is. Cohabitants are instead left to navigate a patchwork of laws that define some of the consequences of cohabiting couples'

2 'Part III: Marriages in Registered Buildings', Marriage Act 1949, www.legislation.gov.uk/ukpga/Geo6/12-13-14/76/part/III/crossheading/marriages-in-registered-buildings/enacted.

3 Ralph Grillo, *Muslim Families, Politics and the Law: A legal Industry in Multicultural Britain* (London: Routledge, 2016).

4 Maya Oppenheim, 'All Religious Marriages Must Be Registered to Protect Women from Abuse and Discrimination, Report Warns', *Independent*, 11 August 2020, www.independent.co.uk/news/uk/home-news/religious-marriages-register-muslim-women-uk-abuse-a9663441.html.

5 The limited empirical data that is available on this issue concerns England, Wales, and Scotland. The jurisdictional focus of this current study is England and Wales only.

relationships.[6] This can result in practical difficulties with pension entitlement, inheritance, and child custody as there are no automatically guaranteed rights if one of the parties dies. Further, upon relationship breakdown, the party with low or no income has no right to claim maintenance or financial support.[7] They also have no housing rights and may be forced to leave the house if the tenancy agreement is not in their name – or joint names.

Furthermore, with no access to the state's legal mechanisms, some Muslim women in particular feel the need to refer to faith-based alternative dispute resolution mechanisms such as Sharīʿa councils to receive expert religious advice or guidance. *Nikāḥ*-only marriages are hence seen by some as 'legal loopholes that compel these women to seek the assistance of the Sharia'.[8] This link to Sharīʿa councils has made the topic of unregistered Muslim marriages highly politicised.

Although exact numbers remain unknown due to the lack of comprehensive statistical data on the phenomenon, much research continues to cite the widespread non-compliance of Muslim marriages with the requirements of the law. In 2016, a study was undertaken as part of a Channel 4 documentary looking at Muslim marriages.[9] The empirical research behind the documentary used questionnaires to seek out information on the registration of *nikāḥ* marriages, or lack of it. From a sample of 903 Muslim women, it was found that 60 per cent had a religious-only marriage.[10] This percentage has been numerously quoted, in the media, policy debates, and academic research, citing the lack of registration as highly prevalent among Muslim communities. Significantly, the report also cites ignorance about the fact that *nikāḥ* was not legally valid (28 per cent out of 60 per cent who had a *nikāḥ*-only marriage).[11]

This is largely the only quantitative research available on the subject and it is important to note that the conclusions drawn from it might not be accurately representative of the actual situation on the ground. For example, as Akhtar notes, the lack of legally binding *nikāḥ*s is more indicative of the low number of mosques that fulfil the criteria to register civil marriages,[12] which points to another challenge associating

6 Kathryn O'Sullivan and Leyla Jackson, 'Muslim Marriage (Non) Recognition: Implications and Possible Solutions', *Journal of Social Welfare and Family Law* 39, no. 1 (2017): 22–41.

7 Ibid.

8 Elham Manea, *Women and Shari'a Law: The Impact of Legal Pluralism in the UK* (London: I.B. Tauris, 2016).

9 Rajnaara C. Akhtar, '"The Truth about Muslim Marriage": 60% of Muslim Women Surveyed Are in Marriages Not Recognised by Law', True Vision, https://assemble.me/uploads/websites/39/files/5a140876945ed.pdf.

10 Ibid.

11 Ibid.

12 Rajnaara C. Akhtar, 'Unregistered Muslim Marriages: An Emerging Culture of Celebrating Rites and Compromising Rights', in *Marriage Rites and Rights*, ed. Joanna Miles, Perveez Mody, and

the lack of registration of Muslim marriages with a lack of engagement of Muslim places of worship in carrying out this duty. Overall, this shows that there are indeed limitations with the inferences made from the above findings about general trends of (non-)marriage registration within Muslim communities and speaks to the need for further research on the extent of *nikāḥ*-only marriages.

In considering the circumstances of entry into and exit from marriage, the welfare of Muslim women falls front and centre of debates on marriage registration because they are very often the ones made vulnerable in the case of relationship breakdown.[13] Commentators cite an increasing number of Muslim women rendered destitute and helpless after divorce or the husband's death because they were not able to avail themselves of legal protection otherwise available to them through civil marriage.[14] Further concerns have been raised about the extent to which the practice of unregistered marriages can be seen as a sign of British Muslims withdrawing from the state's legal system, contracting marriages that are beyond the reach of the state both in their formation and termination. Some have read this as a sign of isolation and a lack of integration of British Muslims into British society.[15]

METHODOLOGY

This paper is based on a research study which consisted of conducting thirty-four semi-structured interviews. These included fifteen interviews with Muslim women who had contracted a religious marriage and had used the services of a Sharīʿa council to obtain a religious divorce, fourteen religious marriage and divorce service providers including imams, muftis, and Sharīʿa council scholars, and five expert interviewees with a wide range of expertise in English law, politics and policy implications, women's issues, and mosque management.

The data obtained from the thirty-four interviews is reduced through the process of creating a coding manual. The interviews were studied using thematic analysis in order to derive meaningful themes and sub-themes from the data. In this interpretive process, I sought to underscore the beliefs, viewpoints, assumptions, and concerns that underly the content of the participants' testimonies.

Rebecca Probert (Oxford: Hart Publishing, 2015), 185.

13 Aina Khan, 'Muslim Marriages Not Protected by British Law', Aina Khan Law, 2018, www.ainakhanlaw.com/muslim-marriages-not-protected-british-law/.

14 Ibid.

15 Maryam Namazie, 'Sharia Law in Britain: A Threat to One Law for All and Equal Rights', One Law for All, 17 June 2010, https://onelawforall.org.uk/new-report-sharia-law-in-britain-a-threat-to-one-law-for-all-and-equal-rights/.

Many participants in my study were of South Asian background (see the Appendix for the participants' profiles). Half of the interviews with women took place in their homes, others in the premises of Apna Haq, who helped recruit those women, and two online via WhatsApp. Most interviews with clerics took place in mosques or Sharīʿa councils, with one conducted in a library and another in a café.

The choice of expert participants was related to their profession and the different roles they play and their proximity in the work that they do to the researched community. Together, their expertise areas include English law (family law more specifically), politics or policy-making, Muslim women's issues and safeguarding, and mosque and Sharīʿa council management. Zlakha Ahmed, MBE, is the founder of Apna Haq and has over twenty-five years of experience working with Muslim and BME (black and majority ethnic) women. Siddique Patel is an Islamic family law specialist solicitor and deputy director of the Register Our Marriage campaign. Naz Shah (Naseem), MP, is a British Labour Party politician and MP for Bradford West and shadow minister in the Ministry of Housing, Communities and Local Government at the time. Hassan Joudi is an elected deputy secretary general and mosque affairs coordinator for the Muslim Council of Britain. Mizan Abdulrouf is a barrister with expertise in Islamic law and matrimonial finance proceedings, and the vice chairman of the UK Board of Sharia Councils.

Through these interviews, I took up the task of testing the views of some of the key groups that are targeted by the proposals seeking to reform and regulate Muslim marriages. Relying on interviewee-specific and open-ended questions with Muslim women, Islamic scholars, and various experts, I am able to offer an appraisal of different avenues for reform and regulation through the opinions and views of Muslims themselves who are at the heart of these proposals.

EXISTING PROPOSALS

Before going into the field to explore the issues at hand, I undertook a document analysis of key sources which have put forward proposals to tackle and potentially 'solve' the issue of unregistered Muslim marriages in Britain. These documents included the Muslim Women's Network UK's (MWNUK) 'Information and Guidance on Muslim Marriage and Divorce in Britain',[16] Baroness Cox's 'Arbitration and Mediation Services (Equality) Bill',[17] the Home Office independent review into the application

16 Shaista Gohir, 'Information and Guidance on Muslim Marriage and Divorce in Britain', Muslim Women's Network UK, January 2016, www.mwnuk.co.uk/resourcesDetail.php?id=156.

17 Arbitration and Mediation Services (Equality) Bill, 2016, https://bills.parliament.uk/bills/1793.

of Sharīʿa law in England and Wales,[18] the Register Our Marriage (ROM) campaign briefing,[19] and the 'Integrated Communities Action Plan' of 2019.[20]

In exploring these proposals as well as their aims and potential instruments, we find a common trend of 'juridifying' the phenomenon of unregistered Islamic marriages,[21] that is, considering the issue to be a solvable technical problem which should be tackled through legislative reforms. The reform would make the registration of all *nikāḥ* marriages compulsory for Muslims. Other proposals include introducing cohabitation rights and reforming and modernising marriage law to make it more convenient, registering mosques to solemnise legal marriages, and raising awareness among Muslim communities to incentivise marriage registration.

RESEARCH FINDINGS

FIQHĪ QUESTIONS ON THE REGISTRATION OF MARRIAGE

In exploring the issues of unregistered *nikāḥ* and civil marriage among Muslims in Britain, three clear positions emerged with differing arguments about the necessity and validity of marriage registration or lack thereof.

One position that was espoused by several participants was that marriage registration was necessary for upholding the terms of Islamic marriage, *nikāḥ*, which is meant to be a binding contract. Drawing on their experience in dealing with Muslim couples in their entry into and exit from marriage, a number of imams and Sharīʿa council scholars stressed the need for an enforcing power for the *nikāḥ* to be binding as a contract. Without a legally recognised marriage, there is no guarantee that either of the parties involved in the relationship will abide by their responsibilities. Even community-based Islamic mechanisms such as Sharīʿa councils that are increasingly working on religious divorce cases do not have any enforcing power to compel or guarantee, for example, that a husband pays for wife and child maintenance or *mahr* (dower).

The second position that emerged from my interviews was the opposite of the first, namely, that civil marriage is neither necessary nor desirable for Muslims in

18 'Applying Sharia Law in England and Wales: Independent Review', Home Office, 1 February 2018, www.gov.uk/government/publications/applying-sharia-law-in-england-and-wales-independent-review.

19 Aina Khan, 'Briefing', Register Our Marriage, 2019, https://registerourmarriage.org/about#mission.

20 'Integrated Communities Action Plan', Ministry of Housing, Communities and Local Government, 9 February 2019, www.gov.uk/government/publications/integrated-communities-action-plan.

21 Patrick S. Nash, 'Sharia in England: The Marriage Law Solution', *Oxford Journal of Law and Religion* 6, no. 3 (2017): 523–43.

Britain. There was a clear prioritisation of the *nikāḥ* as the 'real marriage' by most interviewees, adding that civil marriage adds no particular value. This was evidenced, in the opinion of these participants, by the fact that civil marriage is not even popular among many British people who choose to cohabit. One participant exclaimed that even the prime minister at that time, Boris Johnson, was not married to his partner.

The *nikāḥ* as a contract was described as comprehensive providing Muslims with direct stipulations on marital rights and responsibilities and terms of marriage dissolution if and when necessary. While it was accepted by many participants that the status of civil marriage offers legal protection, some highlighted that civil marriage engenders rights that are not compatible with Islamic law, referring specifically to the equal split of marital assets. Two imams said they were not comfortable to even encourage marriage registration due to this.

Further, by looking at the question of whether civil marriage fulfils the conditions of an Islamic marriage (offer, acceptance, *walī* or legal guardian, *mahr*), proponents of this view believed that Islamic marriage (*nikāḥ*) and civil marriage cannot be equated together.

Another challenge that was highlighted by some participants relates to the dissolution of marriage for those Muslims that have both a *nikāḥ* and civil marriage. Terminating a civil marriage in the English courts was said not to be enough for the termination of an Islamic marriage because the state has no power to end a faith marriage. Civil divorce was hence not legitimate and there remains a need for a religious authority to dissolve the marriage.

The last position which was espoused by most participants, women and clerics, was that marriage registration was not necessary under Islamic law but is to be encouraged considering the specific context within which Muslims are contracting marriage, living as a minority faith group in non-Muslim lands. Civil marriage is encouraged because it is recognised by the state and gives rise to certain rights that would protect the parties involved through recourse to the law in case of marriage breakdown.

Among those who share this opinion are a growing number of mosques in Britain that now encourage or require Muslim couples seeking a *nikāḥ* to also enter into a civil marriage. This is seen as an example of good practice among mosques and Islamic centres. Still, among those who encouraged the registration of marriage, many did not believe that civil marriage could fulfil Islamic marriage conditions and was hence not 'Islamically' valid or legitimate.

A minority view, expressed by two participants, a Shīʿa scholar (*ʿālim*) and Sunnī imam, was that the English civil marriage could in fact be performed in a way that fulfils the conditions of a sound *nikāḥ* which would mean that 'Muslims don't have to marry twice'.[22] Having talked to more Shīʿa scholars outside of the scope of the interviews for my study, this seems not as much a minority view among Shīʿas as it is among Sunnīs in Britain.

A ONE-SIZE-FITS-ALL APPROACH?

it is important to note that the debate on marriage law reform has been going on for several decades now and does not relate to Islamic marriages only. Calls for reform of marriage laws date back to the early 2000s, highlighting how many aspects of family life and relationships had changed in British society which 'make reform a priority'.[23]

Focusing on *nikāḥ*-only marriages, one proposal was to make the registration of all Islamic marriages a legal requirement to 'bring Islamic marriage in line with Christian and Jewish marriage in the eyes of the law'.[24] In the case of marriage breakdown, having a registered marriage means that the couple would be entitled to a civil divorce giving them recourse to the state courts. In order for the compulsory registration requirement to be operational, a duty is to be placed on the celebrant of *nikāḥ* marriages to ensure that a civil marriage had previously been contracted or to fulfil requirements for the *nikāḥ* to be registered on the day of the religious ceremony. Those celebrants that fail to ensure this would be liable to a criminal penalty.[25]

A clear consensus among the research participants in my study is that the proposal to make it compulsory to register all *nikāḥ* ceremonies clearly neglects the diversity within Muslim communities and ignores the many scenarios where non-registration may in fact be a wilful and informed decision by the couple.

One of the implications that needs to be considered is that a significant proportion of unregistered marriages are in fact intended to be religious-only marriages. This could be for many reasons as highlighted in the findings of my study. The main motivations identified by the women participants from their own experiences as well as anecdotal evidence from clerics were protecting financial assets and allowing time to build trust in the marital relationship. Other reasons were attributed to a general complacency to go through cumbersome marriage registration formalities, the practice of *mutʿa* (temporary marriage) among Shīʿas, and leaving the option for a potential second marriage (polygamy) open. In such cases, it was the couple's choice to be in an unregistered marriage, temporarily or indefinitely.

22 Interview, Shīʿa *ʿālim*.

23 'Getting Married: A Scoping Paper', Law Commission, 17 December 2015, 10, https://s3-eu-west-2.amazonaws.com/lawcom-prod-storage-11jsxou24uy7q/uploads/2015/12/Getting_Married_scoping_paper-1.pdf.

24 'Applying Sharia Law', 5.

25 Ibid.

Limited empirical research has been conducted on the motivations behind unregistered Muslim marriages. My interviews help shed light, through experiential and anecdotal evidence, on the various circumstances that give rise to these marriage types.

Examples that were shared in my interviews as to why couples and Muslim women in particular may not wish to contract civil marriage included the desire to build trust first before engaging in a legal commitment that binds the couple, and particularly their financial assets, together by law. This view was articulated by several women interviewees as a valid reason both for men and women who particularly wish to delay the legal marriage by a few years. This was the case for one woman participant who had an arranged marriage and only briefly got to know her husband before the *nikāḥ*. As she explains, civil marriage was something that both of them did not want to engage in at the time. On the other hand, as one Islamic scholar explained, 'some men are afraid because they see horror stories in the news and think "if I had a civil marriage and it ends, I have to give up great sums of money".'

Most participants also felt strongly about the potential introduction of a criminal penalty against religious marriage celebrants if they do not ensure the registration of the marriage. As one Islamic scholar put it:

> putting the onus on imams, it's one thing to say to imams we are going to train you and give you some advice and we're going to trust that you will follow this, but to [say] you are criminally liable, it's a huge step up. And that is remarkably unfair, and I think about possibly putting imams in prison, it's not going to go down well ... I think that kind of criminalising of Muslims is a bad start.

Considering reasons why Muslims engage in religious-only marriages, there was also a discussion with imam participants who performed *nikāḥ*s about a growing section of Muslim youth contracting *nikāḥ* to make romantic and sexual relationships 'halal'. These relationships would not be intended as formally recognised marriages among their families or communities. In some cases, the couple do not necessarily see themselves as husband and wife, but have a *nikāḥ* to be able to cohabit or be together with religious legitimacy. In other cases recounted by some imams, the couple may be very young, for example, university students, whose parents are not aware of their relationship or do not approve of it. In such cases, making it a legal requirement to register the *nikāḥ* as a legally binding marriage was deemed inappropriate for the context in which these *nikāḥ*s are undertaken.

A further prominent example which has been neglected in the literature that would also guard against the introduction of a legal requirement to register *nikāḥ*s is the practice among Muslim Shīʿa communities of *muʿta* or temporary marriage which was cited by a number of imam participants in my study. The proposal for compulsory registration does not take account of this type of marriage. Registration is not appropriate in such scenarios because the essence of *muʿta* marriage is that it is temporary.

A comparative reference with the wider practice of cohabitation in British society was also used by the majority of my participants to protest the perceived targeting and singling out of Muslims for not undertaking legally binding marriages. Indeed, the proposal seems to assume that marriage registration is the norm or mainstream against which Muslims are deviating. Data from the Office for National Statistics shows that families of cohabitating couples continue to increase – from 15.3 per cent to 18.4 per cent – becoming the 'second-largest family type at 3.5 million', while those of married or civil partnered families continue on a declining trend – from 68.6 per cent to 66.8 per cent.[26] There is currently no data to establish whether Muslim couples are statistically more or less likely to be legally married.

Nonetheless, viewing unregistered religious marriages in Muslim communities as an exceptional phenomenon contributes to portraying them as a sign of isolation and parallelism. The findings of my study help to shed light on the interplay of various factors and motivations that may lead to more informal marriage or relationship arrangements.

The interview findings in my study show that there are complex realities that give rise to *nikāḥ*-only marriages; there were no cases that illustrated a lack of awareness as a main factor for having such a marriage. Although many respondents were aware of examples when non-registration may not be considered a well-thought decision, for example, in cases where husbands and in-laws went back on their word,[27] still, civil marriage was not presented as always being in the best interest of women. This position was framed by some women participants in terms of preserving and promoting choice for Muslim couples to regulate their own relationships. There was, however, an apparent contradiction in the views of several women participants with regards to supporting registration of Muslim marriage as a broad aim, but not necessarily always desirable for themselves. They would view their cases as the exception to the rule, for having valid reasons to engage in *nikāḥ*-only marriages, but that overall marriage registration was a positive goal. Some of the exceptional circumstances that these women attributed to their own *nikāḥ*-only marriages were for divorcees or widows undertaking a second or third marriage and wishing to preserve their assets.

The various motivations and circumstances that discourage registration were, however, absent in the Home Office independent review discussion as well as other sources, leaving a general assumption that the choice to have a legal marriage is almost always limited in such contexts. The recommendation would mean that couples who

---

26 'Families and Households in the UK: 2019', Office for National Statistics, www.ons.gov.uk/peoplepopulationandcommunity/birthsdeathsandmarriages/families/bulletins/familiesandhouseholds/2019.

27 Samia Bano, *Muslim Women and Shari'ah Councils: Transcending the Boundaries of Community and Law* (Basingstoke: Palgrave Macmillan, 2012), 161.

voluntarily wish to have a *nikāḥ*-only marriage for whatever purposes will no longer be able to do so; how much of a problem this poses has arguably to do with how valid such purposes are seen to be, and the question is made more complex since there are currently no up-to-date figures to illustrate the extent of unregistered marriages in British Muslim communities.

COHABITATION RIGHTS

in the case of marriage breakdown, Muslim couples in a religious-only marriage are mostly regarded as cohabitees if and when they seek legal support. Under the law, cohabitating couples have fewer rights compared to legally married couples, particularly in the areas of maintenance and property.[28] To redress the potential vulnerability caused by the lack of legal marital status, proposals have been made to bring about reform for greater protection to all cohabitees. Accordingly, those Muslim couples who have not had a legally binding marriage can still be afforded some type of protection under cohabitation laws, particularly in terms of financial claims.

The issue of cohabitation reform has been brought to the fore long before religious-only Muslim marriages became a topical issue. Indeed, with the increasing social shift highlighting a move away from traditional marriage to cohabitation,[29] strengthening cohabitation rights is becoming ever more necessary. Back in 2007, the Law Commission made recommendations to Parliament on laws relating to cohabitation with the view that the latter are 'complex, uncertain, expensive to rely on and, as it was not designed for family circumstances, often give rise to outcomes that are unjust',[30] and that law reform was necessary.[31] More recently, the Law Commission has reiterated this stance arguing for reform that would provide financial relief and ensure protection for a wide range of cohabiting couples, including those in religious-only marriages.[32]

Although most participants seemed to have little knowledge about cohabitation provisions in the legal sense, they were nonetheless more welcoming of this possibility

28 Akhtar, 'Unregistered Muslim Marriages', 183.

29 'Families and Households in the UK: 2016', Office for National Statistics, 6, www.ons.gov.uk/peoplepopulationandcommunity/birthsdeathsandmarriages/families/bulletins/familiesandhouseholds/2016.

30 'Cohabitation: The Financial Consequences of Relationship Breakdown: Executive Summary', Law Commission, 31 July 2007, https://s3-eu-west-2.amazonaws.com/lawcom-prod-storage-11jsxou24uy7q/uploads/2015/03/lc307_Cohabitation_summary.pdf.

31 Ibid., 1.

32 'Getting Married: A Summary of the Weddings Law Consultation Paper', Law Commission, 2020, 34, https://s3-eu-west-2.amazonaws.com/lawcom-prod-storage-11jsxou24uy7q/uploads/2020/09/Weddings-CP-Summary-final-web.pdf.

than other measures such as the requirement to register all *nikāḥ* marriages. Another aspect of this proposal that appealed to some of the respondents was its 'inclusivity', that it would apply to all those in cohabitation relationships, not just Muslims.

Questions about agency and choice are important when talking about registering marriage. This point is particularly relevant in how the choice (to register or not) is discussed. In this current debate where the focus is often said to be on protecting vulnerable or potentially vulnerable people from making unwise or uninformed decisions about their relationships, a double standard becomes apparent. Where *nikāḥ*-only marriage is concerned, it is assumed it mostly arises from a lack of agency or lack of awareness whereas for non-Muslim cohabitants, non-registration is assumed to have arisen from individual choice. This is evident from the strong claim about lack of awareness being a key cause for unregistered religious marriages despite the lack of empirical evidence to substantiate this. *Nikāḥ*-only marriages are also condemned in a way that other cohabiting relationship arrangements are not.

The intentions and circumstances of couples who are considered as cohabitants by the law are bound to be different. As Akhtar et al. note:

> Some cohabitants would like legal recognition, others are cohabiting precisely to avoid legal rights and responsibilities. Similarly, some couples in religious-only marriages want their marriage to be recognized by the law as such, while others have deliberately chosen the option of non-recognition.[33]

In addition to the Law Commission's proposals in the area of cohabitation, the latest scholarly contributions from Akhtar et al.[34] and Sandberg[35] underscore the need to protect choice by providing a mechanism for opt-outs. This is consistent with a more recent contribution from the Women and Equalities Committee in their Rights of Cohabiting Partners report,[36] which specifically references the lack of comprehensive legal protection for ethnic minority women in religious-only marriages. The report calls for the introduction of an opt-out cohabitation scheme as 'a pragmatic approach for reforming cohabitation law'.[37] Indeed, an opt-out scheme would offer more protection as everyone eligible would automatically be covered. Then, if they

33 Rajnaara C. Akhtar, Patrick Nash, and Rebecca Probert, 'Conclusion', in *Cohabitation and Religious Marriage: Status, Similarities and Solutions*, ed. Rajnaara C. Akhtar, Patrick Nash, and Rebecca Probert (Bristol: Bristol University Press, 2020), 158.

34 Ibid.

35 Russell Sandberg, *Religion and Marriage Law: The Need for Reform* (Bristol: Bristol University Press, 2021).

36 'The Rights of Cohabiting Partners', House of Commons, 4 August 2022, https://publications.parliament.uk/pa/cm5803/cmselect/cmwomeq/92/report.html.

37 Ibid., 26.

want to opt-out, they are able to do so after fulfilling certain procedural requirements. Providing a mechanism for opt-out is essential for those who are resolved on avoiding state-sponsored marriage or any sort of marital legal commitment.

It is increasingly seen as an attractive solution for tackling the issue of unregistered Muslim marriages specifically, and to bring more protection for all cohabitees more generally. A tiered model such as that proposed by the Law Commission as far back as 2007 and more recently by Vora,[38] which categorises cohabiting relationships based on length of cohabitation, whether children have been born, and the contribution of parties to shared assets, seems to be workable and appropriate for the set of challenges associated both with unregistered Islamic marriage and cohabitating couples more generally.

MODERNISING REGISTRATION FORMALITIES

Looking back at the reasons behind Muslims not registering *nikāḥ* marriages, we find that couples who want to have a civil marriage, either soon after the *nikāḥ* or sometime in the near future, can be discouraged or put off by bureaucratic hurdles and what are perceived to be complex and needless formalities and procedures according to some of my participants.

While there has been much focus in the solution-oriented debate on the need to bring Muslim marriages under the existing law, the findings of my research illustrate dissatisfaction with current formalities which are described as impractical, complex, cumbersome, and outdated. This is consistent with existing contributions,[39] which have highlighted the inadequacy of the current law on weddings in England and Wales. The latter is described as outdated and 'in desperate need of reform'.[40]

As several participants argued, marriage registration should be simplified and made more convenient. So while the proposal to make civil marriage compulsory was rejected as too simplistic, the legislative route was not ruled out altogether. Most participants felt that legal change would have the swiftest and most direct impact to influence positive change where the non-registration of marriage is not necessarily a clear-cut decision. Since the findings of my research highlight the inadequacy of current law with much dissatisfaction about its impracticality, modernisation becomes imperative. If Muslims and other couples are encouraged to subscribe to the state-sponsored institution of marriage, it is imperative that entry is made more convenient. The focus therefore should not only be on bringing Muslims under existing

38 Vishal Vora, 'The Islamic Marriage Conundrum: Register or Recognize? The Legal Consequences of the Nikah in England and Wales' (PhD diss., SOAS, University of London, 2016).

39 'Getting Married' (2020); Sandberg, *Religion and Marriage Law*.

40 Sandberg, *Religion and Marriage Law*, 1.

regulations but on modernising the current framework of marriage registration to provide more choice instead of restricting it.

REGISTERING MOSQUES TO SOLEMNISE MARRIAGE

The current marriage law in England and Wales places considerable importance on the place where a marriage ceremony is to be held. Hence, another recommendation has been made to have more mosques become registered places to conduct lawful marriages for Muslims. The Marriage Act 1949 allows for a building that is registered as a place of worship to be registered for the solemnisation of marriage and for an authorised person to be appointed to register the marriages in that building.[41] Civil preliminaries would still need to be completed to give formal notice to the local registry office but it would mean that *nikāḥ* ceremonies conducted in such mosques would be legally binding. Given the size of the British Muslim population, there exist relatively few mosques that are registered to conduct legal marriages – out of 1,428 places of worship only 301 were registered in 2021.[42] The question of mosque registration was raised with the imam participants to gauge interest and potentially identify the reasons why mosque registration is not very common.

Imams and mosques play a key role in the facilitation of matrimonial practices and choices within British Muslim communities.[43] Most of the women in my study had their *nikāḥ* performed by an imam (either at home, at the mosque, or in a private venue), and a number of imam participants stated that performing *nikāḥ* and advising on matrimonial issues was high on their list of tasks. The findings from my study as well as existing evidence highlight this key role: some imams and mosques play an active role in encouraging registration, while others may be passive or neutral about the issue seeing only the *nikāḥ* as part of their roles or responsibilities. Only two of the mosques to which the imams interviewed belonged were registered for the purposes of registering marriages.

Three of the imams interviewed were not aware of this possibility, while some others who were aware of it claimed that the registration process can be quite long and complicated and that even if mosques were to be registered, the presence of a registrar would still be needed. To do this, it was claimed, may be more costly than

41 'Guidance: Marriage Ceremonies', HM Passport Office, updated 4 May 2021, www.gov.uk/government/publications/marriage-registration-guidance-for-authorised-persons/marriage-registration-guidance#authorised-persons.

42 'Guidance: Places of Worship Registered for Marriage', HM Passport Office, 17 March 2015, updated 12 June 2023, www.gov.uk/government/publications/places-of-worship-registered-for-marriage.

43 Islam Uddin, 'Islamic Family Law: Imams, Mosques, and Sharīʿa Councils in the UK', *Electronic Journal of Islamic and Middle Eastern Law* 8, no. 1 (2020): 25–36.

to have the couple themselves go to the civil registry office. Some imams felt that this would create more responsibilities for them compared to larger mosques and Islamic centres where the institution may have an administrative team that handles such endeavours.

Overall, there was no sign of commitment or willingness from the imams whose mosques were not already registered for such purposes to potentially pursue this option; this mostly reads as down to the perceived regulatory burden and lack of demand from the communities they serve.

EMPOWERMENT THROUGH RAISING AWARENESS

Lack of awareness as well as misconceptions about the validity of *nikāḥ* marriages have featured as significant factors behind non-registration.[44] Therefore, an important recommendation has emerged encouraging awareness-raising initiatives and activities that build understanding and provide essential information about religious and civil marriage for Muslims in Britain. This recommendation has featured in the Home Office independent review[45] and 'Integrated Communities Action Plan'.[46] Similarly, in their guidance on religious divorce in the British Muslim community, the MWNUK also put forward this recommendation in their report, stating that the government should support a 'Marriage and Divorce Educational Campaign' aimed specifically at Muslim women.[47]

The government's 'Integrated Communities Action Plan' states that the government would indeed support awareness campaigns that will inform and educate on 'the benefits of having a civilly registered marriage'.[48] This materialised when the Register Our Marriage campaign secured funding in early 2019 to run multiple awareness-raising events in major cities in England. The campaign set up 'legal surgeries' held remotely during the COVID-19 pandemic to provide advice and guidance on questions and issues relevant to marital rights and marriage registration.

The state seeking to encourage registration through awareness campaigns was seen as justified for the majority of respondents because the aim is to empower people with knowledge about the implications of either route regarding marriage registration, but it also left the final decision to couples themselves.

Some respondents, however, questioned such campaigns, particularly in terms of impact. One imam highlighted that the issue 'is not just about campaigning, it's about

44 Akhtar, '"The Truth about Muslim Marriage"'.
45 'Applying Sharia Law'.
46 'Integrated Communities Action Plan'.
47 Gohir, 'Information and Guidance', 79.
48 'Integrated Communities Action Plan', 19.

proper teaching'. There was hence more support for a broader approach to awareness raising, putting forward ideas and examples of awareness-raising activities that could take place in many various settings; of these possible settings identified were schools. Several respondents said that basic information on marriage in general and Muslim marriage practices more specifically can be incorporated into school curricula for Islamic schools as well as other schools with a high population of Muslim students, in RE and PHSE education, for example. Indeed, with more than a third of Britain's Muslim population being under fifteen,[49] it is important to consider the advantage of involving younger Muslims in awareness-raising initiatives as opposed to just those whom we think of as at the age of marriage.

Some scepticism arose in the interviews about the topic of raising awareness, particularly, as mentioned earlier, in relation to the exaggeration of claims of how widespread the lack of awareness about the validity of *nikāḥ* among Muslims in Britain is. It can be argued that for many young Muslims in Britain, knowledge and awareness of issues around marriage and divorce largely come from socialisation with family and friends. Such discussions are likely to take place in private, inside the home with family and within social circles. In these settings, the subjects of marriage and divorce are more likely to be approached by focusing on their social and cultural/religious meaning and significance, and procedural or technical details are likely to be overlooked.

All the women interviewed for this study who had a religious-only marriage knew that the *nikāḥ* ceremony would not amount to a legally valid marriage. Two women had plans to have a *nikāḥ* in the near future specifically for that purpose. Commenting on similar findings in her own research, however, Parveen highlights that awareness of this fact does not automatically mean that the women understood the full implications of not having a religious-only marriage.[50] Although the choice to not register is technically open both to men and women, the impact of gender needs to be acknowledged when thinking about avenues for tackling the issue of unregistered Muslim marriages in general and approaches to raising awareness in particular.

The mosque was also recognised by participants as an important setting where education and awareness raising can and should take place, and that it should be done through 'where people go'.[51] Mosques and faith leaders play a key role in the facilitation of matrimonial practices and choices within British Muslim communities. One Sharīʿa council scholar highlighted that 'imams have got a platform every Friday where good, bad, or ugly Muslims turn out for the *khuṭba* [sermon]; the imams have

49 Shelina Janmohamed, *Generation M.: Young Muslims Changing the World* (London: I.B. Tauris, 2016), 7.

50 Rehana Parveen, 'Do Shari'a Councils Meet the Needs of Muslim Women?' (PhD diss., University of Birmingham, 2017), 233.

51 Participant interview, quoting Mizan Abdulrouf, UK Board of Sharia Councils.

[a] ready-built platform for any issues that the Muslim community needs' and that this should be taken advantage of to raise awareness about many issues regarding marriage and divorce. On the other hand, one female participant highlighted that some imams do not always have an understanding of women's issues, which is why input in the mosque setting alone is likely to be limited.

We find that some imams and mosques play an active role in encouraging registration while others seem to be neutral or passive about the issue, seeing only the *nikāḥ* as part of their roles or responsibilities. Other celebrants, however, seem to be 'fast-tracking' *nikāḥ* without proper administration and information for Muslim couples.[52]

CONCLUSION

It is unlikely that any of the 'solutions' and proposals that have been explored in this paper would bring a complete end to unregistered Muslim marriages in Britain. No solution adequately addresses all the questions and concerns raised throughout this paper, particularly about choice and agency, nor appeals to all sections of the debate. The practice of unregistered faith marriages is not a mere technical problem that can be 'solved' by legal reform. Indeed, the proposal for compulsory registration obscures and downplays the plurality of motivations for unregistered *nikāḥ* marriages and neglects the wider socio-cultural norms of marriage and relationships in Britain, which is particularly problematic when potentially 'invasive' proposals to require the registration of all *nikāḥ* marriages gain prominence.

While the objective of incentivising and increasing marriage registration is justifiable considering the state's interest in the institution of marriage, seeking to safeguard individuals against the vulnerability resulting from unregistered marriages should not be at the expense of limiting choice in forming relationships that are meaningful to different people. This is particularly important as, having explored some of the *fiqhī* questions that came up in my interviews, it is clear that there is no clear consensus about the necessity of registration.

Understanding the complex factors and reasons that give rise to unregistered marriages which have been clarified in this paper helps us define the problem more clearly, which is essential for examining proposed solutions. It is the author's view that being in a *nikāḥ*-only marriage is not in itself problematic. The problem is when this arrangement is due to pressure and coercion, lack of awareness of basic legalities on registration and what it entails, and being deterred by the registration process itself being perceived as cumbersome and costly.

52 Uddin, 'Islamic Family Law'.

In appraising different proposals and seeking to identify future avenues, the key focus should be balancing two objectives: safeguarding the vulnerable and protecting choice. This can be done by remedying the inadequacy of existing marriage formalities thus incentivising registration and encouraging more uptake, and strengthening legal protection for those who, for various reasons and circumstances, remain in cohabiting and informal relationship arrangements.

The awareness-raising approach is also important for incentivising registration, the focus being on equipping people with knowledge and information so that they are able to make informed decisions when they are considering marriage. Choosing *nikāḥ*-only marriage does not have to equate to conceding one's rights. Instead, empowering Muslim communities and faith leaders with proper teaching and awareness has greater potential for creating incremental and sustainable change from the bottom up.

Based on the findings in my study, the following recommendations may be made.

GOVERNMENT

1. Reform marriage law to provide more choice for couples on where to get married and modernise marriage preliminaries. Examples include:
    - removing the requirement for exchange of vows in registry office ceremonies
    - removing the obligation to give notice where you live, which has changed for civil ceremonies, Jews and Quakers but not Anglicans and other faiths[53]
    - offering cheaper ceremonies at registry offices, such as the statutory 'two-plus-two' £46 ceremony[54]
2. Strengthen cohabitation rights through a system of categorising cohabiting relationships based on length of cohabitation, children born, and the contribution of parties to shared assets, with an option to opt-out.
3. Instruct relevant agencies (MHCLG, GRO) to put in place and/or support awareness-raising in Muslim communities. The aim should be sharing information and building an understanding of the status of *nikāḥ*-only marriages and the options and formalities required to register a marriage according to the law.
4. Seek cooperation with organisations/actors within the community who are supportive of the role of incentivising marriage registration.

53 Rebecca Probert and Stephanie Pywell, 'Love in the Time of COVID-19: A Case-Study of the Complex Laws Governing Weddings', *Legal Studies* 41, no. 4 (2021): 676–92.

54 Rajnaara C. Akhtar and Rebecca Probert, 'COVID Weddings: Why Some Couples Got Unofficially Married during the Pandemic', The Conversation, 23 June 2021, https://theconversation.com/covid-weddings-why-some-couples-got-unofficially-married-during-the-pandemic-163211.

MOSQUES

Recommendations in this section that relate to conducting *nikāḥ*s are also relevant for Sharīʿa councils and other mechanisms that perform similar work.

1. Register the mosque building for marriage solemnisation.
2. Register mosque imam as authorised person; this would reduce cost of fees to book a registrar from the registry office.
3. Provide printed *nikāḥ* certificate and hold duplicate record.
4. Explicitly highlight non-legal validity of *nikāḥ* during the ceremony and on the certificate.
5. Nikah certificate to state whether couple intend to register marriage.
6. Where pre-marriage counselling is offered by a mosque, include proper sign-posting for information on recognised/unrecognised marriages.
7. Provide information and awareness raising on marriage and divorce; this could be in the form of leaflets provided to couples having their *nikāḥ* at the mosque.

APPENDIX

WOMEN PARTICIPANT INTERVIEW QUESTIONS

Establishing consent

Agree on duration of interview

Personal details

Why did you consult the Sharīʿa council?

Do you have a registered marriage? Why or why not?

If you had already acquired a civil divorce, why did you also resort to a Sharīʿa council?

How did you choose the council?

What were your expectations of the council?

How was your general experience?

How would you rate the services that the council provided for you in relation to the expectations you had before? And how effective were they in helping you solve your problem?

How long did it take to get the *khulʿ*?

Are you aware of some of the concerns and criticisms that Sharīʿa councils face? What do you think about these?

What do you think about demands for regulation and reform?

Are you aware of some recommendations for change concerning Muslim marriage and divorce practices?

Here are some specific measures that have been proposed in order to:

- increase Muslim marriage registration
- strengthen the legal protection for cohabitees
- tackle discrimination against women in Sharīʿa councils
- regulate Sharīʿa councils

- Thoughts on Increasing Registration of Muslim Marriages

What do think about the phenomenon of unregistered Muslim marriages and their effects on families and women in particular?

How widespread do you think it is? And why?

Do you think some degree of reform is needed?

How about making it a requirement for all Muslims get a civil marriage along with the *nikāḥ*?

How about requiring that all imams check whether the couple have had a civil marriage prior to the *nikāḥ*?

How about getting more mosques to register to become official marriage venues?

How about those couples who intentionally want a *nikāḥ*-only marriage?

Consider the implications on polygamy.

What do you think of the initiative to have awareness campaigns to inform or educate Muslims about marriage registration? Who do you think should be involved in such initiatives?

How about training for imams to have a better understanding of legal formalities on marriage and the English legal system?

What measures do you think are likely to reduce unregistered Islamic marriages?

- Improving Legal Protection and Choice for Women

Muslim couples with *nikāḥ*-only marriages are regarded as cohabitees. Do you think the law should offer more protection to cohabitating couples? Would you have found it useful to take advantage of this?

(If in a registered marriage,) what do you think about the proposal to amend Divorce Act 2002 so that one wife/husband could ask for the final divorce document to be delayed until an Islamic divorce is issued from a religious authority?

What kind of impact do you think it would have on Muslim men and women alike?

- Regulating Sharīʿa Councils

What do you think of demands for Sharīʿa councils to be more regulated?

If proposals for regulation is pushed forward, do you think it should better come from the state or from the councils themselves? Who should be involved/take the lead? And why?

Code of conduct – some of the recommendations include:

- the use of a unified marriage contract which delegates the right to divorce to the wife
- uniformity between the councils with regards to marriage and divorce certificates as well as fees
- having more women on the panels/procedures for complaints and appeals
- putting in place safeguarding policies dealing with vulnerable applicants

What are your thoughts on these requirements?

In more general terms, what do you think should be the priority: increasing registration or regulating Sharīʿa councils? And why?

In your opinion, why has reform not materialised yet?

Would any of the above-mentioned proposals have affected your situation? What led you to the council and/or your experience with them?

In addition to the proposals we discussed, what type of improvement would you like to see in Sharīʿa councils?

Do you have anything else you would like to add?

FAITH LEADER INTERVIEW QUESTIONS

Establishing consent

Agree on duration of interview

Personal details

What are your responsibilities as imam/scholar?

What services does your institution provide?

Are you aware of the some of the concerns and criticisms that Sharīʿa councils face? What do you think about these?

What do you think about demands for regulation and reform?

Are you aware of some recommendations for change concerning Muslim marriage and divorce practices?

Here are some specific measures that have been proposed in order to:

- increase Muslim marriage registration
- strengthen the legal protection for cohabitees
- tackle discrimination against women in Sharīʿa councils
- regulate Sharīʿa councils

- Thoughts on Increasing Registration of Muslim Marriages

What do think about the phenomenon of unregistered Muslim marriages and their effects on families and women in particular?

How widespread do you think it is? And why?

Do you think some degree of reform is needed?

How about making it a requirement for all Muslims get a civil marriage along with the *nikāḥ*?

How about requiring that all imams check whether the couple have had a civil marriage prior to the *nikāḥ*?

(If they also perform *nikāḥ*,) how would this affect your work/your institution?

How about getting more mosques to register to become official marriage venues?

How about those couples who intentionally want a *nikāḥ*-only marriage?

Consider the implications on polygamy.

What do you think of the initiative to have awareness campaigns to inform or educate Muslims about marriage registration? Who do you think should be involved in such initiatives?

How about training for imams to have a better understanding of legal formalities on marriage and the English legal system?

What measures do you think are likely to reduce unregistered Islamic marriages?

- Improving Legal Protection and Choice for Women

Muslim couples with *nikāḥ*-only marriages are regarded as cohabitees. Do you think the law should offer more protection to cohabitating couples? Would you have found it useful to take advantage of this?

(If in a registered marriage,) what do you think about the proposal to amend Divorce Act 2002 so that one wife/husband could ask for the final divorce document to be delayed until an Islamic divorce is issued from a religious authority?

What kind of impact do you think it would have on Muslim men and women alike?

- Regulating Sharīʿa Councils

What do you think of demands for Sharīʿa councils to be more regulated?

If proposals for regulation is pushed forward, do you think it should better come from the state or from the councils themselves? Who should be involved/take the lead? And why?

Code of conduct – some of the recommendations include:

- the use of a unified marriage contract which delegates the right to divorce to the wife
- uniformity between the councils with regards to marriage and divorce certificates as well as fees
- having more women on the panels/procedures for complaints and appeals
- putting in place safeguarding policies dealing with vulnerable applicants

What are your thoughts on these requirements?

In more general terms, what do you think should be the priority: increasing registration or regulating Sharīʿa councils? And why?

Would any of these proposals have helped or hindered your work?

In your opinion, why has reform not materialised yet?

In addition to the proposals we discussed, what type of improvement would you like to see in Sharīʿa councils?

Do you have anything else you would like to add?

PARTICIPANTS' PROFILES

Pseudonym	Marriage status	Ethnic origin	Religious orientation	City
Samira	*Nikāḥ* abroad (legal)	Pakistani	Sunnī	Rotherham
Ruqya	*Nikāḥ* abroad (legal)	Pakistani	Sunnī	Rotherham
Sumaya	*Nikāḥ* abroad (legal)	Pakistaní	Sunnī	Rotherham
Nisa	*Nikāḥ* abroad (legal)	Pakistani	Sunnī	Rotherham
Yamina	*Nikāḥ* abroad (legal)	Pakistaní	Sunnī	Rotherham
Nira	*Nikāḥ* abroad (legal)	Pakistani	Sunnī	Rotherham
Nassira	*Nikāḥ* and civil ceremony	Pakistani	Sunnī	Rotherham
Samara	Unregistered *nikāḥ*	Bangladeshi	Sunnī	Burton
Hanane	*Nikāḥ* and civil ceremony	Bangladeshi	Sunnī	London
Reema	*Nikāḥ* and civil ceremony	Pakistani	Sunnī	Bradford
Noura	*Nikāḥ* and civil ceremony	Pakistani	Sunnī	Birmingham
Hala	*Nikāḥ* and civil ceremony	Algerian	Sunnī	London
Zina	1st *nikāḥ* and civil ceremony	Pakistani	Sunnī	Rotherham
Shamima	2nd unregistered *nikāḥ*	Indian	Sunnī	London
Sahra	Unregistered *nikāḥ*	Somali	Sunnī	Bristol
	Nikāḥ abroad			

Razi	Sharīʿa council scholar	Pakistani	Sunnī	London
Mohammad	Mufti	Arab	Sunnī	Cardiff
Muaad	Sharīʿa council scholar	Pakistani	Sunnī	Nottingham
Mounir	Imam	Pakistani	Sunnī	Cardiff
Fadi	Imam and mufti	Pakistani	Sunnī	Birmingham
Sama	Sharīʿa council scholar	Indian	Sunnī	London
Badr	Imam and mufti	Pakistani	Sunnī	Cardiff
Ilyaa	Imam	Indian	Sunnī	Bristol
Chadi	Imam	Pakistani	Sunnī	Bristol
Salem	Imam	Kenyan	Sunnī	London
Kafi	Imam and mufti	Pakistani	Sunnī	London
Fawaz	Mufti	Pakistani	Sunnī	Bristol
Jalil	*ʿĀlim*	Indian	Shīʿa	London
Hani	Sharīʿa council scholar	Arab	Sunnī	London

BIBLIOGRAPHY

Akhtar, Rajnaara C. 'Unregistered Muslim Marriages: An Emerging Culture of Celebrating Rites and Compromising Rights'. In *Marriage Rites and Rights*, edited by Joanna Miles, Perveez Mody, and Rebecca Probert, 167–92. Oxford: Hart Publishing, 2015.

Akhtar, Rajnaara C., Patrick Nash, and Rebecca Probert. 'Conclusion'. In *Cohabitation and Religious Marriage: Status, Similarities and Solutions*, edited by Rajnaara C. Akhtar, Patrick Nash, and Rebecca Probert, 155–60. Bristol: Bristol University Press, 2020.

Akhtar, Rajnaara C., Rebecca Probert, and Annelies Moors. 'Informal Muslim Marriages: Regulations and Contestations'. *Oxford Journal of Law and Religion* 7, no. 3 (2018): 367–75.

Bano, Samia. *Muslim Women and Shari'ah Councils: Transcending the Boundaries of Community and Law*. Basingstoke: Palgrave Macmillan, 2012.

Grillo, Ralph. *Muslim Families, Politics and the Law: A legal Industry in Multicultural Britain*. London: Routledge, 2016.

Janmohamed, Shelina. *Generation M.: Young Muslims Changing the World*. London: I.B. Tauris, 2016.

Manea, Elham. *Women and Shari'a Law: The Impact of Legal Pluralism in the UK*. London: I.B. Tauris, 2016.

Nash, Patrick S. 'Sharia in England: The Marriage Law Solution'. *Oxford Journal of Law and Religion* 6, no. 3 (2017): 523–43.

O'Sullivan, Kathryn, and Leyla Jackson. 'Muslim Marriage (Non) Recognition: Implications and Possible Solutions'. *Journal of Social Welfare and Family Law* 39, no. 1 (2017): 22–41.

Parveen, Rehana. 'Do Shari'a Councils Meet the Needs of Muslim Women?'. PhD diss., University of Birmingham, 2017.

Sandberg, Russell. *Religion and Marriage Law: The Need for Reform*. Bristol: Bristol University Press, 2021.

Uddin, Islam. 'Islamic Family Law: Imams, Mosques, and Sharīʿa Councils in the UK'. *Electronic Journal of Islamic and Middle Eastern Law* 8, no. 1 (2020): 25–36.

Vora, Vishal. 'The Islamic Marriage Conundrum: Register or Recognize? The Legal Consequences of the Nikah in England and Wales'. PhD diss., SOAS, University of London, 2016.

SEYED MOHAMMAD GHARI SEYED FATEMI,
MUNZELA RAZA, AHMAD KAOURI AND ABBAS RAMJI

A Purposive Approach to Islamic Marriage: A Re-assessment of Q. 30:21

> And one of His signs is that He created for you spouses from among yourselves so that you may find tranquillity in them. And He has placed between you compassion and mercy. (Q. 30:21)

In Islamic jurisprudence, marriage is largely considered a contractual relationship between two parties, with no concern as such for the spirit, virtue, and psychology behind matrimonial laws. This is due to a reluctance on the part of jurists to apply a purposive (*maqāṣidī*) approach in the derivation of law given the uncertainty in ascertaining such purposes in the first place. Based on the Qur'anic verse cited above, this paper will argue for *sakīna* (tranquillity) as a specific purpose, in service of more general essential and complementary purposes that help to reveal and establish the spirit behind Islamic law. Such a purpose, in relation to marriage, has been neglected even among orthodox *maqāṣidī* proponents of Islamic law that concentrate mostly on general macro purposes.

In the first instance, the validity of seeing *sakīna* as a purpose from the Qur'an will be established and the pertinent verse will be positioned alongside others to build a clearer picture of the institution of marriage in Islam itself. Then psychological and behavioural data will be brought to show the detrimental effect of marriages lacking in tranquillity upon the spouses themselves as well as any children involved. Following this, the application of both strands will meet in the realm of legal theory where *sakīna* will be proposed as an *'illa* as well as a *maqṣad* to flesh out the broader concept of the institution of marriage. It can then be further argued that a marriage that no longer fulfils this purpose is not consistent with the focal purpose of marriage as conveyed by the Qur'an. Reference will also be made to seeing *sakīna* as a *ḥikma*, that is, the wisdom behind the ruling, a view which reflects current mainstream understanding.

THE CONTRACTUAL NOTION OF MARRIAGE IN ISLAMIC JURISPRUDENCE

According to Islamic jurisprudence, marriage is a contract with both essential and non-essential aspects. In the Imāmiyya, the essential aspect of marriage is only the offer initiated by the female party using a specific formula and the acceptance of it by the male party. Another key, but non-essential part of this contract is the stipulation of the dower (*mahr*) by the female party. The *mahr* is a specified material recompense that the wife asks for upon completion of the recitation of the marriage formula. It is considered a fundamental right of the wife which is obligatory upon the husband to fulfil. Although not the case in the Imāmiyya, *mahr* is generally held to be a consideration (*'iwadh*) in contract law, which signifies receiving something in lieu of another thing. In the Imāmiyya, *mahr* is not a consideration and so is not an essential aspect. The essential aspects remain the offer and acceptance of entering into a marriage. Sufficient to signify offer is for the female to use the words '*ankaḥtu*' or '*zawwajtu*', meaning 'I wed you ...', as part of her formula. For the man, it is sufficient that he merely states, '*qabiltu*', meaning 'I accept', to signify acceptance. Upon such mutual utterances, the marriage is believed to be valid and in effect. Due to the contractual nature of marriage, both parties are permitted to stipulate certain conditions in the contract. Such conditions can serve to determine the balance, power, and privilege in the contractual relationship and in modern Muslim societies is a method by which to make the marriage contract more egalitarian. This can be seen in the cases of women initiating divorce proceedings. In Islamic jurisprudence, divorce remains the unilateral privilege of the husband with the woman only having recourse to it in exceptional circumstances,[1] a fact which creates a significant imbalance in the marriage. Such an imbalance can be mitigated by giving the wife the power of attorney to divorce on his behalf and shift the balance towards the centre.

Although utilisation of the 'conditions' component in marital contracts can help towards a more equitable approach to Islamic marriage, such a conception of marriage, namely, a legal, contractual conception, does little to take into account the philosophy and purpose behind marriage and can even overlook and ignore its sentimental and sacramental nature.

1 S. Mohammad Ghari S. Fatemi, 'Autonomy and Equal Right to Divorce with Specific Reference to Shi'i *Fiqh* and the Iranian Legal System', *Islam and Christian–Muslim Relations* 17, no. 3 (2006): 284.

THE QUR'ANIC CONCEPTION OF MARRIAGE

Unlike the jurisprudential contractual notion of marriage, the Qur'anic conception of marriage is not just one of legal contract. Rather, marriage is a sacred union that fuses two individuals who share in their origin and humanity,[2] as well as worldly burdens and function, as a source of mutual adornment[3] and security.[4] Not only does the Qur'an stress the need for marriage, it goes on to emphasise the manner of interaction between the two parties – both when there is dispute present and not. There is consistent reference to dealing with kindness and amicability in the case of when reconciliation is not possible, namely, divorce,[5] with any attempt at harm during this process being labelled a transgression and violation of God's laws.[6] Rather importantly, kindness and amicability is stressed as the default baseline in dealings between spouses in general.[7] The purpose behind this sacred union can be gleaned from the verse relevant to this paper, namely: 'And of His signs is that He created for you from yourselves mates that you may find tranquillity in them; and He placed between you affection and mercy.'[8] Kindness, mercy, and affection, then, can be thought of as the values underlying an Islamic marriage, the purpose behind which is to create tranquillity and peace in both partners (see Table 1).

Table 1. Some Qur'anic verses related to marriage and interaction between spouses

4:1	O mankind, fear your Lord, who created you from one soul and created from it its mate and dispersed from both of them many men and women.
2:187	They are a clothing for you and you are a clothing for them.
7:189	It is He who created you from one soul and created from it its mate that he might dwell in security with her.
30:21	And of His signs is that He created for you from yourselves mates that you may find tranquillity in them; and He placed between you affection and mercy.
4:19	And live with them in kindness.

2 Q. 4:1. All Qur'anic translations are from Saheeh International (https://quranenc.com/en/browse/english_saheeh).

3 Q. 2:187.

4 Q. 7:189.

5 Q. 2:229.

6 Q. 2:231.

7 Q. 4:19.

8 Q. 30:21.

2:229	Divorce is twice. Then [after that], either keep [her] in an acceptable manner or release [her] with good treatment.
2:231	And when you divorce women and they have [nearly] fulfilled their term, either retain them according to acceptable terms or release them according to acceptable terms, and do not keep them, intending harm, to transgress [against them].

NOTION OF SAKĪNA IN QUR'ANIC TEACHINGS

Etymologically, *sakīna* derives from the Arabic root *s-k-n*, which means to be still, tranquil, peaceful, and at rest. The concept of tranquillity (*sakīna*) is heavily rooted in Islamic scripture with numerous verses of the Qur'an referencing this human state and its bestowal by God unto man as a type of divine aid and blessing,[9] as means of strengthening and enhancing faith,[10] as a sign of God granting man kingship,[11] and, in the case of this paper, the purpose behind matrimony in Islam (see Table 2).

Table 2. Some Qur'anic verses related to *sakīna*	
2:248	And their prophet said to them, 'Indeed, a sign of his kingship is that the chest will come to you in which is **assurance** from your Lord and a remnant of what the family of Moses and the family of Aaron had left, carried by the angels. Indeed in that is a sign for you, if you are believers.'
9:26	Then Allah sent down His **tranquillity** upon His Messenger and upon the believers and sent down soldiers [i.e., angels] whom you did not see and punished those who disbelieved. And that is the recompense of the disbelievers.
9:40	If you do not aid him [i.e., the Prophet – Allah has already aided him when those who disbelieved had driven him out [of Makkah] as one of two, when they were in the cave and he [i.e., Muḥammad said to his companion, 'Do not grieve; indeed Allah is with us.' And Allah sent down His **tranquillity** upon him and supported him with soldiers [i.e., angels] you did not see and made the word of those who disbelieved the lowest, while the word of Allah – that is the highest. And Allah is Exalted in Might and Wise.
48:4	It is He who sent down **tranquillity** into the hearts of the believers that they would increase in faith along with their [present] faith. And to Allah belong the soldiers of the heavens and the earth, and ever is Allah Knowing and Wise.

9 Q. 9:26, 9:40.
10 Q. 48:4.
11 Q. 2:248.

48:14	Certainly, was Allah pleased with the believers when they pledged allegiance to you, [O Muḥammad], under the tree, and He knew what was in their hearts, so He sent down **tranquillity** upon them and rewarded them with an imminent conquest.
48:26	Allah sent down His **tranquillity** upon His Messenger and upon the believers and imposed upon them the word of righteousness, and they were more deserving of it and worthy of it. And ever is Allah, of all things, Knowing.
30:21	And of His signs is that He created for you from yourselves mates that you may find **tranquillity** in them; and He placed between you affection and mercy.

Muḥammad Ḥusayn al-Ṭabāṭabāʾī states in his *al-Mīzān fī tafsīr al-Qurʾān* that *sakīna* is a state particular to the heart of man, and a state which materialises 'when a man is of a stable mind and is not perturbed in taking a firm decision'.[12] This, he argues, happens when there is congruity between man's method of reasoning and his aims in life. If his reasoning is employed to achieve actions that are beneficial and a source of felicity for himself as well as the good of the society at large, then his action and thinking is of the type that it engenders tranquillity in the heart. If, however, he is mired in his low desires and preoccupied with this world, indecision and confusion will reign supreme and there will be little in the way of tranquillity for this person. *Sakīna* for al-Ṭabāṭabāʾī, then, is a virtue indicative of a wise man with a firm will and when present in an individual is a sign of strong faith in God. He goes further to state that *sakīna* can also be understood as a divine spirit or something which associates with a divine spirit to bring man aid and give him peace and tranquillity, as in the case of Q. 9:40 (see Table 2).

From the verses mentioned above, then, it appears that *sakīna* is a state of inner peace and tranquillity which in the case of all verses but one appears to be conferred *upon* man by God as a favour and a means to attaining ease. The exception to this hierarchical endowment is the *sakīna* in Islamic marriage, which is to be attained and mutually sourced when two souls enter into matrimony with each other. *Sakīna*, for the purposes of this paper, therefore, will be translated as a state of peace, tranquillity, and serenity.

MARRIAGE AND TRANQUILLITY IN QURʾANIC TEACHINGS

There appears to be unanimous agreement among exegetes that spousal relationships are created for the purpose of each spouse finding tranquillity in the other. Such a tran-

12 Muḥammad Ḥusayn al-Ṭabāṭabāʾī, *al-Mīzān fī tafsīr al-Qurʾān* (Beirut: Muʾassasat al-Aʿlamī li-l-Maṭbūʿāt, 1932), 2:289.

quillity, they state, is to be acquired by human beings finding completeness through their spouses, and through harmonising as if they are a unified whole, that is, through mutual respect, kindness, compassion, loyalty, and love (see Table 3).

In his exegesis, al-Faḍl b. al-Ḥasan al-Ṭabrisī (d. 548/1153) can be seen in support of the idea that tranquillity is the purpose of God's creation of spouses for man. In his commentary on Q. 30:21, he states that the words 'that you may find tranquillity in them' imply 'so that you find peace with her and ease with each other'.[13] Al-Rāzī (d. 606/1209) adds to this by stating that what in fact allows such a tranquillity to manifest is that women were created of the same genus as men, stating that 'if two differing genera existed, one would not find tranquillity within the other as its spirit is not secured with it and its heart does not incline to it'.[14] The possibility of tranquillity seems, then, to be contingent on belonging to the same genus. Muḥammad Sayyid al-Ṭanṭāwī (d. 2010) echoes al-Rāzī in this stating that men and women are more inclined to each other due to belonging to the same 'kind' and even goes further to state that tranquillity is the purposive intention behind God's creation of spouses.[15]

For the late Muḥammad Ḥusayn Faḍlallāh (d. 2010), marriage signifies a relationship which is a 'living expression that transcends the physical tranquillity that seeks what satisfies the hunger of the instinct and quenches ... the spiritual tranquillity by which a person emerges from the feeling of isolation, loneliness'.[16] He argues that it is a close, intimate bond which alleviates man from isolation and places him in companionship with another, therefore allowing him to fulfil 'a spiritual void'.[17] Al-Ṭabāṭabā'ī takes this notion further by stating that it is in fact the perfection and completion of spouses with each other that marriage signifies. He states that 'every deficient thing yearns for its perfection, and every poor person is inclined to what removes his poverty.'[18] Such a completion can only be actualised when union is achieved with a being who is able to fill what is deficient in us and in doing so, allows us to reach our potential and perfection. It is the very nub of life. The means by which man can and does achieve perfection.

Muḥammad Taqī Mudarrasī, another contemporary exegete, supports the idea that spousal relationships have been created for the purpose of tranquility based on

13 al-Faḍl b. al-Ḥasan al-Ṭabrisī, *Majma' al-bayān fī tafsīr al-Qur'ān* (Beirut: Dār al-Ma'rifa, 1987), 8:470.

14 Muḥammad b. 'Umar al-Rāzī, *al-Tafsīr al-kabīr* (Beirut: Dār Iḥyā' al-Turāth al-'Arabī, 1999), 25:91.

15 Muḥammad Sayyid al-Ṭanṭāwī, *al-Wasīṭ fī al-Qur'ān al-karīm* (Cairo: Nahḍat Miṣr, 2010), 11:76.

16 Muḥammad Ḥusayn Faḍlallāh, *Min waḥī al-Qur'ān* (Beirut: Dār al-Malāk li-l-Ṭibā'a wa-l-Nashr wa-l-Tawzī', 1998), 16:165.

17 Ibid.

18 al-Ṭabāṭabā'ī, *al-Mīzān*, 16:165.

the alleviation of anxieties that he claims to be at play in absence of a spouse.[19] Nāṣir Makārim al-Shīrāzī appears to echo all the above-mentioned exegetes, stating that the goal of marriage is 'spiritual tranquility and psychological calm', where the two spouses complement each other and contribute to individual, social, physical, and spiritual well-being. Finally, he goes on to state that those who 'neglect this divine *sunna* [will] have a defective existence'.[20]

Table 3. Exegetes on Q. 30:21

Exegete (*mufassir*)	**Year**	**Exegesis (*tafsīr*)**	**Considers it a type of rationale (*'illa*) of spousal creation?**	**Considers it the purpose (*maqṣad*)?**
al-Fadl b. al-Ḥasan al-Ṭabrisī	468–548/1075–1153	*Majma' al-bayān fī tafsīr al-Qur'ān*<?>	No	Yes
Fakhr al-Dīn al-Rāzī	543 or 544–606/1149 or 1150–1209	*al-Tafsīr al-kabīr*<?>	No	Yes
Sayyid Muḥammad Ḥusayn Faḍlallāh	1935–2010	*Min waḥī al-Qur'ān*<?>	No	Yes
Sayyid Muḥammad Ḥusayn al-Ṭabāṭabā'ī	1903–81	*al-Mīzān fī tafsīr al-Qur'ān*<?>	No	Yes
Muḥammad Sayyid al-Ṭanṭāwī	1928–2010	*al-Wāsiṭ fī al-Qur'ān al-karīm*<?>	Yes	Yes
Sayyid Muḥammad Taqī Mudarrasī	1945–	*Min hudā al-Qur'ān*<?>	No	Yes

19 Muḥammad Taqī Mudarrasī, *Min hudā al-Qur'ān* (Qom: Dār Muḥibbī al-Ḥusayn 'alayhi al-Salām, 1999), 10:37.

20 Nāṣir Makārim al-Shīrāzī, *al-Amthal fī tafsīr Kitāb Allāh al-munzal* (Qom: Madrasat al-Imām 'Alī, 2000), 12:494.

Nāṣir Makārim al-Shīrāzī	1927–	*al-Amthal fī tafsīr Kitāb Allāh al-munzal*[<?>]	No	Yes

We can see then that all exegetes agree that tranquillity functions as purpose behind marriage.

There is, however, no agreement as to it functioning as a rationale, with the exception of Muḥammad Sayyid al-Ṭanṭāwī, who states that tranquillity can be seen as a kind of rationale.[21] The distinction between a rationale and purpose and the implications of this will be further explored in the final section of this paper. Through assurance (*iṭmi'nān*), by Qur'anic textual indication, both implicit and explicit, we can surmise that key exegetes have seen the foundational purpose (*maqṣad*) behind spousal creation to be that of acquiring tranquillity (*sakīna*). The practical *fiqhī* implication of such a perspective, however, is one not specified by most, bar Muḥammad Ḥusayn Faḍlallāh, who covers the issue more generally from the perspective of deflecting harm (*dafʿ al-ḍarar*) and retaining amicable relations (*imsāk bi-l-maʿrūf*).

PSYCHOLOGICAL LITERATURE ON FACTORS AFFECTING MATRIMONIAL OUTCOMES

Given that tranquillity is deemed to be the purpose in God's creation of spouses from an exegetical point of view, the jurisprudential implications of this become noteworthy, namely, those related to the validity of such a union in the first place. However, this is a bold stance, and it could be argued that reviewing in detail the psycho-social medical evidence is imperative if such a perspective is to have any weight. We therefore turn to what psycho-social literature has to add to the subject.

Literature Search and Results

Studies have long established an association between relationship distress and psychiatric disorders in probability samples and as part of this paper we wished to explore whether the metric of tranquillity or comfort featured in any scientific research. Due to the imprecise and nebulous nature of the term from a scientific perspective, it became easier to define the opposite of tranquillity and look for studies where marital conflict, discord, and dissatisfaction/satisfaction featured. Accordingly, a literature search was performed of the databases Embase and PsycInfo for the period 2003–22. Specifically,

21 al-Ṭanṭāwī, *al-Wasīṭ*, 11:76.

a search was conducted on the subject of marital discord and conflict in heterosexual contracted relationships and the subsequent impact on the couple themselves as well as any children involved. The aim here was to explore whether conflict, trust, comfort, and security, or lack thereof, translated into any positive or negative outcomes for the couple and any children. A total of 109 studies were retrieved, of which many were not directly relevant to the research question and therefore were excluded, leaving only twenty-four studies. The vast majority excluded were those looking at conflict arising from marital dissolution and separation or posed questions not directly relevant to the aims of this paper. The twenty-four relevant studies could be put into four broad categories, namely, those looking at outcomes related to children in marital conflict, those with negative outcomes related to spouses, those with positive outcomes in spouses, and finally predictors for marital quality (see Figure 1). As the findings of all studies cannot be recounted in this paper, a few from each thematic category will be mentioned to illustrate the general trend.

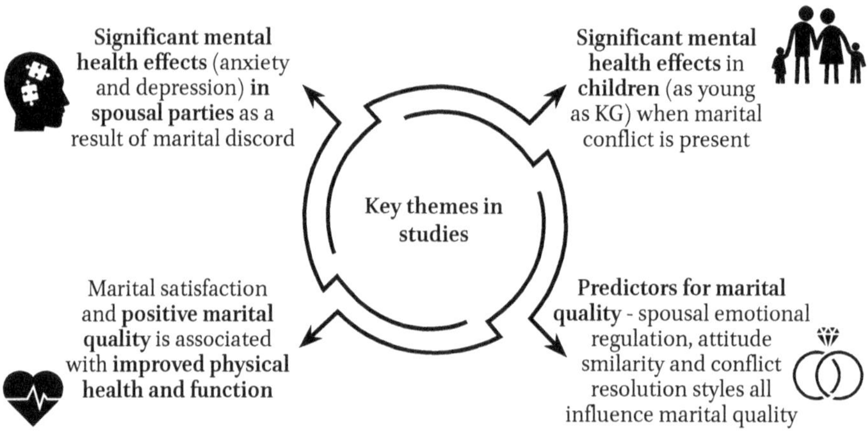

Figure 1. Schematic representation of themes found in relevant studies from the literature search

SIGNIFICANT MENTAL HEALTH EFFECTS IN SPOUSAL PARTIES

Kouros and Cummings conducted an observational study of 296 couples over a period of three years looking at the association between marital conflict and psychological distress as well as the transactional relationship between depressive symptoms and marital conflict.[22] Interestingly, high levels of marital conflict were predictive of depressive symptoms in wives over an extended period of time. This association

22 Chrystyna D. Kouros and E. Mark Cummings, 'Transactional Relations between Marital Functioning and Depressive Symptoms', *American Journal of Orthopsychiatry* 18, no. 1 (2011): 128–38.

appeared transactional in husbands, with depression contributing to marital conflict as well as high levels of marital satisfaction serving as 'a protective mechanism for husbands with regard to depression'.[23] Additionally, Alipour and colleagues were able to demonstrate, through a cross-sectional study of 300 pregnant Iranian women, that 'marital quality is an important predictor of mental health'.[24]

SIGNIFICANT MENTAL HEALTH EFFECTS IN CHILDREN

Lucas-Thompson and colleagues were able to report that marital conflict is indirectly linked to internalising behaviours (anxiety, depression, social withdrawal) in adolescents through self-blame appraisals, which can have long-term consequences on physiological and behavioural regulation.[25] Essex and colleagues also studied marital conflict and maternal depression in 406 families, where American children as young as those in kindergarten demonstrated both internalising as well as externalising behaviours (aggression, bullying, defiance).[26] In addition, they showed that 'presence and timing of marital conflict is important in predicting extremes of externalizing problems among boys and internalizing problems among girls'.[27]

POSITIVE MARITAL QUALITY IMPROVED PHYSICAL HEALTH AND FUNCTION

Holt-Lunstad and colleagues were able to find that better marital quality 'was associated with lower ambulatory blood pressure, lower stress, lower depression and higher satisfaction with life'.[28] However, marriages with lower quality relationships fared worse than singletons which suggests that 'marriage per se is not universally beneficial, rather, the satisfaction and support associated with such a relationship

23 Ibid., 136.

24 Zahra Alipour, Ashraf Kazemi, Gholamreza Kheirabadi, and Ahmad-Ali Eslami, 'Relationship between Marital Quality, Social Support and Mental Health during Pregnancy', *Community Mental Health Journal* 55 (2019): 1064–70.

25 Rachel G. Lucas-Thompson, Erika S. Lunkenheimer, and Adina Dumitrache, 'Associations between Marital Conflict and Adolescent Conflict Appraisals, Stress Physiology and Mental Health', *Journal of Clinical Child & Adolescent Psychology* 46, no. 3 (2017): 379–93.

26 Marilyn J. Essex, Marjorie H. Klein, Eunsuk Cho, and Helena C. Kraemer, 'Exposure to Maternal Depression and Marital Conflict: Gender Differences in Children's Later Mental Health Symptoms', *Journal of the American Academy of Child and Adolescent Psychiatry* 42, no. 6 (2003): 728–37.

27 Ibid., 736.

28 Julianne Holt-Lunstad, Wendy Birmingham, and Brandon Q. Jones, 'Is There Something Unique about Marriage? The Relative Impact of Marital Status, Relationship Quality, and Network Social Support on Ambulatory Blood Pressure and Mental Health', *Annals of Behavioral Medicine* 35, no. 2 (2008): 239.

is important.'[29]

PREDICTORS FOR MARITAL QUALITY

The final group of studies, although not directly relevant to the question of the consequences of marital conflict, shed light on the predictors of marital satisfaction or dissatisfaction. Among them are attitude similarity,[30] conflict resolution styles,[31] and emotional regulation.[32]

CONCLUSIONS AND LIMITATIONS

The evidence demonstrates that there are (i) significant mental health effects (and specifically anxiety and depression) in spousal parties as a result of marital discord; (ii) there are significant mental health effects in children (as young as pre-school) when marital conflict is present; (iii) marital satisfaction and positive marital quality is associated with improved physical health and function; and (iv) predictors of marital quality (spousal emotional regulation, attitude similarity, and conflict resolution styles) all have an effect on marital quality.

However, this review is not an exhaustive one and further research is required, preferably a meta-analysis with clearer definitions and tighter parameters to see any statistical significance. A key limitation here remains the inherent difficulty in defining tranquillity in scientific terms, for which inclusion of the anthropological perspective may offer added depth.

IMPLICATIONS ON LEGAL THEORY

Having established that the presence of marital discord/conflict as well as its absence has significant effects on both the spouses in question as well as their children, we turn to the important question of what effect, if any, this has on the legal framework

29 Ibid.

30 Shannon M. Moore, Bert N. Uchino, Brian R. W. Baucom, Arwen A. Behrends, and David Sanbonmatsu, 'Attitude Similarity and Familiarity and Their Links to Mental Health: An Examination of Potential Interpersonal Mediators', *The Journal of Social Psychology* 157, no. 1 (2017): 77–85.

31 Tina D. Du Rocher Schudlich, Lauren M. Papp, and E. Mark Cummings, 'Relations between Spouses' Depressive Symptoms and Marital Conflict: A Longitudinal Investigation of the Role of Conflict Resolution Styles', *Journal of Family Psychology* 25, no. 4 (2011): 531–40.

32 Unji An, Haeyoung Gideon Park, Da Eun Han, and Young-Hoon Kim, 'Emotional Suppression and Psychological Well-Being in Marriage: The Role of Regulatory Focus and Spousal Behaviour', *International Journal of Environmental Research and Public Health* 19, no. 2 (2022): 973.

surrounding our current conception of marriage in Islam. Marriage in Islam is for the most part viewed as a contractual duty with strict rules, which, if complied with, render it valid and proper. The spirit behind this contract, however, identified here previously as *sakīna*, or tranquillity, is not taken into consideration. Keeping Q. 30:21 front and centre, three possible applications in legal theory become available to us here.

READING 1: SAKĪNA *AS AN* ʿILLA (*RATIO*)

In this instance, *sakīna* is viewed as the ratio behind the law.[33] In *uṣūl al-fiqh*, the discussion of reason behind the law becomes relevant when discussing the subject of analogy or *qiyās*. *Uṣūlīs* typically classify rationale into two categories, namely, *manṣūṣ al-ʿilla* – where the rationale is mentioned explicitly by the Lawgiver – and *mustanbiṭ al-ʿilla* – where the rationale is not explicitly mentioned and is the result of the reasoning of the jurist. The latter is more controversial than the former. In this case, however, bearing in mind *sakīna* is explicitly mentioned in the Qurʾan, the rationale of interest becomes the first one.

Seeing *sakīna* as the *ʿilla* for advocating marriage in the Qurʾan would mean one can then decide on normative situations regarding marriages that do not satisfy the rationale of tranquillity. This could have huge jurisprudential implications on the right of both spouses to terminate a marriage lacking in tranquillity. In this case, the jurist would be able to give considerable room to the expert (*khubra*), perhaps a psychologist, for shedding light on the situation of marriage, as to whether it is a source of tranquillity for both spouses. Methodologically, this also has huge implications on the interaction between science and law, and raises a very sensitive epistemic question, namely, the value of conjecture resulting from an expert's (*khubra*) opinion. We can say, therefore, that a trustworthy expert's view, even though it is shaped by a degree of conjecture, should create a normative authority (*ḥujjiyya*) for a jurist to rely upon. The consequence of taking *sakīna* as the *ʿilla* in a Qurʾanically acceptable marriage is that this would open a new window of co-operation between science and law. It would play a major role in marital conflict resolution, and in particular women's rights in both marriage and divorce. This, however, would depend on a gender-neutral reading of the verse of tranquillity, that is, the Qurʾanic marriage should be a source of tranquillity for both spouses.

READING 2: SAKĪNA *AS A* MAQṢAD (*PURPOSE*)

The second reading of *sakīna* can be as the purpose behind the law as opposed to

33 Here *ʿillā* has been translated as *ratio*, consistent with the usage of Robert M. Gleave, 'Imāmī Shīʿī Refutations of *Qiyās*', in *Studies in Islamic Legal Theory*, Studies in Islamic Law and Society, vol. 15, ed. Bernard Weiss (Leiden: Brill, 2002), 286.

the rationale behind it. The application of this will follow after a brief discussion on the *maqāṣidī* discourse in general.

▪ *Maqāṣid* in *Uṣūlī* Discourse

Maqāṣid al-Sharīʿa are defined as the purposes or objectives behind Islamic law, and although conceived of relatively early in Islamic history, they have remained 'on the fringes of mainstream juristic thought'.[34] Modern times, however, have seen a renewal in this approach, such as in Islamic finance, reflecting the increased need for dynamism and reactive adaptability in Islamic law. Many view it as a means to developing a robust philosophical and methodological framework for 'assessing classic and current juridical theories of Islamic law'.[35] The various iterations of *maqāṣid* have not been extraneously sourced; rather, they are heavily rooted in scripture as well as prophetic practice. The Qur'an contains numerous references to the purposes behind worship, contracts, the basis of law, and even the act of creation. Muslim scholars have, throughout the centuries, aimed to codify and hierarchically classify these purposes, frequently attempting to use these as a driving force behind the changing tides in Islamic law, albeit often unsuccessfully. The first extant treatise on *maqāṣid* appears to be *ʿIlal al-sharāʾiʿ* (*The Reasons behind the Rulings*),[36] by Ibn Bābawayh al-Ṣadūq al-Qummī (d. 381/991), a Shīʿī jurist. Although containing over 300 chapters on the reasons behind doctrinal tenets, acts of worship, historical events, and even ethical qualities, it provides no practical application of these to the field of Islamic law. The next rather significant shift occurs with Abū al-Maʿālī al-Juwaynī (d. 478/1085), whose triumvirate classification remains the most influential and considerable to date, namely: *ḍarūriyyāt* (essential), *ḥājiyyāt* (complementary), and *taḥsīniyyāt* (desirable).[37] Abū Ḥāmid al-Ghazālī (d. 505/1111) further augments his teacher's model by privileging some necessities over others as well as expanding the discussion on *maṣlaḥa* or public interest significantly;[38] however, stopping short of granting any 'independent legitimacy (*ḥujjiyyah*) to any of his proposed *maqāṣid* or *maṣāliḥ*'.[39] Some rather interesting developments follow over the next few centuries as the *maqāṣidī* discourse expands.

Al-ʿIzz b. ʿAbd al-Salām (d. 660/1209) proposes the consequence of invalidity of an

34 Mohammad Hashim Kamali, '*Maqāṣid al-Sharīʿah*: The Objectives of Islamic Law', *Islamic Studies* 38, no. 2 (1999):198.

35 Jasser Auda, *Maqasid al-Shariah as Philosophy of Islamic Law: A Systems Approach* (London: International Institute of Islamic Thought, 2007), xxvii.

36 Jasser Auda, *Maqāṣid al-Sharīʿah: A Beginner's Guide*, Occasional Paper Series 14 (London: International Institute of Islamic Thought, 2008), 17.

37 Kamali, '*Maqāṣid al-Sharīʿah*', 199.

38 Ibid.

39 Auda, *A Beginner's Guide*, 19.

action if it misses its purpose,[40] and Shihāb al-Dīn al-Qarāfī (d. 684/1285) asserts that purposes could be extended to include prophetic practice,[41] and be the means to lawful and good ends, not merely blocking prohibited ones.[42] With Shams al-Dīn b. al-Qayyim (d. 748/1347) we see a push to situate *maqāṣid* as a set of fundamental rules and philosophy behind Islamic law itself,[43] a sentiment echoed by Abū Isḥāq al-Shāṭibī (d. 790/1388). The latter represents the most sophisticated attempt at inclusion of *maqāṣid* into legal theory by placing knowledge of them as a necessary condition for *ijtihād* (juridical effort/reasoning).[44] Crucial to his methodology remains his epistemological foundation of inductive corroboration that allows him to establish the certitude of his purposive framework.[45] This means that each of the necessities individually do not equate to the level of certitude as they 'do not find attestation in any particular piece of conclusive evidence';[46] however, their knowledge is 'enshrined with certainty in the collective mind of the Muslim community ... by virtue of the fact that these principles have been attested to by a wide variety of pieces of evidence, which, in their totality, lead to certitude'.[47] After establishing the validity of his inductive corroboration, namely, his method of arriving at his *maqāṣid*, he is able to position them as fundamentals in the process for deriving legal rulings. Notably for him, public interest or *maṣlaḥa* is 'placed in the service of the aims of the law (*maqāṣid*)'.[48]

In modern times, there is no single universal iteration of *maqāṣid*; rather, we find multiple models based on the levels of necessity, scope of rulings and the people, as well as levels of universality of the *maqāṣid*.[49]

▪ *Maqāsidī* Approach to Islamic Marriage

The incorporation of the concept of *sakīna* in marriage can depend on the framework and hierarchy of *maqāṣid* themselves. Sticking to the prevalent and popular three-tiered *maqāṣidī* framework of *ḍarūriyyāt* (essential), *ḥājiyyāt* (complementary), and *taḥsīniyyāt* (desirable), *sakīna* in marriage can be envisioned both as an essential and a complementary purpose. Traditionally, essential purposes are those that lead to the

40 Ibid.

41 Ibid., 20.

42 Ibid.

43 Ibid., 21.

44 Ibid., 22.

45 Wael B. Hallaq, *A History of Islamic Legal Theories: An Introduction to Sunnī Uṣūl al-Fiqh* (New York: Cambridge University Press, 1997), 166.

46 Ibid.

47 Ibid.

48 Ibid., 169.

49 Auda, *A Beginner's Guide*, 4.

preservation of life, progeny, intellect, religion, and property. From the psychological research previously cited, it becomes apparent that lack of tranquillity (if defined as conflict/discord) in marriage can cause serious adverse effects within children from that marriage and compromise their mental well-being, resulting in internalising/externalising behaviours and emotional dysregulation. Lack of tranquillity, then, calls into question the preservation of healthy progeny.

Research also showed us the significant detrimental mental health effects suffered by spouses who continue in marriages where there is conflict and discord present, in other words, the essential purpose of preservation of the human intellect becomes difficult. Finally, research has also shown that marriages with high quality and satisfaction improve physiological parameters and functionality. Although the reverse has not been demonstrated to be true in this paper, one can say that if tranquillity is present in a marriage, then physical health improves, which furthers the preservation of life.

Therefore, tranquillity in marriage becomes pivotal to conserving the integrity of *three* essential purposes: life, progeny, and intellect. Tranquillity in marriage can also be seen as a complementary purpose. These are those purposes which, although not essential, if enacted, prevent hardship. They serve the fulfilment of the essential purposes. We can say, then, that tranquillity serves to fulfil not only essential but also complementary purposes.

Once one has understood tranquillity in marriage as rudimentary for the preservation of both essential and complementary purposes, the *fiqhī* implications that follow are much the same as when it is seen as *manṣūṣ al-ʿilla.* A jurist having designated it as a purpose would then leave it in the hands of a judge and expert who would apply the ruling to the individual circumstance and allow both spouses the ability and right to terminate their marriage if appropriate.

READING 3: SAKĪNA *AS THE* ḤIKMA (*WISDOM*) BEHIND MARRIAGE

The final reading of this verse can be to view the notion of tranquillity in marriage as the wisdom behind the law. As an Islamic legal term of art, *ḥikma* does not seem to be well defined, and for that reason may not be referred to as a basis for the ruling. Al-Ḥakīm defines *ḥikma* as 'the intended interest of the Legislator in enacting the ruling, namely, what the Legislator intends to achieve in terms of bringing benefit and warding off harm'. Crucially, the difference between *ḥikma* and *ʿilla* is that the *ʿilla* is considered according to a restricted definition, whereas *ḥikma* is not restricted in such a way, and therefore the Legislator does not make it a sign of his rule. Unlike the *ʿilla*, the Lawgiver does not bring about the existence and non-existence of the ruling depending on *ḥikma*.[50] According to Muḥammad Abū Zahra the *ʿilla* is an apparent,

50 Sayyid Muḥammad Taqī al-Ḥakīm, *al-Uṣūl al-ʿāmma li-l-fiqh al-muqāran* (Qom: Mu'assasat Āl

disciplined/defined, limited description, established by the Legislator as a sign for the norm/ruling, while *ḥikma* is an appropriate description for the norm/ruling that is achieved in most cases, and it is undisciplined/undefined and unlimited.[51]

Subḥānī's understanding of the *ḥikma* of a ruling is in line with that of Abū Zahra. To him, things like procreation and formation of the family are not the sole benefits and purposes of marriage; rather, its function is broader.[52] In other words, for Subḥānī, formation of family and hence its sociological consequences, namely, tranquillity, is neither the ratio nor the main purpose of the marriage, and at best is no more than its *ḥikma*. Thus, the validity and other functions and benefits of marriage may still exist in the absence of tranquillity. Subḥānī's position reflects the view of most Muslim orthodox jurists, as it is exceptionally rare to find an orthodox jurist who explicitly permits termination of marriage solely based on the lack of tranquillity in the matrimonial life of a couple. To sum up, we conclude that reading tranquillity in marriage as a *maqṣad* or *ʿilla* or *ḥikma* can have a range of implications in legal theory.

LIMITATIONS

A significant limitation and drawback of this paper remains the insufficiency in defining the term tranquillity itself and its remit. The anthropological and sociological aspects are significantly lacking, which could help enrich the discussion further by adding to our understanding of the concept of tranquillity and its dynamic nature, as it cannot be defined by one or two incidents; therefore, quantity as well as the quality of the behaviour becomes important. Tranquillity may also mean different things at different stages of an individual's life and even vary according to their social status as defined by class and education. In addition, because heavy reliance has been placed on the psychological data, more exhaustive analyses are required in order to create more confidence in the data.

CONCLUSION

We propose that it is only by reflecting on the established psycho-social medical evidence, in collaboration with a deep understanding of the relevant Qur'anic text and jurisprudential considerations, that the discourse on the purpose of marriage in the modern context can progress. It is with this multi-disciplinary approach that one can

al-Bayt, 1979), 296–97

51 Muḥammad Abū Zahra, *Uṣūl al-fiqh* (Cairo: Dār al-Fikr al-ʿArabī, 1997), 223.

52 Jaʿfar Subḥānī, *Uṣūl al-fiqh al-maqāran fī mā lā naṣṣ fīhi* (Qom: Mu'assasat al-Imām al-Ṣādiq, 2004), 96–98.

truly begin to understand the complexity of marriage in the modern era. The medical evidence base is ever evolving, and this is reflective of the changing societal expectations of the marriage partnership. It is therefore a necessity that our understanding of marriage and its purpose is continuously re-assessed, with the foundational jurisprudence and Qur'anic texts providing consistency. This ground-breaking approach invites the incorporation of a multi-disciplinary approach to so many other aspects of Islamic research impacting the Muslim society on a day-to-day basis. This paper has thus fulfilled two aims: the methodological one, where we have demonstrated a dynamic, practical, and multi-disciplinary approach to the institution of Islamic marriage; and the second, more substantive aim, where exegetical and psychological data have been shown to agree that tranquillity is what makes marriage a potential source of social stability. The Qur'an is clear and unambiguous in its declaration that tranquillity is the purpose behind the creation of spouses and indeed marriage itself. Psychological data supports the understanding that marriages lacking in tranquillity produce detrimental effects in both spouses and children. From the perspective of legal theory, we can view *sakīna* in one of three ways: a purpose, a wisdom, or a rationale behind the institution of marriage. Although mainstream opinion has been content to view tranquillity merely as a *ḥikma*, the current paper proposes that this view should shift in light of current psycho-social research regarding marriages that lack this essential quality. It is, however, important to stress that the purpose behind this paper is not to give rulings on the validity of marriages that do not satisfy the condition of tranquillity; rather, it is to demonstrate the viability of a multi-disciplinary approach, one strengthened by current context and understanding. This paper aims to be a proposal of sorts for jurists and policymakers alike to look at the co-operation between science and hermeneutical theories, an approach which has the power to open windows for more healthy families and equality between spouses.

BIBLIOGRAPHY

Abū Zahra, Muḥammad. *Uṣūl al-fiqh*. Cairo: Dār al-Fikr al-ʿArabī, 1997.

Alipour, Zahra, Ashraf Kazemi, Gholamreza Kheirabadi, and Ahmad-Ali Eslami. 'Relationship between Marital Quality, Social Support and Mental Health during Pregnancy'. *Community Mental Health Journal* 55 (2019): 1064–70.

An, Unji, Haeyoung Gideon Park, Da Eun Han, and Young-Hoon Kim. 'Emotional Suppression and Psychological Well-Being in Marriage: The Role of Regulatory Focus and Spousal Behaviour'. *International Journal of Environmental Research and Public Health* 19, no. 2 (2022): 973.

Auda, Jasser. *Maqāṣid al-Sharīʿah: A Beginner's Guide*. Occasional Paper Series 14. London: International Institute of Islamic Thought, 2008.

Auda, Jasser. *Maqasid al-Shariah as Philosophy of Islamic Law: A Systems Approach*. London: International Institute of Islamic Thought, 2007.

Essex, Marilyn J., Marjorie H. Klein, Eunsuk Cho, and Helena C. Kraemer. 'Exposure to Maternal Depression and Marital Conflict: Gender Differences in Children's Later Mental Health Symptoms'. *Journal of the American Academy of Child and Adolescent Psychiatry* 42, no. 6 (2003): 728–37.

Faḍlallāh, Muḥammad Ḥusayn. *Min waḥī al-Qur'ān*. Beirut: Dār al-Malāk li-l-Ṭibāʿa wa-l-Nashr wa-l-Tawzīʿ, 1998.

Fatemi, S. Mohammad Ghari S. 'Autonomy and Equal Right to Divorce with Specific Reference to Shiʿi *Fiqh* and the Iranian Legal System'. *Islam and Christian–Muslim Relations* 17, no. 3 (2006): 281–94.

Gleave, Robert M. 'Imāmī Shīʿī Refutations of *Qiyās*'. In *Studies in Islamic Legal Theory*. Studies in Islamic Law and Society, vol. 15, edited by Bernard Weiss, 267–93. Leiden: Brill, 2002.

al-Ḥakīm, Sayyid Muḥammad Taqī. *al-Uṣūl al-ʿāmma li-l-fiqh al-muqāran*. Qom: Mu'assasat Āl al-Bayt, 1979.

Hallaq, Wael B. *A History of Islamic Legal Theories: An Introduction to Sunnī Uṣūl al-Fiqh*. New York: Cambridge University Press, 1997.

Holt-Lunstad, Julianne, Wendy Birmingham, and Brandon Q. Jones. 'Is There Something Unique about Marriage? The Relative Impact of Marital Status, Relationship Quality, and Network Social Support on Ambulatory Blood Pressure and Mental Health'. *Annals of Behavioral Medicine* 35, no. 2 (2008): 239–44.

Kamali, Mohammad Hashim. '*Maqāṣid al-Sharīʿah*: The Objectives of Islamic Law'. *Islamic Studies* 38, no. 2 (1999): 193–208.

Kouros, Chrystyna D., and E. Mark Cummings. 'Transactional Relations between Marital Functioning and Depressive Symptoms'. *American Journal of Orthopsychiatry* 18, no. 1 (2011): 128–38.

Lucas-Thompson, Rachel G., Erika S. Lunkenheimer, and Adina Dumitrache. 'Associations between Marital Conflict and Adolescent Conflict Appraisals, Stress Physiology and Mental Health'. *Journal of Clinical Child & Adolescent Psychology* 46, no. 3 (2017): 379–93.

Moore, Shannon M., Bert N. Uchino, Brian R. W. Baucom, Arwen A. Behrends, and David Sanbonmatsu. 'Attitude Similarity and Familiarity and Their Links to Mental Health: An Examination of Potential Interpersonal Mediators'. *The Journal of Social Psychology* 157, no. 1 (2017): 77–85.

Mudarrasī, Muḥammad Taqī. *Min hudā al-Qur'ān*. Qom: Dār Muḥibbī al-Ḥusayn ʿalayhi al-Salām, 1999.

al-Rāzī, Muḥammad b. ʿUmar. *al-Tafsīr al-kabīr*. Beirut: Dār Iḥyā' al-Turāth al-ʿArabī, 1999.

Schudlich, Tina D. Du Rocher, Lauren M. Papp, and E. Mark Cummings. 'Relations between Spouses' Depressive Symptoms and Marital Conflict: A Longitudinal Investigation of the Role of Conflict Resolution Styles'. *Journal of Family Psychology* 25, no. 4 (2011): 531–40.

al-Shīrāzī, Nāṣir Makārim. *al-Amthal fī tafsīr Kitāb Allāh al-munzal*. Qom: Madrasat al-Imām ʿAlī, 2000.

Subḥānī, Jaʿfar. *Uṣūl al-fiqh al-maqāran fī mā lā naṣṣ fīhi*. Qom: Mu'assasat al-Imām al-Ṣādiq, 2004.

al-Ṭabāṭabā'ī, Muḥammad Ḥusayn. *al-Mīzān fī tafsīr al-Qur'ān*. Beirut: Mu'assasat al-Aʿlamī li-l-Maṭbūʿāt, 1932.

al-Ṭabrisī, al-Faḍl b. al-Ḥasan. *Majmaʿ al-bayān fī tafsīr al-Qur'ān*. Beirut: Dār al-Maʿrifa, 1987.

al-Ṭanṭāwī, Muḥammad Sayyid. *al-Wasīṭ fī al-Qur'ān al-karīm*. Cairo: Nahḍat Miṣr, 2010.

LAURENS DE ROOIJ

Online Dating for British Muslims and the Relationship with Their Islamic Identities

In Europe and the US, young Muslims are using online matchmaking in growing numbers. Online dating has increasingly become a mainstream activity, at least in Europe and North America. Western Muslims have adapted the idea to suit their needs. For many, online dating offers a low-stress solution to the daunting challenge of finding a partner for marriage in countries where few share their faith, and in communities where matchmaking is considered a family affair. This paper will discuss the relationship between Muslim online matchmaking for British Muslims and their Islamic identities with regards to marriage and romantic relationships. Kecia Ali points out that within the Islamic tradition, marriage was necessarily consensual, but parental – usually paternal – involvement was not limited to the marriage of daughters.[1] This paper highlights the way modern technology interacts with traditional cultural values and shifts the authoritative matchmaking role from an offline actor to an online platform. This provides new insights into how in particular conservative and progressive Muslims use digital technology in order to maintain those identities.

Following a large increase in internet usage, online dating is used for seeking romantic and sexual partners. Using a qualitative approach, eleven people who actively use online dating apps took part in in-depth, online chat interviews. The findings suggest that most of the participants had used multiple dating sites concurrently or at some point in their quest for a partner and used a variety of strategies and mechanisms to engage with their potential romantic interests. In turn, the users employed various standard filter options, as well as some self-selected filters in order to navigate and select potential suitors. Users completed several steps that lead up to potentially meeting their potential partner in person. The first public meeting was always in a public place, and for some women, it was seen as important that she was chaperoned (often by a family member, but not necessarily a male). This is one of many examples where the modern meets the traditional. As a result, this suggests that the traditional–modern or conservative–progressive binaries are complicated and intersected through the affordances of modern technology.

1 Kecia Ali, *Marriage and Slavery in Early Islam* (Cambridge, MA: Harvard University Press, 2010).

For many devout or conservative Muslims marriage is often deemed the cornerstone of not only a person's life but also society as a whole. A variety of web-based services cater to this and allow members to search for partners not only by sect, but also by the particular doctrine of Islam that they follow and the languages they speak. Others market themselves as a place to find a partner with whom they can 'connect' but also of whom their parents approve. In this context, the internet makes meeting easier, culturally, as this group of Muslims would not seek out romantic partners in pubs and clubs. Otherwise, there are very few avenues, apart from family networks, for matchmaking to occur. In addition, using a dating site or phone app makes it easier as the user knows the other users are looking for something similar. As one participant put it:

> It's hard to meet someone you don't know in a school or work setting, because you don't know them and you don't know if they are interested in you romantically. At least if you meet someone on a dating website you know they are looking for a relationship as well. This doesn't guarantee you will find what you are looking for or that you are what they are looking for, but it increases your chances of success.
>
> *Rashid, 32*

As global Islam encompasses a variety of ethnic and geographic boundaries, the apps facilitate the making of connections along more ideological lines, rather than ethno-cultural ones, and perhaps therefore facilitates and democratises the process of meeting potential partners. It offers an avenue of agency to those seeking a partner by narrowing the search to potential partners based on self-selected parameters. This is of increasing interest as in most cases, conservative Islam is not considered empowering, especially for women. But as this paper will show, the apps allow for young people in potentially conservative environments to choose potential matches with greater freedom, finding someone that satisfies all their potential wants and needs. As Heino and colleagues argue, 'the consequences of this type of filtering, enabled by the search functionality of the website, included the tendency to shop for people with the perfect qualifications,'[2] thereby becoming a clinical exercise and removing a lot of the emotional content. However, others felt this was mitigated by the fact that they were seeking for potential love interests to meet in offline settings, rather than having a purely digital-based relationship. For example:

2 Rebecca D. Heino, Nicole B. Ellison, and Jennifer L. Gibbs, 'Relationshopping: Investigating the Market Metaphor in Online Dating', *Journal of Social and Personal Relationships* 27, no. 4 (2010): 437.

> I want to pick someone who has similar values and outlook on life, because that is important for the future. But it can all change when we meet in person. I am looking for someone to hopefully spend the rest of my life with, but if they have a weird vibe or if you don't like how he interacts with others then it won't work, you know. But you can never tell that just from chatting. But it's important to feel things when you are together, and that makes a big difference between just chatting and actually spending time together.
>
> *Aisha, 25*

The apps are a method for managing and producing the image of the participants and their ideas about Islam and being Muslim. While in a European context, Muslim is by no means a self-evident category,[3] it is used to identify oneself and to identify others,[4] simultaneously implemented by both Muslims and non-Muslims as a category of inclusion and exclusion. This project advances beyond studies of the media and ethnicity,[5] since Muslims are a category based on ethnic, social, political, and religious characteristics, depending on what characteristics are highlighted by the person in question. However, there are reservations and potential pitfalls with online dating. The virtual world is potentially a world removed from reality, full of lies and deception, as one can never be certain of whom one is talking to.[6] Simultaneously, where Muslim online matchmaking is made to appeal to (young) people with a strong religious identity, traditional or conservative family environments could mean that those seeking partners face stigmatisation and ridicule while looking to meet future partners online rather than in traditional ways (e.g. via a family introduction). Meeting a partner online, therefore, is not deemed natural and families may be suspicious and wary of matches made this way.

---

3 Ralph Grillo, 'Islam and Transnationalism', *Journal of Ethnic and Migration Studies* 30, no. 5 (2004): 861–78.

4 Richard Jenkins, *Rethinking Ethnicity: Arguments and Explorations* (London: Sage, 1997).

5 Lisa Duke, 'Black in a Blonde World: Race and Girls' Interpretations of the Feminine Ideal in Teen Magazines', *Journalism & Mass Communication Quarterly* 77, no. 2 (2000): 367–92; Justin Lewis, Sut Jhally, and Michael Morgan, *The Gulf War: A Study of the Media, Public Opinion and Public Knowledge* (Amherst: Center for the Study of Communication Research Archives, Department of Communication, University of Massachusetts, 1991); Radhika Parameswaran, 'Western Romance Fiction as English-Language Media in Postcolonial India', *Journal of Communication* 49, no. 3 (1999): 84–105.

6 Catalina L. Toma, Jeffrey T. Hancock, and Nicole B. Ellison, 'Separating Fact from Fiction: An Examination of Deceptive Self-Presentation in Online Dating Profiles', *Personality and Social Psychology Bulletin* 34, no. 8 (2008): 1023–36.

THEORETICAL FRAMEWORK AND RESEARCH QUESTION

Compared to the majority, European Muslims are relatively religious in both institutional affiliation and practice.[7] In the European context, a perceived hostility is seemingly exemplified by media discourse.[8] There is evidence to suggest that Islam-based identities are strengthened if one perceives the local environment as hostile. This would be reflected in user responses, in their desire for a Muslim partner, and in the type of partner desired. However, British Muslims are incredibly diverse, representing many different countries and all major branches of Islam; they are, in fact, not so much of a community as 'joined-by-a-noun' bedfellows.[9] Kim and McKay-Semmler suggest that non-natives' direct social engagement with members of the host society encourages the cross-cultural adaptation process.[10] This would suggest that as dating apps have become more mainstream and used by an increasing number of non-Muslims, they, in turn, will be used increasingly by Muslims as a consequence of the cross-cultural adaptation process. This is in keeping with other computer-mediated communication research,[11] and suggests that Islam-based identities are strengthened in the local environment, reflected in users choosing partners that share those same Islam-based identities.

Dating apps are used most frequently by twenty-five- to thirty-four-year-olds.[12] Katz and colleagues suggest that individuals use certain types of mass media to fulfil specific

7 Hans Schmeets and Saskia te Riele, 'Declining Social Cohesion in the Netherlands?', *Social Indicators Research* 115 (2014): 791–812.

8 Frank Buijs, Froukje Demant, and Atef Hamdy, *Strijders van eigen bodem. Radicale en democratische moslims in Nederland* (Amsterdam: Amsterdam University Press, 2006); Fenella Fleischmann, Karen Phalet, and Olivier Klein, 'Religious Identification and Politicization in the Face of Discrimination: Support for Political Islam and Political Action among the Turkish and Moroccan Second Generation in Europe', *British Journal of Social Psychology* 50, no. 4 (2011): 628–48.

9 Patrick Dunleavy, Richard Heffernan, Philip Cowley, and Colin Hay, eds., *Developments in British Politics*, 8th ed. (London and New York: Palgrave Macmillan, 2006).

10 Young Yun Kim and Kelly McKay-Semmler, 'Social Engagement and Cross-cultural Adaptation: An Examination of Direct- and Mediated Interpersonal Communication Activities of Educated Non-natives in the United States', *International Journal of Intercultural Relations* 37, no. 1 (2013): 99–112.

11 Danielle Couch and Pranee Liamputtong, 'Online Dating and Mating: The Use of the Internet to Meet Sexual Partners', *Qualitative Health Research* 18, no. 2 (2008): 268–79; Patti M. Valkenburg and Jochen Peter, 'Who Visits Online Dating Sites? Exploring Some Characteristics of Online Daters', *CyberPsychology & Behavior* 10, no. 6 (2007): 849–52.

12 Sindy R. Sumter, Laura Vandenbosch, and Loes Ligtenberg, 'Love Me Tinder: Untangling Emerging Adults' Motivations for Using the Dating Application Tinder', *Telematics and Informatics* 34, no. 1 (2017): 67–78.

needs and desires.[13] The dating apps Muzmatch, Ummah Dating, and SingleMuslim will be explored here and satisfy certain specific needs and desires for its users. This is comparable to other research done as to why people use social media.[14] The satisfaction sought from these apps relates to needs, such as establishing new friendships and finding a romantic partner.[15] It has been suggested that online media are an aid to fulfil the need for a specific romantic partner.[16] Although social media platforms may also validate one's own appearance, sex appeal, and lead to an increase of self-worth, lack of success in the online dating environment may of course also lead to it having the opposite effect, and with an environment that is still stigmatised as a place of those who cannot meet anyone in a 'normal' environment, the psychological effects should not be overlooked, even if they are beyond the scope of this paper.[17]

Studies have found that gender and age affects users' physical, social, and psycho-social motivations to use online tools.[18] Gender socialisation literature has emphasised that men and women are socialised towards different physical, social, and psycho-social needs.[19] The developmental literature argues that physical, social, and psycho-social needs change as people grow older.[20] Thus, a user's needs may change

13 Elihu Katz, Jay G. Blumler, and Michael Gurevitch, 'Uses and Gratifications Research', *Public Opinion Quarterly* 37, no. 4 (1973): 509–23.

14 Tracii Ryan, Andrea Chester, John Reece, and Sophia Xenos, 'The Uses and Abuses of Facebook: A Review of Facebook Addiction', *Journal of Behavioral Addictions* 3, no. 3 (2014): 133–48; Guosong Shao, 'Understanding the Appeal of User-Generated Media: A Uses and Gratification Perspective', *Internet Research* 19. no. 1 (2009): 7–25; Mark A. Urista, Qingwen Dong, and Kenneth D. Day, 'Explaining Why Young Adults Use MySpace and Facebook through Uses and Gratifications Theory', *Human Communication* 12 (2009): 215–29.

15 Matt Hart, 'Youth Intimacy on Tumblr: A Pilot Study', *Young* 23, no. 3 (2015): 193–208.

16 David Gudelunas, 'There's an App for That: The Uses and Gratifications of Online Social Networks for Gay Men', *Sexuality & Culture* 16, no. 4 (2012): 347–65.

17 Jacqueline Nesi and Mitchell J. Prinstein, 'Using Social Media for Social Comparison and Feedback-Seeking: Gender and Popularity Moderate Associations with Depressive Symptoms', *Journal of Abnormal Child Psychology* 43, no. 8 (2015): 1427–38; Jennifer Yurchisin, Kittichai Watchravesringkan, and Deborah Brown McCabe, 'An Exploration of Identity Re-creation in the Context of Internet Dating', *Social Behavior and Personality: An International Journal* 33, no. 8 (2005): 735–50.

18 Valerie Barker, 'Older Adolescents' Motivations for Social Network Site Use: The Influence of Gender, Group Identity, and Collective Self-Esteem', *CyberPsychology & Behavior* 12, no. 2 (2009): 209–13.

19 Nina Haferkamp, Sabrina C. Eimler, Anna-Margarita Papadakis, and Jana Vanessa Kruck, 'Men Are from Mars, Women Are from Venus? Examining Gender Differences in Self-Presentation on Social Networking Sites', *Cyberpsychology, Behavior, and Social Networking* 15, no. 2 (2012): 91–98.

20 Jeffrey Jensen Arnett, 'Emerging Adulthood: A Theory of Development from the Late Teens through the Twenties', *American Psychologist* 55, no. 5 (2000): 469–80; Dan P. McAdams and Bradley D. Olson, 'Personality Development: Continuity and Change over the Life Course', *Annual Review of Psychology* 61 (2010): 517–42.

when they grow older, and their motivations for using the application may also change. Research supports this reasoning as an influence of age on motivations to use online media has been found.[21] Differences exist in relationships between different motivations to use online media and offline outcomes, such as arranging offline meetings with an online partner or engaging in casual sex adventures with online partners.[22] Therefore, the body of research suggests that the motivations for using the application will result in different gratifications and may result in different offline outcomes.

METHODOLOGY

This paper will examine how British Muslims use Muslim smartphone dating apps, and how this relates to their ideas about the nature of marriage, romantic relationships, and Islam. This project addresses the following research question: To what extent does the use of Muslim smartphone dating apps by British Muslims reflect their opinion on matters of marriage and relationships, and its relationship to their religious beliefs? In order to answer this question, participants were sought out, and their personal narratives on how they use the apps were collected. This allows for the analysis of the construction of meaning(s) and understanding(s) for the consumer using participant responses. In turn, this will enable me to demonstrate the relationship between Islam and participants' views of marriage and relationships through the lenses of how people choose to engage with Muslim dating apps.

The research presented here involved online ethnographic observation and in-depth interviews and follows other studies of religious practice,[23] and the members studied are mostly second- or third-generation economic migrants that spoke English

21 Robert J. Stephure, Susan D. Boon, Stacey L. MacKinnon, and Vicki L. Deveau, 'Internet Initiated Relationships: Associations between Age and Involvement in Online Dating', *Journal of Computer-Mediated Communication* 14, no. 3 (2009): 658–81.

22 Gudelunas, 'There's an App for That'.

23 Safet Bectovic, 'Studying Muslims and Constructing Islamic Identity', *Ethnic and Racial Studies* 34, no. 7 (2011): 1120–33; Marta Bolognani, 'Islam, Ethnography and Politics: Methodological Issues in Researching amongst West Yorkshire Pakistanis in 2005', *International Journal of Social Research Methodology* 10, no. 4 (2007): 279–93; Vered Kahani-Hopkins and Nick Hopkins, '"Representing" British Muslims: The Strategic Dimension to Identity Construction', *Ethnic and Racial Studies* 25, no. 2 (2002): 288–309; Seán McLoughlin, 'Researching Muslim Minorities: Some Reflections on Fieldwork in Britain', in *Studies in Islamic and Middle Eastern Texts and Traditions in Memory of Norman Calder*, ed. Gerald Richard Hawting, Jawid Ahmad Mojaddedi, and Alexander Samely (Oxford: Oxford University Press, 2000), 175–94; Emma Tarlo, *Visibly Muslim: Fashion, Politics, Faith* (London: Bloomsbury, 2010); Daniel Winchester, 'Embodying the Faith: Religious Practice and the Making of a Muslim Moral Habitus', *Social Forces* 86, no. 4 (2008): 1753–80.

and had little-to-no experience of living in their country of heritage. I sought out members who were willing to discuss their religious values as well as their views on marriage. An important factor to consider was the effect of extra-familial culture, as well as parents,[24] because if the larger social structure strongly influences them this would be borne out in their religious values and the type of partner they desire, though it might be difficult to detect an understanding of marriage alone. In addition, Nelson and colleagues found that understandings of morality contribute to the sense of well-being and success in a marriage.[25] Even expressing marital commitment for religious couples is understood in moral terms. This builds on what Johnson and colleagues defined as the sense that one is morally obligated to behave in a certain way when in a relationship.[26] In such instances, the matching up of religious values is important for participants as it places the same moral implications on similar acts, as well as providing for compatibility in one's outlook on life. For example, the importance of commitment is not understood by participants as a commitment to one another, and therefore if one breaks that commitment by having an affair, it is not seen as solely an interpersonal problem, but rather due to understanding marriage in religious terms it is a commitment to God that would also be broken by having an affair and would have moral implications.

The sample was produced through asking for volunteers from users of the apps. A total of eleven adults, aged eighteen to thirty, took part in the study. Of the eleven, six had used Ummah Dating at least once, and two had used SingleMuslim at least once. Four were current Ummah Dating users and seven were current Muzmatch users. The gender distribution was six male users and five female. On average, users were twenty-five years old, and most were students. The data is part of a larger study looking at Muslim media use in the UK, and its relationship with identity formation practices. The project received approval from the University of Durham Ethics Committee in 2013. All participants are practising Muslims of varying ethnicities: four were of Indian heritage, one Palestinian, five Pakistani, and one Iraqi. This paper will describe specific data gathered during the winter of 2014 through the spring of 2015.

The method further limits the scope of the study to people who (1) consider themselves Muslim; (2) consider their religiosity as an important factor in their search

24 Dean R. Hoge, Gregory H. Petrillo, and Ella I. Smith, 'Transmission of Religious and Social Values from Parents to Teenage Children', *Journal of Marriage and the Family* 44, no. 3 (1982): 569–80.

25 Judith A. Nelson, Amy Manning Kirk, Pedra Ane, and Sheryl A. Serres, 'Religious and Spiritual Values and Moral Commitment in Marriage: Untapped Resources in Couples Counseling?', *Counseling and Values* 55, no. 2 (2011): 228–46.

26 Michael P. Johnson, John P. Caughlin, and Ted L. Huston, 'The Tripartite Nature of Marital Commitment: Personal, Moral, and Structural Reasons to Stay Married', *Journal of Marriage and the Family* 61, no. 1 (1999): 160–77.

for a partner; and (3) desire to find a partner using digital mechanisms. Therefore, the research focus is on a certain segment among young Muslims. This selection of Muslims cannot be easily identified as 'devoted', 'traditional', 'conservative', or similar, because, while they may hold values similar to others in these categories, they choose a mechanism for finding a partner that is not traditional, but modern, and potentially taboo. This suggests these individuals are challenging certain cultural norms and boundaries, despite desiring partners that may hold similar and potentially conservative views on life; thereby adding empirical data to what Kalliny and Hausman consider theoretically might be the case.[27]

The participant responses are evaluated precisely in terms of their capacity to answer the main question – were participants using the apps to transcend spatial, religious, and social constraints, or to find a partner with similar attitudes in a social environment deemed not Islamic enough? Therefore, profiles that expressed such sentiments were contacted, as well as an equal number of profiles who did not, so as to see whether people who do not express these perspectives on their profile still share these sentiments. In total forty-seven users were contacted, and I engaged with people through the applications whereby the volunteers were selected based on their willingness to participate. This engagement was based on a series of semi-structured interviews, whereby I had some set questions on the nature of relationships and their understanding of marriage, but also followed up on user responses and their narratives.

The research looks at the links between different religious values and understandings of marriage in participants and use of mobile dating apps to satisfy their need for a partner. Their religious practices are understood to be ritualistic acts that are self-identified and described by the participants. In understanding what these practices are we can follow Rappaport's highly condensed definition of ritual, namely, 'the performance of more or less invariant sequences of formal acts and utterances not entirely encoded by the performer'.[28] Using this understanding of religious ritual, we can see later how the dating apps function as a mediator between the subjective and personal acts and utterances that are encoded by the actor, as defined by their social constraints and simultaneously challenge those constraints, as well as, on the other hand, enabling users to consume and select suitable partners based on certain (formal) acts and utterances. In this particular case, the successful participation in the Islamic ritual of marriage that is largely encoded in religious terms. The research focus is therefore on how these acts that are committed by the participants in their (public or private) lives signify, symbolise, and make present their faith in Islam with

27 Morris Kalliny and Angela Hausman, 'The Impact of Cultural and Religious Values on Adoption of Innovation', *Academy of Marketing Studies Journal* 11, no. 1 (2007): 125–36.

28 Roy A. Rappaport, *Ritual and Religion in the Making of Humanity* (Cambridge: Cambridge University Press, 1999), 137.

regards to marriage and finding a partner.[29] Importantly, this will represent an organic understanding of what religion means to the participants and how it is practised within their personal context. This is especially pertinent as mosque attendance or predetermined rituals, as relevant indicators of religious practice, are increasingly questioned.

MARRIAGE IN THE ISLAMIC TRADITION

For many Muslims marriage is an important milestone. Among the more traditional it is seen as a religious duty for Muslims to get married. The family is the cornerstone of relationships, and marriage is seen as the basis from which Muslim people, communities, and society engages with one another. The Qur'an reads:

> And marry those among you who are single ... If they are needy, God will make them free from want out of His grace. (Q. 24:32)
>
> And He it is who has created man from water; then He has made for him blood-relationship and marriage-relationship. And thy Lord is ever Powerful. (Q. 25:54)

As a result, some have described marriage as 'half of faith', and even recommended it for those who cannot afford it. In such cases, marriage, for those who are financially or socially disadvantaged, is an Islamic ritual that can benefit all those who get married regardless of status, but is extra important for those who might not be able to afford other ritual practices.[30]

The Qur'an provides the basis for Islamic law on marriage, and it is complemented by provisions in the Sharīʿa. Such provisions vary by region, legal school, or division of Islam, but fundamentally, marriage is a contract between a man and a woman over the age of consent (potentially with the consent of her *walī* or legal guardian). Polygamy is permitted by the Qur'an, but restricted by rules of fairness and equity; this position has been incorporated into state law by some Muslim countries such as Tunisia.[31] Some scholars argue for women to be accorded higher social status, political freedom, and autonomy and demand a reforming of the traditional Islamic marriage laws. Yet in dating apps these calls for progressive social needs or values can be met, while preserving the conservative theology, as will be shown later.

29 Webb Keane, 'The Evidence of the Senses and the Materiality of Religion', in 'The Objects of Evidence: Anthropological Approaches to the Production of Knowledge', special issue, *Journal of the Royal Anthropological Institute* 14, no. S1 (2008): S110–S127.

30 Muḥammad b. ʿAlī al-Shawkānī, *Nayl al-awṭār* (Lahore, 1967).

31 Jamal A. Badawi, *Gender Equity in Islam: Basic Principles* (Chicago: American Trust Publications, 1995).

Historical practices were sometimes incorporated into the Sharīʿa during the history of Islam, and so too contemporary developments are influencing modern marriage practices by Muslims who have incorporated both regional customs and Western practices. Shīʿa Islam legally permits temporary marriage, called *mutʿa*, whereby the marriage ends at a predetermined time according to the terms agreed at the start of the marriage, rather than via divorce. Aside from its social and religious benefits, the institution of marriage is also recognised for its personal and physical benefits of providing a religiously endorsed outlet for sex. This is highly relevant within the framework of this paper because sexual satisfaction is seen as particularly important to men,[32] who 'more often attach importance to the physical need of sexual gratification as an explanation for their social media use'.[33]

The Islamic tradition considers it permissible for a Muslim man to marry a woman of any religious tradition, but not vice versa.[34] Thus these apps potentially allow for women to operate with a greater sense of agency and with more potential matches available to them. Despite this difference, both Muslim men and women are encouraged to base their choice of partner on matching ideology (the most important being piety). 'Muzmatch is the app for anyone seeking a halal Muslim marriage' – the headline to the welcome page also contains a link to the app's terms and conditions. Although the Prophet is reported to have said that partner selection is based on four qualities, namely, beauty, noble lineage, wealth, and piety, it is piety that is the best quality upon which to base that decision.[35]

MARRIAGE WITHIN THE BRITISH MUSLIM COMMUNITY

To speak of a British Muslim community is somewhat of a misnomer as Muslims in Britain are not monolithic in their sectarian or ethnic identities. The British Muslim community defies heterogeneity and transcends it, while still claiming a core of individuals who confess to a single faith but stem from a variety of ethnic and cultural backgrounds. Although mainly from South Asia, the statistics from the 2011 census reveal that the number of Muslims in Britain had grown to 4.8 per cent of the total population (2.7 million people).[36] As a result, Muslims made up the second largest

32 Deborah L. Tolman, Meg I. Striepe, and Tricia Harmon, 'Gender Matters: Constructing a Model of Adolescent Sexual Health', *Journal of Sex Research* 40, no. 1 (2003): 4–12.

33 Sumter et al., 'Love Me Tinder', 7.

34 Alex B. Leeman, 'Interfaith Marriage in Islam: An Examination of the Legal Theory behind the Traditional and Reformist Positions', *Indiana Law Journal* 84, no. 2 (2009): 743–71.

35 See Muḥammad b. Ismāʿīl al-Bukhārī, *Ṣaḥīḥ al-Bukhārī* (Cairo: Dār al-Fikr, 1966), *ḥadīth* no. 3.

36 Office For National Statistics, 'Key Statistics for Local Authorities in England And Wales – Religion Statistics', 2011, www.ons.gov.uk/ons/rel/census/2011-census/key-statistics-for-localau-

religious group within Britain. The Muslim population is 'a fast growing and young population', with 60 per cent being below thirty years of age.[37] Their diversity is borne out in their outlook, values, and attitudes, and further reflected in income and education levels. The 2011 census data also reveals that Muslims were considered more ethnically diverse than other religious groups. Two-thirds of Muslims (68 per cent) were from an Asian background (within this group, the 38 per cent Pakistani and 15 per cent Bangladeshi were the largest groups). The proportion of Muslims reporting as white was around 8 per cent; mixed ethnicity reported 4 per cent; those belonging to Black/African/Caribbean British communities made up about 10 per cent of the Muslim population; and this was a similar reporting size to those identifying as belonging to another ethnic group (around 11 per cent).[38] In 2011, 53 per cent of all Muslims were born outside Britain and the number of such Muslims had almost doubled between 2001 and 2011 with a rise of 599,000 from 828,000 in 2001 to 1.4 million in 2011.

This diversity in backgrounds and economic status has challenged the unity within the community, and some find the challenges of reconciling their cultural heritage with their adopted land a problematic experience. Nyang has pointed out how Muslim immigrants' self-identification and self-differentiation contribute significantly to shaping ethnic identities within the Muslim community.[39] Because of this diversity, there is no universal mechanism for marital dating used by Muslims, either in Britain or elsewhere. Marriage as a social institution is constrained by the practices and customs that regulate it. Those regulations (whether religious or legal codes) affect how members react towards the available pool of potential spouses.

An official marriage registration provides tax benefits as well as the right to perform recognised marriage ceremonies. Up until 30 June 2012 there were 973 certified Muslim places of worship in England and Wales, and 213 of these premises were registered for the solemnisation of marriages.[40] It is estimated that at least as many unregistered mosques exist as well. It is not possible to determine how many marriages took place at the 213 Muslim places of worship in England and Wales prior to 2011, as the data does not include a venue code. However, it is possible to determine that the number

thorities-in-england-and-wales/sty-religion.html.

37 Patrick Dunleavy, 'The Westminster Model and the Distinctiveness of British Politics', in Dunleavy et al., *Developments in British Politics*, 317.

38 Office For National Statistics, 'Full Story: What Does the Census Tell Us about Religion in 2011?', 2013, www.ons.gov.uk/ons/dcp171776_310454.pdf.

39 Sulayman S. Nyang, 'Convergence and Divergence in an Emergent Community: A Study of Challenges Facing U.S. Muslims', in *The Muslims of America*, ed. Yvonne Z. Haddad (New York: Oxford University Press, 1991), 236–49.

40 Office For National Statistics, 'Number of Muslim Weddings', 2012, www.ons.gov.uk/ons/about-ons/business-transparency/freedom-of-information/what-can-irequest/previous-foi-requests/population/number-of-muslim-weddings/index.html.

of marriages solemnised in England and Wales in 2015 (most recent data release) is 301.[41] Marriage statistics by denomination can be misleading, however, as Muslim marriages can take place at unregistered premises. For that marriage to be recognised as legal, the couple must undergo a further marriage ceremony in a registry office or approved building. Such weddings are classed as civil marriages because only the civil marriage certificate is received.

Despite Islamic law not distinguishing between civil and religious marriages, the British state wishes to supervise the actual process of marriage in order to prevent abuse. Therefore, should a religious ceremony take place in England without fulfilling the preliminary civil requirements, the official law will not recognise this marriage as legally valid. In other words, the civil ceremony is the only marriage which English law recognises. The Marriage (Registration of Buildings) Act 1990 and the Marriage Act 1994 are two amendments to the Marriage Act 1949 that allow buildings to become registered and allow for their own Muslim officials to perform a fully legalised marriage according to both Muslim law and English law. Only after an Islamic marriage ceremony (*nikāḥ*) is a marriage regarded as legitimate from a religious and cultural perspective. This further suggests that the religious marriage determines the nature of the relationship. In addition, Muslims fortify the strength of *nikāḥ* by incorporating official legal rules into their unofficial laws.[42] For some traditional Muslims 'arranged' marriages are relatively common and such marriages may be arranged by a family member, through a service, through friends, or by a *walī* (guardian). Pressure is also apparently exerted by close relatives in Pakistan, who use marriage as a route for their children to migrate legally to Britain.[43]

Finding love in this traditional setting is a complex matter because the traditional methods often presuppose expectations, and opportunities for the couple in question to discuss marital views may be limited if restricted to a few meetings. Traditional practices also uphold the heteronormativity of the Islamic understanding of marriage. These existing structures and institutions dictate how people choose potential spouses. For example, Muslim women living in a mostly non-Muslim society are subject to the religious constraint that a Muslim woman can only marry a Muslim male, and therefore there are many women who are reliant on outside help in order to find an

41 Office For National Statistics, 'Religious Marriages in England and Wales, 2004 to 2015', www.ons.gov.uk/peoplepopulationandcommunity/birthsdeathsandmarriages/marriagecohabitationandcivilpartnerships/adhocs/008310religiousmarriagesinenglandandwales2004to2015.

42 Ihsan Yilmaz, 'Marriage Solemnization among Turks in Britain: The Emergence of a Hybrid Anglo-Muslim Turkish Law', *Journal of Muslim Minority Affairs* 24, no. 1 (2004): 57–66.

43 Pnina Werbner, 'Veiled Interventions in Pure Space: Honour, Shame and Embodied Struggles among Muslims in Britain and France', *Theory, Culture & Society* 24, no. 2 (2007): 161–86.

appropriate spouse.[44] These mechanisms also provide participants with potentially more outside involvement for finding a spouse, such as needing to rely on a social network consisting of extended family members.

MUSLIM ONLINE DATING APPS

Online dating sites essentially offer personal ads. The three Muslim dating apps in question, Muzmatch, Ummah Dating, and SingleMuslim, are no different. These apps were selected because they are available for free, explicitly Muslim, the most popular (measured by number of downloads at the time of research), and accessible on both iPhone and Android platforms. In comparison to other dating apps, individuals post their own profile and then search and read profiles before contacting a person on the site to learn more about them and to gauge whether the other was also interested in them. The amount of information and detail people can add differs from site to site, but most will enable users to show at least one photograph of themselves and some enable them to add video and voice files to their profiles. Online daters can present information about themselves in a number of ways. They can either fill in small text boxes (OkCupid, SingleMuslim), rate themselves (Match.com), or check boxes indicating attributes (Muzmatch) such as their age, gender, location, job, and physique (e.g. a choice ranging from slim to overweight). Some questions are a compulsory requirement (e.g. age and gender). Users are usually given an opportunity and encouraged to expand upon this information by sharing their hobbies and interests. Finally, and perhaps most importantly, there is a section where users can describe the type of person they are attempting to attract and what would be their ideal match. Some online dating sites do the matching for the client by claiming to be able to 'scientifically' match individuals. The assumption is that there is a formula to matching appropriate people – usually generating a compatibility percentage based on overlapping responses to the questions answered on one's profile.

In addition to general online dating sites such as eHarmony, True.com, Match.com, there are also more specialised online dating sites which gather like-minded individuals together. For example, there are sites designed specifically for Christians, Jews, Vegans, Goths, and, for the purpose of this study, Muslims. Such sites are similar to social groups which one might join in the hope of finding others that share the same values or interests. Moreover, it potentially cuts out some of the work associated with the search for the perfect other, and it puts a person in the position whereby everyone they contact is also looking for a connection. This makes it different from other social

44 Jemima Khan, 'The Marriage Business', *New Statesman*, 15 March 2012, 32–35.

encounters where individuals may not be available for the type of relationship that the online dater is looking for.

Notably, such platforms provide a liminal stage between a non-sexualised and a sexualised interaction, where flirtation is described as an interaction and practices relevant to a current role and a possible future one are simultaneously presented. This allows users to potentially engage one another without concerns for chastity or the need to involve family members. Thus, elements such as bodily alignment, the tone of voice, and even the occasional touch of flirting interactions are borrowed from a possible future, in which they are already engaged in a sexualised or intimate encounter.[45] Online dating in this regard facilitates the courting process, enabling the related discussions and interactions, both in cyberspace and in planning a potential future offline, but not limited by traditional structures and mechanisms. However, one difference with 'offline' dating is the difficulty in getting across the tone of voice, body language, and other subtle cues from face-to-face encounters into text-based interactions. One mitigating factor is the use of emoticons which help in getting across certain meanings in text form; the other is video chatting which gives users the ability to see each other across distances and still pick up visual cues from the body language of the correspondents.

The desire for spousal specificity with regards to the ethnic or communal association may depend on different notions of tradition. For many Muslims, a potential spouse is not necessarily similar in religious orthodoxy, but rather religious homogeneity. Therefore, Muslims with a less orthodox and more traditionalist or ethnically tinted interpretation of Islam may be going back to their country of heritage to look for spouses who share in their religious practices, rather than searching for a partner within the British Muslim community that might have a different Muslim identity. However, Muzmatch, one of the dating apps in question, offers another opportunity. While users can identify themselves and potential partners via nationality, ethnic background, and country of origin, the app also requires every member to answer the following questions with regards to religion: 'Sect (Sunni, Shia, Other), How Religious (Not Practising, Moderately Practising, Fairly Practising, Very Practising), Praying (Never Pray, Sometimes Pray, Usually Pray, Always Pray), Eat Only Halal (yes/no), Drink Alcohol (yes/no), Smoker (yes/no), Convert/Revert (yes/no), and Marriage Plans (as soon as possible, 1–2 years, 3–4 years, 4+ years)'.

Although the creation of Muslim internet dating sites is the result of market opportunities following the technological and medialisation advances and further com-

45 Iddo Tavory, 'The Structure of Flirtation: On the Construction of Interactional Ambiguity', in *Studies in Symbolic Interaction*, vol. 33, ed. Norman K. Denzin (Bingley: Emerald, 2009), 59–74.

mercialisation of pre-existing methods of securing marital partners, in recent years, online romance, marriage, and dating have become an increasingly popular if not a mainstream activity with regards to meeting potential love interests. The new modes of establishing relationships are an extension of new modes of social interaction (chatrooms, instant messaging, and email) that have become commonplace. The result is that they challenge the traditional methods of courting and selecting a spouse. The concept of courting and in turn love and marriage, whether initiated online or offline, is related to the post-modern discourse on freedom and agency. The increasingly mainstream nature and prevalence of online dating also challenges the assumption that anyone who would turn to a computer for love must be a desperate individual, unable to find love in more traditional ways. In addition, the Muslim community often contains strict protocols for interaction between genders, especially in formal settings. In return, it makes it difficult for free interaction and socialisation between genders. Some of these protocols extend themselves online, as Muzmatch has the option for women to not show their picture to men until they allow them to view it. This may have a religious underpinning but could also be to elicit a response from a user who likes the profile and sends the person in question a message, rather than basing their decision on physical appearance. Furthermore, if the context is more ethnic or language based, it further decreases the potential partners and reduces the chances of finding love outside of that particular group. This is something that the apps cater for by allowing users to restrict members based on their location, ethnicity, or linguistic background, but simultaneously it also helps users find members beyond their immediate location, ethnic or linguistic communities.

One major difference between apps is that Muzmatch will not allow you to search for members of the same sex or gender, meaning there is an implied heteronormative understanding of (sexual) relationships that underpins the site. It also appears as a much more professional app, when compared to SingleMuslim, for example. While both use the swipe function to indicate likes and dislikes, Muzmatch is a far more formal app with questions to determine who is a match, rather than a list of likes and dislikes and a swipe function for users to show interest. This is comparable to the difference between Match.com and Tinder. As a result, some social constraints that users may be seeking to escape are perpetuated by the characteristic of the apps. So if users were seeking to transcend certain potential social constraints as Lo and Aziz suggest, by seeking out a homosexual relationship, for example, they would be unable to do so because they were unable to search profiles that would correspond to the characteristics they are looking for.[46] This suggests that dating apps may be more

46 Mbaye Lo and Taimoor Aziz, 'Muslim Marriage Goes Online: The Use of Internet Matchmaking by American Muslims', *The Journal of Religion and Popular Culture* 21, no. 3 (2009): 5–5.

attuned to individuals who are looking for Islamic identities that are strengthened by a local environment perceived as hostile.

Although some specialised commercial sites have a number of sites under their umbrella that provide matchmaking services for specific groups, they differ in terms of target demographics, location, and the language they use. Their common denominator is that the target demographic is Muslim and single. The apps aim at Muslims of all types, and thus allow for users to self-identify according to sect. However, the fact that sect becomes a selection criterion means that it will allow users to screen out those belonging to sects they would not like to be partnered with. As such it can emphasise sectarian divisions within the Muslim community and restrict partner choices. Some apps allow for non-Muslim women who want to date or marry Muslim men, or non-Muslim males dating or marrying Muslim women to sign up (although the latter two may be highly unlikely). Although the sites are characterised by Muslim orientation, love cards, greetings, smiles, and other dating criteria tailored to meet Muslims, they follow mainstream trends. However, this allows users to apply their own ideas on love and relationships. Despite there being many suggested motives for using Muslim dating sites, such as marrying someone in the Islamic tradition or physical appearance, the reasons that Muslims want to marry are diverse, and cannot easily be captured in these lenses.[47] The language of love, caring, loneliness, and so forth seems to be the main feature of online dating and dating sites. In addition, a desire to travel and see the world, ideally with a partner, is something most users expressed in their interviews and many state as much on their profiles. While this may be characteristic of the user demographic, in this study eighteen- to thirty-four-year-olds, who are mostly students, it is something that may reflect other factors present in society.[48]

47 Lo and Aziz, 'Muslim Marriage Goes Online'; Smeeta Mishra, Mathukutty M. Monippally, and Krishna P. Jayakar, 'Self Presentation in Online Environments: A Study of Indian Muslim Matrimonial Profiles', *Asian Journal of Communication* 23, no. 1 (2013): 38–53; Jiban K. Pal, 'Social Networks Enabling Matrimonial Information Services in India', *International Journal of Library and Information Science* 2, no. 4 (2010): 54–64; Detlev Zwick and Cristian Chelariu, 'Mobilizing the *Hijab*: Islamic Identity Negotiation in the Context of a Matchmaking Website', *Journal of Consumer Behaviour* 5, no. 4 (2006): 380–95.

48 Gitte du Plessis, 'Enjoy Your Vacation!', *Ephemera* 15, no. 4 (2015): 755–72; Jan Moller Jensen, 'The Relationships between Socio-demographic Variables, Travel Motivations and Subsequent Choice of Vacation', 2nd International Conference on Economics, Business and Management, 2011, 37–44; David T. Ory and Patricia L. Mokhtarian, 'When Is Getting There Half the Fun? Modeling the Liking for Travel', *Transportation Research Part A: Policy and Practice* 39, no. 2–3 (2005): 97–123; Jan Vidar Haukeland, 'Motives for Holiday Travel', *The Tourist Review* 47, no. 2 (1992): 14–17.

ONLINE DATING BY MUSLIMS

Research suggests that the motivations for using these apps will result in different gratifications and may result in different offline outcomes.[49] Online dating can offer a space for people to meet others with the same values, and to also allow a user to change their search parameters as their values change and develop over time. In doing so, a service that caters specifically to Muslims simultaneously offers them a space online if they seek to liberate themselves from potentially constricting boundaries and traditional values, as well as offering an alternative space for those seeking someone with those same traditional values. The services aim to accommodate people and their personal convictions.[50] What is most important is assuring themselves that a potential partner has similar attitudes towards Islam.[51]

Therefore, online dating blurs the lines between the traditional family formation and modern practices. Historically, love and sexual attraction were potentially highly disruptive emotions. There is the potential for a tension to form between the emotive and what is considered proper. 'Therefore love was absent from the family formation process, not because it was denied that this sentiment existed, but because it was considered a strong and unpredictable force that had to be contained.'[52] It has sprung up out of a need to balance a highly formalised modern marriage ritual,[53] with a desire for emotive content and sentimental connections with a potential partner. The dating apps provide an online third space for users to develop and present their own identities, negotiate and contest (cultural) values within a space that is outside the boundaries that may restrict such negotiation and contestation, and to form and belong to a community – the larger community of users – as well as the desire to form a partnership with other users.

---

49 Barker, 'Older Adolescents' Motivations'; Gudelunas, 'There's an App for That'; Haferkamp et al., 'Men Are from Mars'.

50 Lincoln Dahlberg, 'The Internet and Democratic Discourse: Exploring the Prospects of Online Deliberative Forums Extending the Public Sphere', *Information, Communication & Society* 4, no. 4 (2001): 615–33; Terera Davis, 'Third Spaces or Heterotopias? Recreating and Negotiating Migrant Identity Using Online Spaces', *Sociology* 44, no. 4 (2010): 661–77; Constance A. Steinkuehler and Dmitri Williams, 'Where Everybody Knows Your (Screen) Name: Online Games as "Third Places"', *Journal of Computer-Mediated Communication* 11, no. 4 (2006): 885–909; Scott Wright, 'From "Third Place" to "Third Space": Everyday Political Talk in Non-political Online Spaces', *Javnost – The Public* 19, no. 3 (2012): 5–20.

51 Leen Sterckx, 'The Self-Arranged Marriage: Modern Muslim Courtship Practices in the Netherlands', in *Everyday Life Practices of Muslims in Europe*, ed. Erkan Toğuşlu (Leuven: Leuven University Press, 2015), 113–26.

52 Ibid., 121.

53 Ibid.

In doing so, users select characteristics that define their values, and in turn their Muslimness, in order to sift through personalised criteria for potential mates online. By increasing the customisation, these internet dating sites are able to attract more users. This is due to their ability to combine both Islamic marriage culture and modern aspirations of individual freedom and personal choices. They give users the ability and opportunity to express their personal views, values, concerns, ambitions, and feelings. Expressing this range of choices is not often available or allowed in the traditional marriage system, either through direct interpersonal contact, along with traditional Muslim dating values, or via the use of an intermediary.

Lo and Aziz observed regionally or communally based sites and mailing lists that catered to small 'like-minded groups and local communities', whose correspondences are reliant largely upon individual blogs, mailing lists, and the internet. In these groups, marriage seekers often send emails to a mailing list or an affiliated community mosque where the imam matches that request with requests for similar needs.[54] Eventually, candidates interested in pursuing an offline relationship will meet. Imams and community organisers may play a role in facilitating such dating efforts, by offering a safe neutral space or having a gathering where prospective couples can meet.[55] They provide services in exchange for either small fees, or as a free public service within their socio-cultural mission. Most of these spaces are administered by advocacy groups and umbrella organisations. Their marital services are usually offered in conjunction with other services they provide, and demographic information is usually the main indicator of potential matches. The service is usually open to members only, and these spaces do not reflect the typical places open to everyone.

Online dating spaces usually cater to a very specific user, and are largely oriented along professional and ethnic lines. Since the dominant Muslim ethnicity in the UK is South Asian, Muslims from Pakistan, India, and Bangladesh have much in common, including primarily religious ideology and practice. Traditional modes of supervised courtship characterise the potential meetings of people, and these sites have become another avenue for parents to maintain continuity with their homeland's traditions by reaching out to their country of heritage to look for 'ideal' marriage candidates for their British-born children. An alternative is using the internet to search for a prospective partner, and because to my participants it was presupposed that the partner be Muslim, it was important for all the users interviewed that their partner also be Muslim. It was seen as common sense that if one was looking for a Muslim partner to use a Muslim dating app. While participants understood there were alternatives out there that could provide a similar service, the ones that had used an alternative

54 Lo and Aziz, 'Muslim Marriage Goes Online'.

55 Adam B. Ellick, 'Speed-Dating, Muslim Style', *New York Times*, 13 February 2011, www.nytimes.com/2011/02/13/nyregion/13dating.html.

application or website felt that a Muslim app was better suited to meeting their needs. For example:

> I tried using other apps, but I only found people who were not serious or who I could not really connect with spiritually. Religion is important to me and I would like to share that with my partner and share in the religious experience. I think this app has more chance helping me find that person.
>
> *Samira, 22*

> The primary motivations for users to select using this app were related to meeting a potential partner in a respectful way, and for finding a user with similar cultural-religious values which were deemed important to the user. For example:

> A nice and cool way to respectfully contact the other gender.
>
> *Ali, 23*

> I would like both my partner and I to encourage each other to become the best versions of ourselves spiritually and intellectually. So, I think that an app that caters to people with a specific religious background will help me find someone that I can bond with spiritually.
>
> *Aisha, 25*

> I'm looking for a pious Salafi man, honest, kind, loyal, and funny to build a family with. A man who will treat his wife like a princess. If I cannot find someone in my immediate network, then maybe online I can find that perfect someone.
>
> *Laila, 25*

Communication mechanisms in this regard allow users to develop relationships beyond spatial and social constraints – something that Lo and Aziz identify as one of the findings in their research.[56] As fake profiles exist, users who portrayed unrealistic expectations, or were too good to be true, were approached with caution.[57] In addition, users adopted several strategies to overcome such issues, such as 'using their communication skills to study others carefully, doing "police work" to uncover any inconsistencies in their statements, "interrogating" them using a pre-developed list of questions and involving their family members in their negotiations'.[58] This is high-

56 Lo and Aziz, 'Muslim Marriage Goes Online'.

57 Yeslam Al-Saggaf, 'Males' Trust and Mistrust of Females in Muslim Matrimonial Sites', *Journal of Information, Communication and Ethics in Society* 11 (2013): 174–92.

58 Al-Saggaf, 'Males' Trust and Mistrust of Females', 90.

lighted by Nazira who is happy with how the app allows her to connect with someone and find out if they are compatible without needing to engage in the organised ritual of meeting a potential partner as described by Moors.[59]

> The app allows for people to talk and potentially connect in a manner that is respectful but doesn't need for a lot of complicated planning. You can message each other when it's convenient and then only when you know the person is interesting and interested in you as a person can you meet them. You don't need to worry about covering your hair or so when the message comes in, or what people may think. When you meet someone of the opposite sex in public things are always a bit awkward and complicated. This app lets you get straight to the point and find out if you are compatible.
>
> *Nazira, 24*

Online dating offers users the ability to find emotional adventures, potential casual relationships, and love and marriage in cyberspace. The flexibility of online dating lends itself to offering its product to all kinds of consumers and the non-committal nature of the websites or the correspondents gives users the utmost feeling of agents of their own fate. While the apps 'host' the activities, and act as an intermediary much like the imam or the mailing list, the apps also now provide a much more direct service. In doing so, the media acts as the intermediator, but the users are given direct access to other users, possibly for a fee. This allows for greater freedom in the selection process by the individual seeking a partner, and it also allows for the person to present themselves in a way that suits their wishes.

> Living in Europe and people back in Egypt always assume you behave and act like a European. That is why we were raised very strict but we are a very close family.
>
> *Semi, 20*

> For my study, I have to spend at least six months abroad. I love to travel and experience different cultures (as I am part of two different cultures). I am not in a rush and very patient and I believe that Allah has a plan for all of us.
>
> *Meryema, 20*

With it being reported that coerced and forced marriages are a reality for many young Muslims in Britain, the individual agency that these apps provide is important

59 Annelies Moors, 'Unregistered Islamic Marriages: Anxieties about Sexuality and Islam in the Netherlands', *Applying Sharia in the West: Facts, Fears and the Future of Islamic Rules on Family Relations in the West*, ed. Maurits S. Berger (Leiden: Leiden University Press, 2013), 141–64.

to consider. According to the Muslim Arbitration Tribunal report on forces marriages, 70 per cent of marriages between a Muslim British citizen and a foreign national from the Asian subcontinent entailed some level of coercion. The report concludes, 'Young Muslims in Britain are under siege from their elders and parents because of the generational and cultural gap.'[60] This could have been exacerbated before the advent of the internet, because the main methods of finding a spouse utilised for many Muslims in Britain were through personal contact, an institution, or a social connection acting as an intermediary. Through personal contact, a person will meet a potential spouse that they eventually marry following a period of courtship. That potential spouse may be someone with whom he or she interacts in their social or professional spheres, perhaps someone they know from work, a social club, sports organisation, or from their Muslim community whom they propose marriage to directly. Muslims also use institutions as intermediaries in finding spouses, such as mosques or Islamic centres. Some local imams and community leaders keep a list of those who are interested in finding a spouse and use the social network of the mosque to introduce interested parties. Another possibility is the social network of friends and family back in one's country of heritage. Using intermediaries within this type of network suggests a desire for a spouse having the same heritage. The intermediary, then, is the 'middleman' between the individual looking for a spouse and a potential pool of spouses. This traditional system of 'arranging' marriage through a network of family and friends, usually the parents and their contacts, could include individuals from one's native country and/or from the same (ethnic) community in Britain.

In turn, the greater individualism in partner selection gives the user greater freedom and liberties in seeking out the partner of their choice. This is evidenced by user responses:

> Someone simple, kind, and funny, who likes to travel and doing sports. Someone in between *dīn*[61] and *dunyā*.[62]
>
> *Aisha, 25*

60 Muslim Arbitration Tribunal, 'Forced Marriages Initiative', www.matribunal.com/forced-marriages-intiative.php.

61 'Often translated as "religion." *Deen* (or *Din*) implies that living in obedience to God is an obligation owed to Him, for which people will be held account. It encompasses beliefs, thoughts, and deeds. From this perspective the peaceful submission to God, as demonstrated through belief in Islam and its rituals, is termed the "way of truth" (*din al-haqq*). The worship of Allah is termed the "straight path" and established for human life (*al-din al-qayyim*).' John L. Esposito, ed., *The Oxford Dictionary of Islam* (New York: Oxford University Press, 2004), 71. In this context the participants see their potential match as their true match and a way for serving God in the proper manner. Further suggesting that for these participants marriage is seen as a core part of their religious duties.

62 'In matters of religious belief and practice, [*dunyā*] refers to earthly concerns, contrasted with those of God or heavenly concerns (din).' Ibid.

> Looking for someone interesting, practising, and easy-going and someone who can hold a conversation, and who will be my *dīn*.
>
> *Samira, 22*

Although consisting primarily of Muslims, the demography of consumers is larger and more diverse. It is designed to cater to the needs of Muslims that are searching for (marriage) partners. In addition, traditional parental inclusion has remained evident in online dating as well. Some had asked their parents or siblings to help with their self-presentation, or when they had met a potential match discussed this with their family to gauge their opinion on the potential match.

> When I wrote my profile, I wasn't really sure what I should write or how to write it. I am not really good at that stuff. Plus, what do women want to know? So, I had asked my sisters to help me write it and put something together that is attractive but realistic too.
>
> *Mohammed, 23*

> I am here to find someone specific that will be good for me in the long term. It is only natural I think that you then ask people around you that know you best. Especially if you want your parents to like them and think you made a good choice. So, when I get to the point that I want to meet someone I ask my mum and dad to see what they will think.
>
> *Nazira, 24*

In the context of Muslim male users, the study finds comparable data with that conducted by Lo and Aziz, in that these users tend to be ambiguous in articulating their desired attributes beyond generalities and that their ideal matches would be more 'traditional' in their views on marriage.

> Honest, practising Muslim.
>
> *Nabil, 28*

> Someone to talk, to travel with, to eat out, and watch movies.
>
> *Rashad, 23*

> Someone who looks nice, is a true person to get married, and spend my life with.
>
> *Ali, 23*

Al-Saggaf adds that males' willingness to use online tools was reliant on their willingness to take risks, abilities, and confidence.[63] Women, on the other hand, are motivated to marry but are much more specific in the type of person they are looking for. Also, even in such online settings, women are active users of the applications, but simultaneously pursued by potential suitors, much more than male users.[64] As a result, female users reported that they spent significant time actively filtering out attention received in addition to actively searching themselves. Whether the need for being more specific in the person they are looking for is a result of filtering out the prompts from potential suitors, or a reflection of larger social aspects, requires further research at this stage. However, female participants were better at articulating their desires, as compared to their male counterparts. For example:

> I'm looking for someone like-minded, educated, down to earth, and open-minded with a good sense of humour. Someone that is a gentleman, who is confident without being cocky and doesn't take life too seriously. I am open to anyone from any walks of life as long as they are Muslim. I'd like to meet someone that is wanting to travel to new places and to try different things. Although I am pretty independent I'm looking for someone to be a provider and protector, someone to be the man in the relationship and look after me so if you are looking for a woman to sort your life out, in other words, a mother figure; I am not the lady for you.
>
> *Meryema, 20*

While seeking out users that share their aspirations and inspirations, the sites reflect the type of individuality and customisation that enables almost every user to find their type. For example, in questions related to visual appearance and the level of religiosity in the context of wearing hijab, participants are given the options of choosing: (1) always; (2) often; (3) occasionally; (4) rarely; (5) never; (6) prefer not to answer. Similar questions are asked with regards to personal interests, hobbies, political outlook, favourite music, films, books, entertainers, food, and so on. This offers users the ability to present themselves and their desires in ways that they may not otherwise have the opportunity to provide in such detailed answers, with regards to the choices they make, and their ability to express their preferences and desires.

In other contexts, the imam is the most evident and effective marital intermediary for individuals who consider religious affiliation or piety a predominant value and for those who lack any other kind of social network. Family (and sometimes friends) is the most utilised marital intermediary for individuals who consider other values more important to religious affiliation and for those whose primary concern is not a

63 Al-Saggaf, 'Males' Trust and Mistrust of Females'.

64 Based on participant self-reporting.

practising Muslim but rather someone that shares a similar outlook and ideology as well as their Muslim faith (albeit nominally). Based on informal surveys and observations, women seem to make use of an intermediary in facilitating a marriage more often than men. This is most likely due to a conservative devout Muslim woman's role (as she sees herself and in the community), such as not being allowed to marry non-Muslims, and also restrictions placed on physical appearances and limits as a result of social protocol that affect women's ability to use public space to meet, interact, and engage with the opposite sex.[65]

CONCLUSION

The use of Muslim smartphone dating apps by British Muslims reflects their opinion on matters of marriage and relationships, because rather than finding a spouse based solely on sectarian affiliation, the consumer is able to customise their searches to reflect a desire for a 'Muslim' spouse based on compatibility of what they believe in and aspire to within a multicultural society. This is opposed to earlier attempts that would match people based a definition of what they are rather than their values. However, this research shows that this is only possible within the 'acceptable' doctrinal parameters as defined by the app, and users are unable to be radically free in their choices within the app.

The success of a dating site is in its ability to cater to those who are searching for their partner according to their personal (religious) desires, which are not necessarily shared by the institutions they belong to, the authorities in their lives (imams, family, etc.), or other avenues through which they seek love and a spouse. However, the apps in question shift that authority from the offline authorities that may place spatial and cultural restrictions on them to the restrictions placed on them by the digital platform of choice, providing greater autonomy and freedom of choice, but often seen as providing total autonomy and freedom of choice. This research shows that Muslim users do not necessarily have specific motivations that can be identified as being different from non-Muslims, in that they seek someone with compatible values. The use of a 'Muslim' dating app is to guarantee that the potential partners are Muslim, which is important to the users as a religion-cultural resource. However, what Muslims are seeking to find using the app may be expressed using cultural or religious language that would potentially look out of place in another space. This further supports the

65 For more on how that may play out among Salafi women, see Anabel Inge, *The Making of a Salafi Muslim Woman: Paths to Conversion* (New York: Oxford University Press, 2016).

analysis of Muslim dating apps as a third space,[66] and allows for users to develop relationships based on the criteria they negotiate and employ in their quest for love.

The movement follows a mainstream trend where the internet is used to liberate people from the restrictions of traditional practices while still enabling adherence to traditional values, as well to explore new horizons for self-expression and freedom of choice. Therefore, online dating sites are a means of affirming personal desires while remaining true to personal religious values and finding someone who possesses those values too. Evidence suggests that individuals with common Islam-based identities are better served by the dating apps as their ability to seek out a partner who meets their religious values is easier satisfied. However, some seeking to transcend local restrictions, such as homosexuals, may not be served as well by the dating apps, because of their inherent structure.

Yet in this regard, what Boellstorff writes in his discussion of gays and lesbians in Indonesia may be of relevance too.[67] He notes that their identity may be exercised intermittently, 'first at one place and then at another, but not in the space between'; their subjectivity is not reliant on a 'unified, unchanging identity in all situations'.[68] Their structure is 'archipelagic', and this would be reflected in user responses, in their desire for a Muslim partner, and in the type of partner desired. Closeted gays and lesbians may still seek out heterosexual relationships for a variety of reasons. For example, in order to meet social norms, or fulfil their own desires for offspring. But those looking for gay or lesbian relationships would be excluded by the Muslims dating apps, and are therefore still constrained online in their choice of partner. This challenges the findings by Lo and Aziz,[69] and highlights the presupposed heteronormativity of Muslim relationships, but the internet does offer alternatives like 'Grindr', a dating app for homosexuals.

While the findings were based on eleven conversations that were carried out over online chats, as a preliminary study, one must consider what the impact is without either longer-term participant observation (including perhaps offline) with the interlocutors or a larger sample size. Future research could build on this by exploring how the relationship between spouses continues after marriage and if there are differences

66 Comparable to the discussions in Homi K. Bhabha, 'In the Cave of Making: Thoughts on Third Space', in *Communicating in the Third Space*, ed. Karin Ikas and Gerhard Wagner (New York: Routledge, 2008), ix–xiv; Davis, 'Third Spaces or Heterotopias?'; Wright, 'From "Third Place" to "Third Space"'.

67 Tom Boellstorff, 'Between Religion and Desire: Being Muslim and Gay in Indonesia', *American Anthropologist* 107, no. 4 (2005): 575–85.

68 Tom Boellstorff, *The Gay Archipelago: Sexuality and Nation in Indonesia* (Princeton: Princeton University Press, 2005), 174.

69 Lo and Aziz, 'Muslim Marriage Goes Online'.

between couples that met online vs offline, or if they feel connected in a different way given their digital mediation in the matchmaking process. In this sense, Muslim dating sites are a product of the general trends; they are selective of what fits their religious beliefs and cater to a user's specific desires. It is obvious in the findings that many sites are using the new technologies to maintain traditional methods of marriage. Thus, Muslim online dating networks serve as platforms through which users preserve their identity. However, these sites are also indicative of an existing problem as many Muslim users, who are a part of the socio-cultural fabric of Britain, have often felt like they have exhausted the opportunities available offline. Therefore, we could reason and ask questions about whether that is indicative of a change in relationships or dynamics within the Islamic community of Britain as a whole. Since opportunities to meet potential matches may be through their social network, professional life, family members, and religious institutions, but if they are being exhausted more than before, what does that tell us about social and family dynamics of Muslims in the UK today? As the apps limit the options available to users, and therefore force users seeking non-traditional relationships to use alternative mechanisms even more, they implicitly suggest that only the types of relationships or searchable characteristics are Islamic. This in turn could reinforce traditional gender roles, and limits a user's ability to find a partner only according to the traditional rules of marriage. It could be fruitful, for example, to compare the visions and values of Muslims using generic/non-Muslim dating apps (e.g. Match.com, Tinder, OkCupid) with explicitly Islamic ones such as those used in this study. In previous studies it remains unclear whether Muslim users have specific motivations that can be identified. Yet in this study, people with Islamic identities, strengthened by the cross-cultural adaptation process, are increasingly using the internet to overcome existing spatial and cultural barriers to develop relationships to better fit their religious outlook. However, with such a small sample size it would be worth exploring this question on a larger scale, possibly with other platforms and thus not limited to dating or relationships, but mapping the use of (mobile) technology among Muslims to gauge this process further. This would be in keeping with other research on computer-mediated communication.[70] However, despite these limitations and questions that arise from this study, this paper suggests that Muslims with strong Islamic identities, who would be considered within the parameters of traditional Islam, are using the apps to find partners that possess the same Islam-based identities.

70 Couch and Liamputtong, 'Online Dating and Mating'; Valkenburg and Peter, 'Who Visits Ona line Dating Sites?'.

BIBLIOGRAPHY

Al-Saggaf, Yeslam. 'Males' Trust and Mistrust of Females in Muslim Matrimonial Sites'. *Journal of Information, Communication and Ethics in Society* 11 (2013): 174–92.

Ali, Kecia. *Marriage and Slavery in Early Islam*. Cambridge, MA: Harvard University Press, 2010.

Arnett, Jeffrey Jensen. 'Emerging Adulthood: A Theory of Development from the Late Teens through the Twenties'. *American Psychologist* 55, no. 5 (2000): 469–80.

Badawi, Jamal A. *Gender Equity in Islam: Basic Principles*. Chicago: American Trust Publications, 1995.

Barker, Valerie. 'Older Adolescents' Motivations for Social Network Site Use: The Influence of Gender, Group Identity, and Collective Self-Esteem'. *CyberPsychology & Behavior* 12, no. 2 (2009): 209–13.

Bectovic, Safet. 'Studying Muslims and Constructing Islamic Identity'. *Ethnic and Racial Studies* 34, no. 7 (2011): 1120–33.

Bhabha, Homi K. 'In the Cave of Making: Thoughts on Third Space'. In *Communicating in the Third Space*, edited by Karin Ikas and Gerhard Wagner, ix–xiv. New York: Routledge, 2008.

Boellstorff, Tom. 'Between Religion and Desire: Being Muslim and Gay in Indonesia'. *American Anthropologist* 107, no. 4 (2005): 575–85.

Boellstorff, Tom. *The Gay Archipelago: Sexuality and Nation in Indonesia*. Princeton: Princeton University Press, 2005.

Bolognani, Marta. 'Islam, Ethnography and Politics: Methodological Issues in Researching amongst West Yorkshire Pakistanis in 2005'. *International Journal of Social Research Methodology* 10, no. 4 (2007): 279–93.

Buijs, Frank, Froukje Demant, and Atef Hamdy. *Strijders van eigen bodem. Radicale en democratische moslims in Nederland*. Amsterdam: Amsterdam University Press, 2006.

al-Bukhārī, Muḥammad b. Ismāʿīl. *Ṣaḥīḥ al-Bukhārī*. Cairo: Dār al-Fikr, 1966.

Couch, Danielle, and Pranee Liamputtong. 'Online Dating and Mating: The Use of the Internet to Meet Sexual Partners'. *Qualitative Health Research* 18, no. 2 (2008): 268–79.

Dahlberg, Lincoln. 'The Internet and Democratic Discourse: Exploring the Prospects of Online Deliberative Forums Extending the Public Sphere'. *Information, Communication & Society* 4, no. 4 (2001): 615–33.

Davis, Teresa. 'Third Spaces or Heterotopias? Recreating and Negotiating Migrant Identity Using Online Spaces'. *Sociology* 44, no. 4 (2010): 661–77.

du Plessis, Gitte. 'Enjoy Your Vacation!'. *Ephemera* 15, no. 4 (2015): 755–72.

Duke, Lisa. 'Black in a Blonde World: Race and Girls' Interpretations of the Feminine

Ideal in Teen Magazines'. *Journalism & Mass Communication Quarterly* 77, no. 2 (2000): 367–92.

Dunleavy, Patrick, Richard Heffernan, Philip Cowley, and Colin Hay, eds. *Developments in British Politics*. 8th ed. London and New York: Palgrave Macmillan, 2006.

Dunleavy, Patrick. 'The Westminster Model and the Distinctiveness of British Politics'. In *Developments in British Politics*, 8th ed., edited by Patrick Dunleavy, Richard Heffernan, Philip Cowley, and Colin Hay, 315–41. London and New York: Palgrave Macmillan, 2006.

Esposito, John L., ed. *The Oxford Dictionary of Islam*. New York: Oxford University Press, 2004.

Fleischmann, Fenella, Karen Phalet, and Olivier Klein. 'Religious Identification and Politicization in the Face of Discrimination: Support for Political Islam and Political Action among the Turkish and Moroccan Second Generation in Europe'. *British Journal of Social Psychology* 50, no. 4 (2011): 628–48.

Grillo, Ralph. 'Islam and Transnationalism'. *Journal of Ethnic and Migration Studies* 30, no. 5 (2004): 861–78.

Gudelunas, David. 'There's an App for That: The Uses and Gratifications of Online Social Networks for Gay Men'. *Sexuality & Culture* 16, no. 4 (2012): 347–65.

Haferkamp, Nina, Sabrina C. Eimler, Anna-Margarita Papadakis, and Jana Vanessa Kruck. 'Men Are from Mars, Women Are from Venus? Examining Gender Differences in Self-Presentation on Social Networking Sites'. *Cyberpsychology, Behavior, and Social Networking* 15, no. 2 (2012): 91–98.

Hart, Matt. 'Youth Intimacy on Tumblr: A Pilot Study'. *Young* 23, no. 3 (2015): 193–208.

Heino, Rebecca D., Nicole B. Ellison, and Jennifer L. Gibbs. 'Relationshopping: Investigating the Market Metaphor in Online Dating'. *Journal of Social and Personal Relationships* 27, no. 4 (2010): 427–47.

Hoge, Dean R., Gregory H. Petrillo, and Ella I. Smith. 'Transmission of Religious and Social Values from Parents to Teenage Children'. *Journal of Marriage and the Family* 44, no. 3 (1982): 569–80.

al-Shawkānī, Muḥammad b. ʿAlī. *Nayl al-awṭār*. Lahore, 1967.

Inge, Anabel. *The Making of a Salafi Muslim Woman: Paths to Conversion*. New York: Oxford University Press, 2016.

Jenkins, Richard. *Rethinking Ethnicity: Arguments and Explorations*. London: Sage, 1997.

Jensen, Jan Moller. 'The Relationships between Socio-demographic Variables, Travel Motivations and Subsequent Choice of Vacation'. 2nd International Conference on Economics, Business and Management, 2011, 37–44.

Johnson, Michael P., John P. Caughlin, and Ted L. Huston. 'The Tripartite Nature of Marital Commitment: Personal, Moral, and Structural Reasons to Stay Married'. *Journal of Marriage and the Family* 61, no. 1 (1999): 160–77.

Kahani-Hopkins, Vered, and Nick Hopkins. '"Representing" British Muslims: The Strategic Dimension to Identity Construction'. *Ethnic and Racial Studies* 25, no. 2 (2002): 288–309.
Kalliny, Morris, and Angela Hausman. 'The Impact of Cultural and Religious Values on Adoption of Innovation'. *Academy of Marketing Studies Journal* 11, no. 1 (2007): 125–36.
Katz, Elihu, Jay G. Blumler, and Michael Gurevitch. 'Uses and Gratifications Research'. *Public Opinion Quarterly* 37, no. 4 (1973): 509–23.
Keane, Webb. 'The Evidence of the Senses and the Materiality of Religion', in 'The Objects of Evidence: Anthropological Approaches to the Production of Knowledge'. Special issue, *Journal of the Royal Anthropological Institute* 14, no. S1 (2008): S110–S127.
Khan, Jemima. 'The Marriage Business'. *New Statesman*, 15 March 2012, 32–35.
Kim, Young Yun, and Kelly McKay-Semmler. 'Social Engagement and Cross-cultural Adaptation: An Examination of Direct- and Mediated Interpersonal Communication Activities of Educated Non-natives in the United States'. *International Journal of Intercultural Relations* 37, no. 1 (2013): 99–112.
Leeman, Alex B. 'Interfaith Marriage in Islam: An Examination of the Legal Theory behind the Traditional and Reformist Positions'. *Indiana Law Journal* 84, no. 2 (2009): 743–71.
Lewis, Justin, Sut Jhally, and Michael Morgan. *The Gulf War: A Study of the Media, Public Opinion and Public Knowledge*. Amherst: Center for the Study of Communication Research Archives, Department of Communication, University of Massachusetts, 1991.
Lo, Mbaye, and Taimoor Aziz. 'Muslim Marriage Goes Online: The Use of Internet Matchmaking by American Muslims'. *The Journal of Religion and Popular Culture* 21, no. 3 (2009): 5–5.
McAdams, Dan P., and Bradley D. Olson. 'Personality Development: Continuity and Change over the Life Course'. *Annual Review of Psychology* 61 (2010): 517–42.
McLoughlin, Seán. 'Researching Muslim Minorities: Some Reflections on Fieldwork in Britain'. In *Studies in Islamic and Middle Eastern Texts and Traditions in Memory of Norman Calder*, edited by Gerald Richard Hawting, Jawid Ahmad Mojaddedi, and Alexander Samely, 175–94. Oxford: Oxford University Press, 2000.
Mishra, Smeeta, Mathukutty M. Monippally, and Krishna P. Jayakar. 'Self Presentation in Online Environments: A Study of Indian Muslim Matrimonial Profiles'. *Asian Journal of Communication* 23, no. 1 (2013): 38–53.
Moors, Annelies. 'Unregistered Islamic Marriages: Anxieties about Sexuality and Islam in the Netherlands'. *Applying Sharia in the West: Facts, Fears and the Future of Islamic Rules on Family Relations in the West*, edited by Maurits S. Berger, 141–64. Leiden: Leiden University Press, 2013.

Nelson, Judith A., Amy Manning Kirk, Pedra Ane, and Sheryl A. Serres. 'Religious and Spiritual Values and Moral Commitment in Marriage: Untapped Resources in Couples Counseling?'. *Counseling and Values* 55, no. 2 (2011): 228–46.

Nesi, Jacqueline, and Mitchell J. Prinstein. 'Using Social Media for Social Comparison and Feedback-Seeking: Gender and Popularity Moderate Associations with Depressive Symptoms'. *Journal of Abnormal Child Psychology* 43, no. 8 (2015): 1427–38.

Nyang, Sulayman S. 'Convergence and Divergence in an Emergent Community: A Study of Challenges Facing U.S. Muslims'. In *The Muslims of America*, edited by Yvonne Z. Haddad, 236–49. New York: Oxford University Press, 1991.

Ory, David T., and Patricia L. Mokhtarian. 'When Is Getting There Half the Fun? Modeling the Liking for Travel'. *Transportation Research Part A: Policy and Practice* 39, no. 2–3 (2005): 97–123.

Pal, Jiban K. 'Social Networks Enabling Matrimonial Information Services in India'. *International Journal of Library and Information Science* 2, no. 4 (2010): 54–64.

Parameswaran, Radhika. 'Western Romance Fiction as English-Language Media in Postcolonial India'. *Journal of Communication* 49, no. 3 (1999): 84–105.

Rappaport, Roy A. *Ritual and Religion in the Making of Humanity*. Cambridge: Cambridge University Press, 1999.

Ryan, Tracii, Andrea Chester, John Reece, and Sophia Xenos. 'The Uses and Abuses of Facebook: A Review of Facebook Addiction'. *Journal of Behavioral Addictions* 3, no. 3 (2014): 133–48.

Schmeets, Hans, and Saskia te Riele. 'Declining Social Cohesion in the Netherlands?'. *Social Indicators Research* 115 (2014): 791–812.

Shao, Guosong. 'Understanding the Appeal of User-Generated Media: A Uses and Gratification Perspective'. *Internet Research* 19. no. 1 (2009): 7–25.

Steinkuehler, Constance A., and Dmitri Williams. 'Where Everybody Knows Your (Screen) Name: Online Games as "Third Places"'. *Journal of Computer-Mediated Communication* 11, no. 4 (2006): 885–909.

Stephure, Robert J., Susan D. Boon, Stacey L. MacKinnon, and Vicki L. Deveau. 'Internet Initiated Relationships: Associations between Age and Involvement in Online Dating'. *Journal of Computer-Mediated Communication* 14, no. 3 (2009): 658–81.

Sterckx, Leen. 'The Self-Arranged Marriage: Modern Muslim Courtship Practices in the Netherlands'. In *Everyday Life Practices of Muslims in Europe*, edited by Erkan Toğuşlu, 113–26. Leuven: Leuven University Press, 2015.

Sumter, Sindy R., Laura Vandenbosch, and Loes Ligtenberg. 'Love Me Tinder: Untangling Emerging Adults' Motivations for Using the Dating Application Tinder'. *Telematics and Informatics* 34, no. 1 (2017): 67–78.

Tarlo, Emma. *Visibly Muslim: Fashion, Politics, Faith*. London: Bloomsbury, 2010.

Tavory, Iddo. 'The Structure of Flirtation: On the Construction of Interactional Ambiguity'. In *Studies in Symbolic Interaction*, vol. 33, edited by Norman K. Denzin, 59–74. Bingley: Emerald, 2009.

Tolman, Deborah L., Meg I. Striepe, and Tricia Harmon. 'Gender Matters: Constructing a Model of Adolescent Sexual Health'. *Journal of Sex Research* 40, no. 1 (2003): 4–12.
Toma, Catalina L., Jeffrey T. Hancock, and Nicole B. Ellison. 'Separating Fact from Fiction: An Examination of Deceptive Self-Presentation in Online Dating Profiles'. *Personality and Social Psychology Bulletin* 34, no. 8 (2008): 1023–36.
Urista, Mark A., Qingwen Dong, and Kenneth D. Day. 'Explaining Why Young Adults Use MySpace and Facebook through Uses and Gratifications Theory'. *Human Communication* 12 (2009): 215–29.
Valkenburg, Patti M., and Jochen Peter. 'Who Visits Online Dating Sites? Exploring Some Characteristics of Online Daters'. *CyberPsychology & Behavior* 10, no. 6 (2007): 849–52.
Vidar Haukeland, Jan. 'Motives for Holiday Travel'. *The Tourist Review* 47, no. 2 (1992): 14–17.
Werbner, Pnina. 'Veiled Interventions in Pure Space: Honour, Shame and Embodied Struggles among Muslims in Britain and France'. *Theory, Culture & Society* 24, no. 2 (2007): 161–86.
Winchester, Daniel. 'Embodying the Faith: Religious Practice and the Making of a Muslim Moral Habitus'. *Social Forces* 86, no. 4 (2008): 1753–80.
Wright, Scott. 'From "Third Place" to "Third Space": Everyday Political Talk in Non-political Online Spaces'. *Javnost – The Public* 19, no. 3 (2012): 5–20.
Yilmaz, Ihsan. 'Marriage Solemnization among Turks in Britain: The Emergence of a Hybrid Anglo-Muslim Turkish Law'. *Journal of Muslim Minority Affairs* 24, no. 1 (2004): 57–66.
Yurchisin, Jennifer, Kittichai Watchravesringkan, and Deborah Brown McCabe. 'An Exploration of Identity Re-creation in the Context of Internet Dating'. *Social Behavior and Personality: An International Journal* 33, no. 8 (2005): 735–50.
Zwick, Detlev, and Cristian Chelariu. 'Mobilizing the *Hijab*: Islamic Identity Negotiation in the Context of a Matchmaking Website'. *Journal of Consumer Beh*

Marital Disputes and the Pursuit of Justice

'In Islam, raising one's voice against cruelty (*ẓulm*) is the greatest jihad,' the judge (*qāżī*) said.[1] It was January 2020, and we were sitting in the qazi's empty room, he behind his desk and I on the bench in front of it. Between us, piles of case files were neatly stacked awaiting the qazi's attention. I had asked the qazi what sustained him in his work, which primarily entails hearing and adjudicating marital disputes. His response was that this work of marital dispute adjudication was part of a struggle against *ẓulm* and for justice. 'Allah does not like cruelty,' he had told me, 'and in our department we struggle and raise our voices against cruelty and for justice (*inṣāf*). For this reason, I like my work.'

The qazi works at an Islamic institution called the Imarat Shariah, which is located in Bihar, India. The Imarat Shariah was founded in 1921 to serve Muslims in the region and it remains an important Islamic institution.[2] The Imarat Shariah runs a hospital that offers inexpensive treatment to anyone in need of care; its treasury department raises money and provides relief to those affected by natural disasters such as flooding that are a regular part of life in Bihar. Education is another key area of intervention, and the Imarat Shariah supports a large number of madrasas throughout Bihar, and the neighbouring states of Orissa and Jharkhand. The legal department of the Imarat Shariah offers authoritative advice in fatwas and helps Muslim families to settle disputes in its *dār ul-qażā*s ('Sharīʿa courts').[3] The *dār ul-qażā* in which I was sitting with the qazi is the centre of a network of sixty-five courts scattered throughout Bihar, Orissa and Jharkhand, for which it also serves as an appellate court. The *dār ul-qażā* at the Imarat Shariah is in practice a matrimonial court specialising in cases of women-initiated separation and divorce, though occasionally Muslims bring conflicts over inheritance

1 '*ẓulm ke khilāf āwāz uṫhānā sabse baṙā jihād hay*'.

2 Papiya Ghosh, *Community and Nation: Essays on Identity and Politics in Eastern India* (New Delhi: Oxford University Press, 2008); Mohammad Sajjad, *Muslim Politics in Bihar: Changing Contours* (New Delhi: Routledge, 2014).

3 The Imarat Shariah maintains an informative website that outlines its aims and activities: www.imaratshariah.com/.

and other kinds of property.[4] According to my analysis of the *dār ul-qażā*'s case registry, it heard 1888 cases, at a rate of between 300 and 450 per year, between 2014 and 2019. Of these cases, the majority were women-initiated divorces while about 35 per cent were cases initiated by husbands who wanted their wives to return home. As the qazi said to me, 'many of the cases at the *dār ul-qażā* are brought by women because they suffer a great deal of cruelty in India.'[5] The qazi cited a recent case to illustrate this point. He told me that a brother and a sister approached the *dār ul-qażā* because the brother was denying the sister her share (*ḥiṣṣa*) of the inheritance. During the course of the hearing, the qazi explained that according to fiqh the sister was entitled to her share and that failing to give her this share created *ẓulm*. The qazi thus alleviated *ẓulm* at two levels: he convinced the brother that his sister should also receive her due, thereby addressing some of her financial hardships; and he educated both brother and sister on their entitlements according to fiqh, which has the potential to impact other inheritance disputes.

The qazi with whom I was speaking has worked in the *dār ul-qażā* for about twenty years, having received his training to become both a mufti and a qazi at the Imarat Shariah. From his perspective, the court's main aim is to increase the justice in people's lives. He told me that many people think that in preparation for the hereafter (*ākharat*) it is most important to pray or to give money to the poor. But this, he insists, is not the only way to achieve reward (*thawāb*) in the hereafter. He quoted a *ḥadīth* that says that giving a single just judgement is equivalent to seventy years of worship (*'ibādat*). The reason for the importance of hearing cases justly is that unlike prayer, which is for yourself (*āp ke liye*), the work of increasing justice is for society as a whole (*samaj ke liye hay*).

In this paper, I argue that in the face of the conditions of immiseration in which many litigants live, the qazis seek justice by helping women to address concerns about their individual marriages. An analysis of case hearings provides insight into the expectations men and women have of marriage and of the resources on which the qazi draws to provide greater justice in marriage. Because marriage as an institution bears on emotional and material relations between spouses and family members it is a site of negotiation. The notion of *inṣāf* reflects and responds to changing wishes for and assumptions about marriage as well as to Islamic understandings of rights and responsibilities in marriage; yet the possibility of providing justice is circumscribed by material conditions. In what follows, the paper offers an account of the overall

4 The *dār ul-qażā* does sometimes hear property disputes concerning inheritance and land. However, the vast majority of the cases that they adjudicate are marital disputes. See also Jeff Redding, *A Secular Need: Islamic Law and State Governance in Contemporary India* (Seattle: University of Washington Press, 2020).

5 *'India main unka ẓulm zyāda hota hay'.*

situation of Muslims in this part of India and of the relationship between the Imarat Shariah and the Indian legal system to situate the *dār ul-qażās*' work and the divorce disputes they hear. It then develops an outline of expectations in marriage derived from litigants' claims and qazis' responses and shows how rights and justice in marriage link emotional and material conditions, making the two interdependent. Ultimately, the paper suggests that because marriage as an institution is at once individual and individualising and also inextricably bound up with broader socio-economic conditions, the qazis' work to increase the justice in individual marriages (often by helping spouses to negotiate a divorce) is essential but limited in its possible effects.

MATERIAL CONDITIONS AND LAW

Indian qazis adjudicate cases within a context where they and the individuals they serve are marginalised: while Muslims in general are among the most disenfranchised of India's citizens, qazis are marginalised in relation to the legal system. Muslims comprise 14.2 per cent of the population of India, with a population of 172 million.[6] The most recent Indian census, from 2011, found that 43 per cent of Indian Muslims are illiterate, 48 per cent of Muslim women and 38 per cent of Muslim men.[7] *The Times of India* has reported that 30 per cent of the prison population are Muslim,[8] while they are statistically disadvantaged when it comes to employment and housing.[9] In Bihar, Muslims constitute 16.5 per cent of the population but only 6 per cent of the

6 Stephanie Kramer, 'Religious Composition of India', 21 September 2021, Pew Research Center, www.pewresearch.org/religion/2021/09/21/population-growth-and-religious-composition/. It is important to note that Bihar is a state with a slightly larger proportion of Muslims. The 2011 census found that 16.8 per cent of the population of Bihar, 17.5 million people, identify as Muslim (www.census2011.co.in/data/religion/state/10-bihar.html).

7 The census found that 44 per cent of Indian women overall and 30 per cent of Indian men overall are illiterate.

8 Vignesh Radhakrishnan and Jasmin Nihalani, 'Over 30% of Detainees in Indian Prisons Are Muslims, Double Their Share in Population', The Hindu, 13 September 2022, https://www.thehindu.com/data/over-30-of-detainees-in-indian-prisons-are-muslims-double-their-share-in-population/article65882525.ece.

9 Amit Pandya writes: 'In the Indian Administrative Service, the elite officers of the public services, Muslims account for less than 3 percent as compared with their 13.5 percent proportion of the Indian population. Among district judges in a sample of 15 states surveyed, Muslims again constituted less than 3 percent. These figures improve slightly for the Indian Police Service (the centrally recruited and assigned elite officer cadre for police forces throughout India—4 percent), high court judges (more than 4 percent), and judicial officers (more than 6 percent), but are still short of their share of the population.' Amit A. Pandya, *Muslim Indians: Struggle for Inclusion* (Washington, DC: Stimpson, 2010), 18.

police force.[10] Zoya Hasan and Ritu Menon's 2004 study of Muslim women in India found that in spite of the diversity between Muslim women, studies on them 'reiterate that the majority are among the most disadvantaged, economically impoverished, and politically marginalized sections of Indian society today'.[11] The overall picture painted by these statistics is reflected in the *dār ul-qażā*, where most litigants have little property, are unemployed, or perform low-wage work, live in precarious housing, often with inadequate and unreliable electricity and sanitation, and are illiterate or semi-literate. At the same time, this is not true of all litigants, some of whom are wealthy, high status, and highly educated. The qazis at the Imarat Shariah thus attend to people most of whom struggle to make ends meet.

Qazis occupy a marginal place in relation to the legal system.[12] Beginning in the eighteenth century, and accelerating in the nineteenth and early twentieth centuries, British colonial administrators introduced significant legal reforms in India, both centralising the legal system as a whole and limiting the jurisdiction of religious law to family matters.[13] Concomitant with these centralisation efforts, British legal reforms removed both qazis and Hindu religious authorities from their posts. These authorities were replaced with British judges trained in common law and in the state's version of religious personal law. At independence in 1947, the reconfigured and secularised legal system was incorporated into the constitution and the religious personal law system remains in force.[14] Partly as a consequence of this legal organisation, family law,

10 Ibid.

11 Zoya Hasan and Ritu Menon, *Unequal Citizens: A Study of Muslim Women in India* (New Delhi: Oxford University Press, 2004), 3.

12 This even though – as Redding, *Secular Need*, and Katherine Lemons, *Divorcing Traditions: Islamic Marriage Law and the Making of Indian Secularism* (New York: Cornell University Press, 2019), have both argued – the secular state relies on *dār ul-qażā*s and other religious adjudication institutions to help respond to marital disputes.

13 The literature documenting and analysing these changes is immense and important. Several significant studies of Muslim personal law reforms in particular include Scott Alan Kugle, 'Framed, Blamed and Renamed: The Recasting of Islamic Jurisprudence in Colonial South Asia', *Modern Asian Studies* 35, no. 2 (2001): 257–313; Julia Stephens, *Governing Islam: Law, Empire, and Secularism in Modern South Asia* (Cambridge: Cambridge University Press, 2018); Rachel Sturman, *The Government of Social Life in Colonial India: Liberalism, Religious Law, and Women's Rights* (New York: Cambridge University Press, 2012); Rina Verma Williams, *Postcolonial Politics and Personal Laws: Colonial Legal Legacies and the Indian State* (New Delhi: Oxford University Press, 2006).

14 For some of the many excellent studies of postcolonial personal law, see Flavia Agnes, *Family Law*, vol. 1, *Family Laws and Constitutional Claims* (New Delhi: Oxford University Press, 2011); Flavia Agnes, *Family Law*, vol. 2, *Marriage, Divorce and Matrimonial Litigation* (New Delhi: Oxford University Press, 2012); Gerald James Larson, *Religion and Personal Law in Secular India: A Call to Judgment* (Bloomington: Indiana University Press, 2001); Werner Menski, *Modern Indian Family Law* (Richmond, England: Curzon Press, 2001); B. Sivaramayya, Archana Parashar, and

and Muslim divorce in particular, has been deeply politicised in postcolonial India, especially since the 1980s, with several consequences.[15] On the one hand, as Hasan and Menon have noted, inequality in personal law is often treated as the single relevant explanation of Muslim women's overall marginality, belying the significance of material immiseration.[16] Secondly, politicisation of divorce has made Muslim women reticent to approach state courts with their marital disputes.

However, in spite of their efforts to centralise and control legal processes, neither colonial administrators nor postcolonial legislators have exhaustive reach. As the British worked to consolidate a centralised legal system, religious legal authorities established their own forums. These included Hindu panchayats but also Islamic legal institutions such as *dār ul-qażās*.[17] The Imarat Shariah is one such institution. While the Imarat Shariah and other religious institutions do not issue legally binding judgements, *dār ul-qażās*' right to provide mediation and advice to people who approach them has recently been upheld in the Indian Supreme Court.[18]

In contemporary India, materially and legally marginalised and struggling with gender inequality both in their families and in courts, many women in unworkable marriages turn not to the state's family courts but instead to non-state institutions like the *dār ul-qażā*. Some approach the institution because they wish to secure a religiously recognised divorce, but they also choose to approach it because it is more

---

Amita Dhanda, *Redefining Family Law in India: Essays in Honour of B. Sivaramayya* (New Delhi: Routledge, 2008); Narendra Subramanian, *Nation and Family: Personal Law, Cultural Pluralism, and Gendered Citizenship in India* (Stanford: Stanford University Press, 2020); Gopika Solanki, *Adjudication in Religious Family Laws: Cultural Accommodation, Legal Pluralism, and Gender Equality in India* (Cambridge: Cambridge University Press, 2011).

15 One watershed moment of politicisation was the 1986 Supreme Court decision in the so-called Shah Bano case, which entailed a large public debate about Muslim women's rights in marriage. On this important topic, see e.g. Zakia Pathak and Rajeswari Sunder Rajan, 'Shahbano', in *Feminists Theorize the Political*, ed. Judith Butler and Joan W. Scott (New York: Routledge, 1992), 257–79. On the politics of Muslim personal law more generally, see e.g. Flavia Agnes, *Law and Gender Inequality: The Politics of Women's Rights in India* (New Delhi: Oxford University Press, 2001).

16 Hasan and Menon, *Unequal Citizens*.

17 On the history of such legal practices in the eighteenth century, see Elizabeth Lhost, *Everyday Islamic Law and the Making of Modern South Asia* (Chapel Hill: University of North Carolina Press, 2022). On later colonial and postcolonial Muslim legal institutions, see Mengia Hong Tschalaer, *Muslim Women's Quest for Justice: Gender, Law and Activism in India* (Cambridge: Cambridge University Press, 2017); Lemons, *Divorcing Traditions*; Solanki, *Adjudication*; Sylvia Vatuk, 'Extra-Judicial *Khul'* Divorce in India's Muslim Personal Law', *Islamic Law and Society* 26, no. 1–2 (2019): 111–48; Sylvia Vatuk, *Marriage and Its Discontents: Women, Islam and the Law in India* (New Delhi: Women Unlimited, 2017).

18 Vishwa Lochan Madan v. Union of India (2014), Writ Petition 386 of 2005, SC. For analyses, see Lemons, *Divorcing Traditions*; and Redding, *Secular Need*.

affordable and efficient than Indian state courts, and because clerks and other staff assist litigants as they make their way through the bureaucracy. In many ways, then, the Imarat Shariah is an institution for the disenfranchised and the *dār ul-qażā* their court.[19]

METHODS

I have carried out ethnographic and archival research at the Imarat Shariah from 2017 through 2022. The research has taken place during regular visits of several weeks to a month each and continuity has been made possible with the help of my research assistant, Nadia Hussain, who is trained in law and is herself from Patna. During this time, I have observed about forty cases, taking notes on the hearings, interviewing litigants, studying case files, and talking with judges once decisions were finalised. My research assistant and I have been able to follow a handful of cases throughout their entire trajectory and to talk with litigants months and years after their cases were decided. My ethnographic research is complemented by a careful study of the *dār ul-qażās*' case archives, in which I have read over a hundred case files. I have also systematically studied the Imarat Shariah's weekly newspaper and biographies of the institution's leaders, giving me a sense of its broader aims and work. While informed by this broad swath of research, this paper focuses on several cases I have studied in order to draw out a granular account of women's and men's expectations of and disappointments with marriage.

WOMEN-INITIATED DIVORCE IN THE DĀR UL-QAŻĀ

Women can file for two different types of divorce at the *dār ul-qażā*: *faskh* and *khul*ʿ. Although both *faskh* and *khul*ʿ are women-initiated divorces, they are juridically distinct. A *faskh* is a judicial divorce given for cause, which means that it is the qazi who executes the divorce once he has established, by means of an adversarial court process, that the wife has grounds for divorce.[20] At the time of divorce by *faskh* the

19 Catherine Larouche and I have shown in a small-scale study of family courts that Muslim women rarely file personal law cases in these courts, demonstrating their marginality to the formal legal system. See Catherine Larouche and Katherine Lemons, 'The Narrowness of Muslim Personal Law: Practices of Legal Harmonization in a Delhi Family Court', *The Journal of Legal Pluralism and Unofficial Law* 52, no. 3 (2020): 308–29.

20 According both to the qazis and to the scholarship on Muslim divorce in India, the grounds for *faskh* are: a husband has gone missing for a period of time; failure to provide maintenance; abuse/danger to the wife's life; severe illness; lengthy imprisonment; or a woman's unyielding refusal to live with her husband. See Tahir Mahmood, *The Muslim Law of India, 3rd ed.* (Delhi:

husband owes his wife any of her *mahr* (dower) that has not yet been paid, property or jewellery that she brought with her to the marriage, and monetary support during *ʿiddat*, the three-month waiting period during which she may not remarry (*ʿiddat kharch*), for her and for any minor children while they remain in her custody.

Khulʿ, on the other hand, is executed not by the qazi but by the husband. As long as husband and wife agree that they are not able to live up to the ethical and legal requirements of marriage and agree on the terms of the divorce, the husband is authorised to pronounce a divorce. In India it is usual that the wife forgives some portion of what is owed to her, either in order to convince her husband to grant her a *khulʿ* or in exchange for it.[21] At the Imarat Shariah, wives divorced by *khulʿ* typically give up their *mahr* and *ʿiddat kharch*, and not infrequently also forfeit any property still in the marital family's possession. Generally, women retain custody of any children in both *faskh* and *khulʿ*.[22] Formally, then, *faskh* is a divorce in the course of which women receive some material or financial settlement, whereas *khulʿ* is a divorce for which she must compensate her husband. Based on patterns of petitions at the *dār ul-qażā* women more readily apply for *faskh* than *khulʿ*.

UNHAPPY MARRIAGES

The women and men who approach the *dār ul-qażā* usually do so because their marriages are not working.[23] As noted earlier, most cases at the *dār ul-qażā* stem from marriages to which wives object. They express these objections either by filing cases for divorce or by moving out of their marital homes, following which their husbands have filed cases with the *dār ul-qażā* in an effort to bring them back. An overview of the reasons for which women leave or file for divorce offers insight into spouses' views of and expectations for marriage; because this data was collected in a court

LexisNexis Butterworths, 2002). Although the *dār ul-qażā* follows the Ḥanafī legal tradition of the majority of Indian Muslims, these grounds are based on Mālikī law. Notably, these are the grounds for divorce provided under the 1939 Dissolution of Muslim Marriages Act (DMMA). The overlap is not a coincidence but is because both the DMMA and the *dār ul-qażā* refer to the collaborative fatwa collection *al-Ḥīla*, composed by Ashraf Ali Thanwi during the colonial period. See Lemons, *Divorcing Traditions*; and Muhammad Qasim Zaman, *Ashraf ʿAli Thanawi: Islam in Modern South Asia* (New York: Oneworld, 2012).

21 Mahmood, *Muslim Law of India*.

22 Husbands do, sometimes, argue that they want to have custody of children with whom they have no relationship in order to pressure their wives to agree to financial terms beneficial to the husband.

23 Married couples do also approach the Imarat Shariah's legal wing to register their marriages. The steady flow of newly-weds coming to register their marriages means that the corridors of the *dār ul-qażā* contain the many sides of marriage: as a promise, the site of disillusionment, or the source and object of the full range of human emotion.

setting, the allegations also provide insight specifically into the kinds of issues litigants think will be compelling to Islamic judges. The consequence is that they teach us about ordinary Muslims' understandings of rights and responsibilities in marriage. The most common allegations raised by wives are that their husbands fail to support them materially, that they are subjected to violence by their husbands and/or their families, and that their husbands fail to be sexually or emotionally present. Women also approach the *dār ul-qażā* with complaints that their mobility and autonomy are unjustly constrained by their husbands or marital kin or that their husbands have married several wives whom they fail to treat equally.[24] The following cases offer specific examples of each type of complaint.

CASE 1: ABANDONMENT

One exemplary case, which I observed in the summer of 2017, illustrates both the significance of material abandonment and its entanglement with violence and with other forms of loss. In the afternoon of this case, I had been called into the chief judge's (*qāżī sharīʿat*) room to observe a divorce hearing. Prior to entering the judge's room, I had met Zeenat – the complainant in the case – and her mother who, like me and my research assistant, had been biding their time in the Ladies' Waiting Room down the hall over the lunch break. They told us that Zeenat had married in 2006 but had rarely lived with her husband during the intervening eleven years. Initially, Zeenat's husband worked in Jaipur in the state of Rajasthan selling shoes, stones, and costume jewellery, while Zeenat lived with her new in-laws in a village in Bihar. Zeenat had a particularly tense relationship with her *bahābī* (her husband's older brother's wife), whom she accused of having a long-standing affair with her husband. According to Zeenat, a year following her marriage and fed up with the feeling that her husband was avoiding her, she went unannounced to Jaipur. To her husband's apparent annoyance, she stayed for several months. During this time, she became pregnant by him, with twins. The children did not help her relationship with her in-laws and seemed to displease her husband. After another year with her in-laws, Zeenat returned to her parents' home where she lived until 2017 when she approached the *dār ul-qażā* for a *khulʿ* divorce.

Between 2008, when she moved out of her in-laws' home, and 2017, when she approached the *dār ul-qażā*, Zeenat and her husband periodically brought cases against one another in state courts. In 2009, Zeenat told us she sued in civil court for her husband to return from Jaipur.[25] She won this case, but her husband never

24 In India, Muslim men are legally entitled to marry up to four wives.

25 This claim is somewhat difficult to understand because restitution of conjugal rights case law grants Muslim men but not Muslim women the right to petition for it. I have also never seen

obeyed the court's order. Zeenat had also brought a case under the Criminal Procedure Code 125 – for maintenance[26] (material support to which a wife is entitled, and which includes money, housing, clothing, food) – and one under 498A – for protection against domestic violence.[27] The maintenance claim had yielded an order with which the defendant never complied, and the domestic violence suit was ongoing. Zeenat's husband, meanwhile, had filed a case for guardianship of the children that had been through several stages of appeal. The Jaipur High Court had granted the defendant custody but, according to Zeenat, her appeal to the Supreme Court had stayed that order. At the time of the *dār ul-qażā* case, it seemed that her chief worry was that she would lose custody of her children.

The hearing at the *dār ul-qażā* lasted two days. The second day, when my research assistant and I were present, both parties and their family members appeared before the qazi. They had already decided on a *khulʿ* divorce, and the qazi helped them negotiate the terms. Once the terms of this *khulʿ* had been decided, the qazi wrote out the divorce agreement, or *khulʿanāma*. The agreement was provisional, divorce contingent on the parties withdrawing all other cases against each other in state courts. In exchange for the *khulʿ*, Zeenat relinquished her *ʿiddat* maintenance, but not the part of the *mahr* she was promised at marriage (25,000 Indian rupees or 243 pounds sterling). She promised to petition to close the domestic violence case. The one thing that was left hanging, to Zeenat's great chagrin, was the matter of custody, which the qazi opaquely said they would deal with at a later date, 'according to the Sharīʿa'.

In our conversations with Zeenat, it was never clear why in 2017 she had decided to bring the case to the qazi. She did suggest, though, that she wished to end the drawn-out and fruitless series of court cases that kept her tied to her husband. The other possibility, which several women stated explicitly in discussions of their cases, was that she no longer wanted to be in limbo – neither in a relationship with her husband nor divorced from him. Whatever the specific reason, when she turned to the qazi it was no longer with property or domestic violence complaints but to obtain a divorce. Her complaints both in the *dār ul-qażā* and in the state courts suggest that her dissatisfaction was both material and emotional. Her husband had abrogated on his responsibility to provide for her and had also failed to live with her or to offer emotional support to her or their children.

a case of *rukhsatī* (a petition for the spouse to return) initiated by a wife in the *dār ul-qażās*. As I did not have access to the full case file in this case, and do not know if it included the civil court petition, I do not know what legal statute this refers to.

26 CrPC 125 allows 'destitute and abandoned or deserted wives or children to claim maintenance from their husbands or children, respectively'.

27 CrPC 498A stipulates: 'Whoever, being husband or the relative of the husband of a woman, subjects women to cruelty shall be punished with imprisonment for a term which may extend to three years and shall also be liable to fine.'

CASE 2: MARITAL RIGHTS

While the question of material support is an overwhelming factor in divorce cases, sex is also frequently an issue. Litigants and qazis invoke *ḥaqīqat zaujiyat* or 'rights in marriage' to refer to spouses' obligation to be sexually available to one another. Sometimes, discussions of *ḥaqīqat zaujiyat* entail allegations that a polygynous husband is treating his wives unequally. Here, the allegation that he is not providing his wife with her marital rights has emotional overtones. In other cases, though, the discussion touches on wives' right to sex, which is sometimes linked to the expectation that one outcome of marriage should be biological reproduction.

I observed one such case at the Imarat Shariah's branch court in Ranchi, Jharkhand, about 400 kilometres south of the Patna headquarters in September 2019. The plaintiff in the case had married five months before approaching the qazi for a divorce. The qazi sought information about the case from the litigants, their families, and the head of the village committee in the place where the couple lived. Quickly, the discussion turned to the allegation that the husband was unable to have sexual intercourse. In order to pursue this allegation more discreetly, the qazi dismissed everyone but the plaintiff, with whom he spoke alone (though my research assistant and I were permitted to stay in the room). The qazi asked the plaintiff why she did not want to live with her husband. She argued that no woman should be expected to live with this man, as he was not only unable to establish a sexual relationship, but he also had other disabilities, including problems with his memory and an inability to travel independently. After trying to convince the plaintiff to stay with her husband, arguing that appropriate medical interventions could help him, the qazi accepted the plaintiff's statement that she was not able to live with her husband.[28] Before he called her husband and the spouses' families back into his room, the plaintiff raised another issue with the qazi. She told him that her family was poor, and that she therefore wanted her husband's family to return the goods (*sāmān*) that her family had given to them at the time of the marriage. She also asked to receive her *ʿiddat kharch*, money to support her during the three-month period following divorce during which she cannot remarry. This request highlights women's awareness of the financial entailments of marriage and of the material consequences of divorce, which often put them and their families at a disadvantage.

The qazi called everyone back into his office and informed them that the plaintiff was unwilling to reconcile with her husband and that she requested that her property be returned and *ʿiddat kharch* paid. The news infuriated her father-in-law, who raised his voice in indignation, asking why they should return anything when the marriage

28 She said, '*mayn tayyār nahīn hūnh*' (I am not ready).

had never even been consummated. In reply, the qazi politely asked the families and committee head to go to the adjacent waiting room and together figure out what they were going to do about the property. When they returned, twenty minutes later, the defendant's father agreed to return the wedding gifts and the property the bride had brought into the marriage; she forgave the interim maintenance (*ʿiddat kharch*) and her dower (*mahr*). The qazi printed the divorce agreement (*khulʿanāma*) he had typed on his computer, and as the document reported, the defendant pronounced a *ṭalāq ul-bȧin* (unilateral divorce), ending the marriage. The qazi collected signatures or fingerprints from everyone present and recorded next to each signature the relationship between the signatory and the litigants.

This is one of many cases that highlight the significance of marriage as an arrangement of sexuality. The inability or unwillingness to provide *ḥaqīqat zaujīyat* is an adequate ground for women to seek divorce. In this case the allegation is of impotence, while in other instances women allege that their husbands do not treat multiple wives equally. During the course of divorce procedures, women and men regularly claim that their spouses have had affairs, which is also a betrayal of the sexual rights of and in marriage.

CASE 3: AUTONOMY AND PARTNERSHIP

Marriage and expectations that men and women have of it are also a site for negotiating changing aspirations, as I have argued elsewhere. Some women approach the *dār ul-qażā* because their aspirations are incompatible with the demands their husbands or in-laws make on them.[29] In one such case, a litigant I call Rukhsana was summoned to the *dār ul-qażā* by her husband because she had moved out of the marital household; during the course of the *dār ul-qażā* hearings, she sought to establish an ethical marriage predicated on a partnership between spouses.[30] In this case, Rukhsana challenged the management of the household economy, and in particular her husband's efforts to control that economy. She also argued for the right to work for wages outside of the home, which she saw as necessary to a good life for herself, her husband, and their children. In my interpretation, this case concerns women's changing expectations for their relationship to their spouses and children, one that is more of a partnership than a relation of dependence.

In other cases, the significance of the male breadwinner ideal, the view that one of a husband's primary duties is to financially support his wife (and children), is

29 Katherine Lemons with Nadia Hussain, 'The Ends of Divorce: Marital Dispute as a Locus of Social Change in India', in *Islamic Divorce in the Twenty-First Century: A Global Perspective*, ed. Erin E. Styles and Ayang Utriza Yakin (New Brunswick: Rutgers University Press, 2022), 187–203.

30 Ibid.

debated in other ways.[31] For example, in one case a woman's parents encouraged her to seek *khulʿ* because her husband was unable to earn a sufficient income to support her and their children. After a brief separation the woman was able to reunite with her husband. At the time of their reunion, she expressed regret that she had not sought training to do some kind of piecework from home to help increase the family's earnings but more than that she was relieved and happy to be reunited with her husband. Notably, in both of these cases ideals of autonomy or of romance cannot be disentangled from financial concerns.

In each type of case, marriage appears to be an entanglement of economic and emotional concerns. Unlike other, more specialised institutions, marriage is tasked with providing emotional, physical, educational, and material well-being of its members. In the cases that come before the *dār ul-qażā*, extended families are often involved, yet the married couple is treated as the centre of these kin relations. Both the relation between spouses and relations with the larger kin group entail gendered hierarchy that is itself often a source of strife, as becomes particularly evident in cases that revolve around wives who wish to pursue their studies or work for wages outside the home. Marriage, then, at once entails relationships with the broader kin group while being the focal point of most allegations of cruelty.

THE INSTITUTION OF MARRIAGE: INDIVIDUAL AND SOCIAL

The three cases discussed above show that each marriage is individual, with its own characteristics, the site of unique relationships and conflicts. Inasmuch as they are exemplary, they also indicate how individual marriages are located within and affected by broader socio-economic circumstances. Whereas the specific issues in the three cases are distinct, it is not coincidental that all three concern finances, or what I have elsewhere referred to as the economy of the household.[32] Each of the women's claims around household economics is affected by an overall condition of economic insecurity. In each case, this broader condition of economic insecurity manifests itself differently: it is a question of whether the husband does or can earn (Case 1), of what kind of property settlement the wife will receive (Case 2), and of whether the wife is allowed to work for wages outside the home (Case 3).

Although less explicitly stated, all three of these cases also provide insight into how a broader context of gender inequality both plays out and elicits contestation in

31 This ideal, which I have discussed in Lemons, *Divorcing Traditions*, and Lemons with Hussain, 'Ends of Divorce', is pervasive in north India. For more, see Shalini Grover, *Marriage, Love, Caste, and Kinship Support: Lived Experiences of the Urban Poor in India* (Abingdon: Routledge, 2018).

32 Lemons with Hussain, 'Ends of Divorce'.

individual marriages. Case 1 is indicative of the assumed gendered divisions of labour that underwrite cases in the *dār ul-qażā* and most litigants' views of the entitlements of marriage. Thus, the plaintiff filed a case for maintenance because of the state's and *dār ul-qażās*' shared view that husbands are required to materially support their wives. Case 3, by contrast, where the plaintiff and wife performed waged work, most clearly illustrates how *dār ul-qażās* can be sites for contesting assumed gendered divisions of labour between spouses, and in particular the so-called male breadwinner ideal.[33] This does not mean that all women are satisfied with the outcomes of their cases. On more than one occasion, women litigants told me that they felt the qazis were not granting gender just decisions because, as in Case 2, they had to give up more property than they felt was fair in order to secure a divorce. Case 2 is a good illustration of this dynamic: the plaintiff was granted the divorce she requested, and the *dār ul-qażā* hearings served a place for the plaintiff to argue for property entitlements; yet she had to make financial compromises.

Finally, Case 2 draws attention to a prevalent theme in marital disputes in the *dār ul-qażā*: domestic violence. In this case, we have little information about the situation other than Zeenat's decision to file for relief under state law. She did tell the qazi that her husband treated her poorly and that she did not get along with her in-laws, with whom she was expected to live. These are common complaints, and domestic violence is often the reason women give for leaving their marital homes. Like the state courts, qazis consider domestic violence to be a ground for divorce, as it is an explicit form of cruelty. Each case of domestic violence is unique, but collectively allegations of domestic violence suggest that this is a significant aspect of marriage for many women and is thus also a broader social phenomenon.[34]

CONCLUSION

Faced with the particular conjunction of unique individual troubles and broader social dynamics, qazis who adjudicate marital disputes among Indian Muslims provide an essential but limited form of justice. Marriage, which is expected to offer financial and physical security, is often instead a site of insecurity – financial as well as physical and emotional. Divorce cases bring out these aspects of marriage. Those cases initiated by women at the same time draw attention to the possibilities that are available when women resist these conditions. As noted earlier, sometimes such resistance takes the form of simply leaving the marital home, often with children. But

33 I discuss this in ibid. at greater length.

34 See Srimati Basu, *The Trouble with Marriage: Feminists Confront Law and Violence in India* (Oakland: University of California Press, 2015).

at other times, it involves seeking divorce. Both types of resistance to marital distress are visible in the *dār ul-qażā*.

Qazis who hear divorces at the *dār ul-qażā* seek to help couples 'separate with kindness', and are in this way trying to alleviate cruelty and to increase justice. The qazi quoted at the beginning of the paper makes the important point that in a context of gender inequality, women are often the plaintiffs in these cases, as they are the ones seeking a fair settlement. For women in particular, divorce is essential because it enables them to exit violent households with the approval of religious authorities and because it enables them to remarry. Unlike men, women cannot marry multiple husbands. One consequence of this is that they can be left hanging – neither treated as wives nor divorced and therefore not authorised to remarry or to pursue other life goals. The qazis' willingness and ability to adjudicate divorce cases is, therefore, an essential service even though they are not in a position to address the broader conditions, in particular material immiseration, that surround and often shape these disputes.

Even though qazis are not in a position to address the material conditions of litigants, and in spite of the ways in which their assumptions reinscribe prevailing gender and kinship norms, the *dār ul-qażā* process can itself offers procedural justice. I have argued elsewhere that the *dār ul-qażā* is a place in which litigants, in particular women, can argue their cases and through them can seek to alter household arrangements.[35] Ziba Mir-Hosseini has made an analogous argument in her work on Iranian divorce courts: women who approach these courts argue vociferously with the judges, seeking particular outcomes.[36] In the *dār ul-qażā*, qazis insist that respect for one another's rights in marriage is crucial, and they therefore grant divorces in cases where such rights are denied. This reflects the sort of revision to the '*qiwama* postulate' that Mir-Hosseini has discussed: marriage is no longer only considered to be a matter of maintenance and obedience but also, even primarily, requires affection between spouses.[37] Inasmuch as the *dār ul-qażā* offers a place for negotiation and challenge for women in troubled marriages, it is a locus for the pursuit of *inṣāf*. Like other family law forums, the justice it can offer is important but limited.

BIBLIOGRAPHY

Agnes, Flavia. *Family Law*. Vol. 1, *Family Laws and Constitutional Claims*. New Delhi: Oxford University Press, 2011.

35 Lemons with Hussain, 'Ends of Divorce'.

36 Ziba Mir-Hosseini, *Marriage on Trial: Islamic Family Law in Iran and Morocco*, rev. ed. (London: I.B. Tauris, 2011).

37 Ziba Mir-Hosseini, Kari Vogt, Lena Larsen, and Christian Moe, eds., *Gender and Equality in Muslim Family Law: Justice and Ethics in the Islamic Legal Tradition* (London: I.B. Tauris, 2013).

Agnes, Flavia. *Family Law*. Vol. 2, *Marriage, Divorce and Matrimonial Litigation*. New Delhi: Oxford University Press, 2012.

Agnes, Flavia. *Law and Gender Inequality: The Politics of Women's Rights in India*. New Delhi: Oxford University Press, 2001.

Basu, Srimati. *The Trouble with Marriage: Feminists Confront Law and Violence in India*. Oakland: University of California Press, 2015.

Ghosh, Papiya. *Community and Nation: Essays on Identity and Politics in Eastern India*. New Delhi: Oxford University Press, 2008.

Grover, Shalini. *Marriage, Love, Caste, and Kinship Support: Lived Experiences of the Urban Poor in India*. Abingdon: Routledge, 2018.

Hasan, Zoya, and Ritu Menon. *Unequal Citizens: A Study of Muslim Women in India*. New Delhi: Oxford University Press, 2004.

Kugle, Scott Alan. 'Framed, Blamed and Renamed: The Recasting of Islamic Jurisprudence in Colonial South Asia'. *Modern Asian Studies* 35, no. 2 (2001): 257–313.

Larson, Gerald James. *Religion and Personal Law in Secular India: A Call to Judgment*. Bloomington: Indiana University Press, 2001.

Lemons, Katherine. *Divorcing Traditions: Islamic Marriage Law and the Making of Indian Secularism*. New York: Cornell University Press, 2019.

Lemons, Katherine, with Nadia Hussain. 'The Ends of Divorce: Marital Dispute as a Locus of Social Change in India'. In *Islamic Divorce in the Twenty-First Century: A Global Perspective*, edited by Erin E. Styles and Ayang Utriza Yakin, 187–203. New Brunswick: Rutgers University Press, 2022.

Lhost, Elizabeth. *Everyday Islamic Law and the Making of Modern South Asia*. Chapel Hill: University of North Carolina Press, 2022.

Mahmood, Tahir. *The Muslim Law of India*. 3rd ed. Delhi: LexisNexis Butterworths, 2002.

Menski, Werner. *Modern Indian Family Law*. Richmond, England: Curzon Press, 2001.

Mir-Hosseini, Ziba. *Marriage on Trial: Islamic Family Law in Iran and Morocco*. Revised ed. London: I.B. Tauris, 2011.

Mir-Hosseini, Ziba, Kari Vogt, Lena Larsen, and Christian Moe, eds. *Gender and Equality in Muslim Family Law: Justice and Ethics in the Islamic Legal Tradition*. London: I.B. Tauris, 2013.

Pandya, Amit A. *Muslim Indians: Struggle for Inclusion*. Washington, DC: Stimpson, 2010.

Pathak, Zakia, and Rajeswari Sunder Rajan. 'Shahbano'. In *Feminists Theorize the Political*, edited by Judith Butler and Joan W. Scott, 257–79. New York: Routledge, 1992.

Redding, Jeff. *A Secular Need: Islamic Law and State Governance in Contemporary India*. Seattle: University of Washington Press, 2020.

Sajjad, Mohammad. *Muslim Politics in Bihar: Changing Contours*. New Delhi: Routledge, 2014.

Sivaramayya, B., Archana Parashar, and Amita Dhanda. *Redefining Family Law in India: Essays in Honour of B. Sivaramayya*. New Delhi: Routledge, 2008.

Solanki, Gopika. *Adjudication in Religious Family Laws: Cultural Accommodation, Legal Pluralism, and Gender Equality in India*. Cambridge: Cambridge University Press, 2011.

Stephens, Julia. *Governing Islam: Law, Empire, and Secularism in Modern South Asia*. Cambridge: Cambridge University Press, 2018.

Sturman, Rachel. *The Government of Social Life in Colonial India: Liberalism, Religious Law, and Women's Rights*. New York: Cambridge University Press, 2012.

Subramanian, Narendra. *Nation and Family: Personal Law, Cultural Pluralism, and Gendered Citizenship in India*. Stanford: Stanford University Press, 2020.

Tschalaer, Mengia Hong. *Muslim Women's Quest for Justice: Gender, Law and Activism in India*. Cambridge: Cambridge University Press, 2017.

Williams, Rina Verma. *Postcolonial Politics and Personal Laws: Colonial Legal Legacies and the Indian State*. New Delhi: Oxford University Press, 2006.

Zaman, Muhammad Qasim. *Ashraf 'Ali Thanawi: Islam in Modern South Asia*. New York: Oneworld, 2012.

www.ingramcontent.com/pod-product-compliance
Lightning Source LLC
Chambersburg PA
CBHW041312110526
44591CB00022B/2892
* 9 7 8 1 9 1 5 5 5 0 0 3 3 *